Beiträge zum
ausländischen öffentlichen Recht und Völkerrecht

Edited by

the Max Planck Society
for the Advancement of Science
represented by Prof. Dr. Armin von Bogdandy
and Prof. Dr. Anne Peters

Volume 349

Jannika Jahn | Moritz Vinken
Khaled El Mahmoud [eds.]

The ICJ Advisory Opinion on Climate Change

At the Forefront of the Structural Transformation of International Law

A Collection of Essays

Nomos

Open Access funding provided by Max Planck Society

The Deutsche Nationalbibliothek lists this publication in the Deutsche Nationalbibliografie; detailed bibliographic data are available on the Internet at http://dnb.d-nb.de

1st Edition 2026

Published by
Nomos Verlagsgesellschaft mbH & Co. KG
Waldseestraße 3–5 | 76530 Baden-Baden
www.nomos.de

Production of the printed version:
Nomos Verlagsgesellschaft mbH & Co. KG

Waldseestraße 3–5 | 76530 Baden-Baden

ISBN (Print): 978-3-7560-3694-3
ISBN (ePDF): 978-3-7489-6837-5

DOI: https://doi.org/10.5771/9783748968375

Online Version
Nomos eLibrary

Table of Contents

Conclusion

Introduction

Climate Change at the Forefront of the Structural Transformation of International Law

Moritz Vinken, Jannika Jahn**, Khaled El Mahmoud****

I. Introduction

On 23 July 2025, the International Court of Justice (ICJ or Court) delivered its long-awaited Advisory Opinion on the *Obligations of States in respect of Climate Change.*[1] The Court was faced with a complex task. Amid vigorous debates over the efficacy and relevance of international law, it was called upon to define and reaffirm international law's capacity to guide state conduct in tackling an increasingly – in the Court's own words[2] – 'urgent' and 'existential' issue whose planetary proportions have arguably led to the emergence and solidification of a new geological epoch, the Anthropocene.[3]

The widely hailed landmark Opinion has just begun to spark an academic and political debate on the manner and the extent to which it strengthens

* Research Fellow at the Max Planck Institute for Comparative Public Law and International Law.

** Senior Research Fellow at the Max Planck Institute for Comparative Public Law and International Law.

*** Law Clerk at the Higher Regional Court of Berlin.

1 ICJ, *Obligations of States in Respect of Climate Change*, Advisory Opinion of 23 July 2025.

2 ICJ, *Obligations of States in Respect of Climate Change* (n. 1), paras. 73, 456.

3 While it is still geologically disputed, the Anthropocene has firmly established itself in critical reflections and re-conceptualisations of international law. Among the many, see Jorge E. Viñuales, *The Organisation of the Anthropocene. In Our Hands?* (Brill Nijhoff 2018); Louis J. Kotzé, 'Earth system law for the Anthropocene: rethinking environmental law alongside the Earth system metaphor' TLT 11 (2020), 75-104.
For a social scientific perspective, see Eva Horn and Hannes Bergthaller, *The Anthropocene. Key Issues for the Humanities* (Key Issues in Environment and Sustainability, Routledge 2019).

the role of international law in global climate governance.[4] Shortly after the publication of the Advisory Opinion, our blogpost symposium on *Völkerrechtsblog*, which forms the basis of this edited volume, aimed at intervening in this debate by emphasising the Opinion's systemic and structural implications for international law.[5] This volume intends to highlight that the decisive '*ecologisation*' of international law[6] undertaken by the Court in this Advisory Opinion both reflects and advances the ongoing structural transformation of international law. It shapes a comprehensive legal order that reinforces the shared value of long-term, science-based climate protection grounded in multilateral cooperation. To this end, the Advisory Opinion clarifies that the Paris Agreement is not merely an isolated instrument of political coordination and interaction. Instead, it is embedded in a coherent international legal order, together with which it constrains state discretion and imposes concrete obligations on states to pursue a transition away from greenhouse gas emissions, in particular CO_2.

This edited volume is organised into four thematic clusters that illuminate how the Advisory Opinion constitutes a significant step in the structural transformation of international law. Each cluster addresses one foundational tension of the discipline of international law – some might say fault lines[7] – which are at the heart of that transformation: the recalibration of international law between the co-existential protection of state

4 For the growing body of early commentary, in particular in the form of blog posts, see for instance a series of blogposts on EJIL:Talk! as well as the carefully curated blog-debate from the *Verfassungsblog* in cooperation with the Sabin Centre, Maria Antonia Tigre, Maxim Bönnemann & Antoine De Spiegeleir (eds.), *The ICJ's Advisory Opinion on Climate Change* (Verfassungsbooks, 2025) or online, https://verfassungsblog.de/category/debates/the-icjs-advisory-opinion-on-climate-change-debates/.

5 Cf. Khaled El Mahmoud, Jannika Jahn and Moritz Vinken (eds.), *Systemic Impacts and Structural Shifts: Climate Change and the Role of the ICJ Advisory Opinion*, Völkerrechtsblog Symposium, available at https://voelkerrechtsblog.org/symposium/symposium-on-the-icj-climate-change-advisory-opinion/.

6 Louise du Toit and Louis J. Kotzé, 'Reimagining international environmental law for the Anthropocene: An earth system law perspective' ESG 11 (2022), 1–10.
For a similar terminological approach to this ongoing process, see Sandrine Maljean-Dubois and Jacqueline Peel, 'The progressive "climatization" of international law', in Sandrine Maljean-Dubois and Jacqueline Peel (eds.), *Climate Change and the Testing of International Law* (Brill Nijhoff, 2023), 3–39.

7 Moritz Vinken, 'International Law's Fault Lines and Sediments: Geology as Method', *Max Planck Institute for Comparative Public Law & International Law (MPIL) Research Paper Series*, No. 2025–09, available at https://papers.ssrn.com/sol3/papers.cfm?abstract_id=5274030.

sovereignty and the cooperative regulation and management of community interests (II.), the continued contestation of the public-private divide (III.), the increasing reliance on the epistemic authority of science in international law and governance (IV.), and the ongoing re-negotiation of an increasingly heterogeneous postcolonial international legal order[8] (V.). The volume also offers elements of comparative analysis of the three Advisory Opinions on climate matters handed down in 2025: those of the ICJ, the International Tribunal of the Law of the Sea (ITLOS) and the Inter-American Court of Human Rights (IACtHR). This enables the volume to identify the broader structural trends underlying these successive pronouncements and to highlight the specific role these Advisory Opinions have come to play in the development of international (climate) law. The introduction draws on the contributions to this volume and references them in the footnotes.

II. Recalibrating the Sovereignty/Community Interest Divide

At the centre of the ongoing structural transformation of international law lies its recalibration towards the protection of global (environmental) commons as an interest shared by the *community* of states. Prior to the Advisory Opinion(s), this process appeared to have stalled, especially with regard to climate change. Within the climate regime established under the UNFCCC, the 'bottom-up' architecture of the Paris Agreement seemed to confine the normative reach of international law primarily to procedural obligations, geared towards aspirational targets, rather than imposing substantive legal constraints.[9] Moreover, customary international law and specialised areas of international law were often regarded as fragmented and contested in their applicability to the phenomenon of climate change. Indeed, many states conceived of the climate treaty regime as a *lex specialis* displacing other rules of international law. The ICJ's Advisory Opinion repudiates these lines of argument, thereby (re-)positioning international law at the forefront of climate governance.

---

8 The use of the term of *postcolonial* international order attempts to encapsulate the simultaneity of the aspirations of the international legal order to overcome its colonial past but which is caught in – and to some extent perpetuates and translates – the lingering reverberation of past forms of colonial domination. In this sense, Sundhya Pahuja, 'The Postcoloniality of International Law' HarvIntlLJ 46 (2005), 459-469.

9 For critical assessments of the qualification of the Paris Agreement as a bottom up structure, see for instance Christina Voigt, 'The ICJ and the UN Climate Regime: Clarifying mitigation obligations under the Paris Agreement', in this volume.

A first sub-cluster of contributions addressing the recalibration between state sovereignty and community interests accordingly focuses on the Advisory Opinion's identification and interpretation of the relevant subfields of international law and examines the manner in which the Court derived concrete climate obligations through the technique of systemic integration (1.). A second sub-cluster explores the further proceduralisation of international environmental law through the extension and refinement of procedural obligations[10] and its future-oriented regulatory turn, and examines to what extent this reflects a normative commitment to the cooperative pursuit of shared interests (2.).

1. The Advisory Opinion and the Systemic Integration of International Law in the Context of Climate Change?

> '[T]he Court considers that the argument according to which the climate change treaties constitute the only relevant applicable law cannot be upheld and finds that the principle of *lex specialis* does not lead to a general exclusion by the climate change treaties of other rules of international law.'[11]

This reasoning enables the derivation of climate-related obligations beyond the Paris Agreement, drawing on other applicable rules of international law through systemic integration. It is on this basis, that the Court articulates a coherent legal framework composed of the 'most directly relevant' norms, from which a set of complementary obligations can be derived. These obligations do not flow solely from climate change treaties, but also from a broad spectrum of international legal sources: custom[12], the law of the sea[13] and human rights.[14] Through systemic integration, the Court identifies 'a single set of compatible obligations'[15], and thus constructs an integrated international order with respect to climate change obligations.[16]

10 Cf. Heike Krieger and Anne Peters, 'Due Diligence and Structural Change in the International Legal Order', in: Heike Krieger, Anne Peters and Leonhard Kreuzer (eds.), *Due Diligence in the International Legal Order* (Oxford University Press, 2020), 382.

11 ICJ, *Obligations of States in Respect of Climate Change* (n. 1), para. 171.

12 Phillip Paiement and Corina Heri, 'Strengthening International Climate Obligations Beyond Paris: Situating the ICJ's Opinion within a Comparative Legal Context', in this volume.

13 Rozemarijn Roland Holst, 'Climate Change Law and the Law of the Sea: Systemic Impacts of the ICJ and ITLOS Advisory Opinions Read Together', in this volume.

As far as the climate change treaties are concerned, the ICJ intervenes on a number of intensely debated questions. It clarifies the relationship between the existing climate change treaties[17] and strengthens the role of decisions taken by the Conference of the Parties (COP) serving as the meeting of the Parties to the Paris Agreement (CMA) by acknowledging their potential legal bindingness.[18] In this context, the Court dispels uncertainty regarding the Paris Agreement's dual temperature goal by considering 'the 1.5°C threshold to be the parties' agreed primary temperature goal [...] under the Paris Agreement'[19]. More importantly, the Court clarifies the obligations arising from the Paris Agreement, especially with regard to mitigation. It limits the discretion of parties in defining their nationally determined contributions (NDCs) and in implementing them by a set of concrete obligations of conduct and of result, which must be exercised with *stringent* due diligence.[20]

Moreover, the Advisory Opinion engages in an in-depth cross-judicial dialogue with the ITLOS and the IACtHR. Several contributions to this volume take a comparative perspective on the three Advisory Opinions and demonstrate that the ICJ sought to produce an Advisory Opinion that is in harmony with the two others. They reveal how cross-judicial dialogue not only fosters normative integration across jurisdictions, but also acts as a powerful tool in the construction of a more coherent body of international climate law.[21] Moreover, they highlight the merit of a more detailed investigation into the evolving normative function of Advisory Opinions and their normative influence on the development of the international legal order, specifically in relation to climate change. Through persuasive legal reasoning, careful management of stakeholder expectations, and robust engagement with the jurisprudence of other international bodies, the Court

14 Helen Keller, 'A Right to a Clean, Healthy and Sustainable Environment – or Perhaps not (yet)?', in this volume; Malavika Rao, 'Climate Displacement in the ICJ's Advisory Opinion: Recognised but not Resolved', in this volume.

15 ICJ, *Obligations of States in Respect of Climate Change* (n. 1), para. 165.

16 Andrej Lang and Denise Koecke, 'Rising to the Occasion: The World Court as Architect of a Harmonious International Climate Law Framework', in this volume.

17 ICJ, *Obligations of States in Respect of Climate Change* (n. 1), paras. 194, 225.

18 ICJ, *Obligations of States in Respect of Climate Change* (n. 1), paras. 140, 184.

19 ICJ, *Obligations of States in Respect of Climate Change* (n. 1), para. 224.

20 Voigt (n. 9), in this volume.

21 For instance, Khaled El Mahmoud, 'One Climate, Many Courts: The ICJ Advisory Opinion on Climate Change, Systemic Integration, Cross-Judicial Law-Making, and Interjudicialism', in this volume.

has laid a normative foundation that may guide future litigation and policymaking efforts in the area of climate change law.[22] For instance, both the ICJ and the IACtHR affirm the justiciability of climate harm and the applicability of international legal responsibility to climate-related breaches of international obligations, albeit through distinct lines of reasoning. While the ICJ places emphasis on strengthening the doctrinal foundation of climate obligations, the IACtHR focusses on enhancing the accessibility and effectiveness of climate justice through procedural innovations and rights-based reasoning.[23]

2. The Proceduralisation of International Environmental Law and its Turn to the Future

Early manifestations of the proceduralisation of international environmental law date back several decades.[24] While proceduralisation has often been depicted as a means of substituting substantive agreement with diplomacy,[25] thereby diluting the substance and force of international law, others have argued, conversely, that it may exert a stabilising effect on the international legal order.[26] In this view, proceduralisation can help redress power imbalances, enhance legal and political accountability, and, importantly, create space for the incremental development of substantive norms.[27] As contributions to this volume suggest, the Advisory Opinion further advances proceduralisation through its pronounced reliance on due diligence.[28] At the same time, proceduralisation in this context reinforces substantive obligations and enables international law to assume a more future-oriented regulatory role.

---

22 Andreas Kulick, 'Great Expectations', in this volume.
23 Juan Auz, 'The Legal Consequences of Climate Harm: Complementarity Between the Advisory Opinions of the International Court of Justice and the Inter-American Court of Human Rights', in this volume.
24 Cf. Martti Koskenniemi, 'Peaceful Settlement of Environmental Disputes', Nord. J. Int'l L. 60 (1991), 73.
25 Koskenniemi (n. 24), 78, 85.
26 See Krieger and Peters (n. 10), 382-384.
27 See Krieger and Peters (n. 10), 382-384.
28 See Jutta Brunnée, 'The Advisory Opinion on Obligations of States in Respect of Climate Change: Harm Prevention under Customary International Law', in this volume; elaborating the close connection between due diligence and international law's proceduralisation, Krieger and Peters (n. 10), 363-364.

Due diligence functions as a cross-cutting regulatory technique governing all legal climate obligations of states arising under international law.[29] In fact, the core of the obligations identified by the Court require parties to act with due diligence – whether it concerns the obligation to prepare NDCs under Article 4(1) of the Paris Agreement, the duty to pursue domestic mitigation measures under Article 4(2), or other obligations of conduct enshrined in the Paris Agreement.[30] A due diligence standard also underpins customary international duties, such as the obligation to prevent significant environmental harm and the duty to cooperate.[31]

The Court offers a reading of due diligence that refines the substantive dimensions of the procedural obligations under the Paris Agreement and customary international law. It recognises that the procedural obligations of the Paris Agreement and of the harm prevention rule are constitutive for the pursuit of the substantive goals of harm prevention and the 1.5°C temperature goal. Vice versa the procedural obligations are normatively charged with these substantive goals. This leads to a form of proceduralisation that acknowledges the deep intertwinement of substance and procedure.[32]

This form of proceduralisation is also a legal response to climate change's futurity, which necessitates regulation under factual uncertainty. While climate law as interpreted by the Court requires timely action, it nevertheless leaves flexibility in reacting to future challenges and does not foresee substantive obligations of result. There are many areas of international law that are characterised by international law's turn to the future, but climate governance is one of the most prominent examples. The ICJ's Advisory Opinion marks the latest effort to operationalise this regulatory turn to the future.[33] Most strikingly in this context, the Court recognises intergenerational equity as an interpretative principle:

---

29 On the proliferation of due diligence standards beyond international environmental law, see Anne Peters, Heike Krieger and Leonhard Kreuzer (eds), *Due Diligence in the International Legal Order* (Oxford University Press, 2020).
The use of the notion of 'regulatory technique' in regard to due diligence aims at underscoring its impact on the overall structure of the legal framework. For this use, see Krieger and Peters (n. 10) 351.

30 ICJ, *Obligations of States in Respect of Climate Change* (n. 1), paras. 245 et seq., 252 et seq., 258, 262.

31 Brunnée (n. 28), in this volume.

32 Jutta Brunnée (n. 28), in this volume.

33 Jochen Rauber, 'Custom, Entrenchment, Interpretation – How the ICJ's Advisory Opinion on Climate Change Contributes to International Law's Turn Toward the Future', in this volume.

> '[...] intergenerational equity is a manifestation of equity in the general sense and thus shares its legal significance as a guide for the interpretation of applicable rules.'[34]

This entails a future-oriented regulatory turn which refines the traditional conception of state sovereignty, recasting States as trustees of future generations' interests in the functioning of the climate system and subjecting carbon sovereignty to justification under international law.[35] This interpretive refinement is driven by a normative vision of the cooperative pursuit of common interests.

In support of this normative vision, the ICJ's Advisory Opinion as well as the Advisory Opinions by ITLOS and the IACtHR rely on certain narratives on the temporality of international climate law. [36] By embracing a specific understanding of climate change's temporal situatedness, through the creation of temporal boundaries of the phenomenon of climate change, the Advisory Opinions delimit the jurisdictional scope for international law and strongly influence our climate 'imaginaries'.

III. International Law beyond the State: A Careful Recalibration of the Public/Private Divide

At first glance the Advisory Opinion the Court seems to move within the classical confines of the Public / Private distinction. It does not address the private sector directly. Instead, it importantly recognises that the obligations of States in light of climate change include the obligations to regulate the conduct of private actors.[37]

Another central manifestation of the Public / Private divide that the advisory proceedings seem to challenge more fundamentally, concerns modes of public participation. In this context the divide appears as the

34 ICJ, *Obligations of States in Respect of Climate Change* (n. 1), para. 157.

35 Jannika Jahn and Nele Suchantke, 'The ICJ Advisory Opinion on Climate Change: From Carbon Sovereignty to Trusteeship of the Climate Commons', in this volume.

36 David Scott, 'Timing the Environment in International Law: Reflections on Temporality in the Three Advisory Opinions on Climate Change', in this volume.

37 Harro van Asselt, 'The Private Life of the ICJ Advisory Opinion on Climate Change', in this volume.

distinction between public norm-setters and private norm-takers.[38] A number of contributions to this volume investigate how this distinction is cautiously softened, as non-State actors have shaped both the process and the substance of the Advisory Opinion. In this regard, the Advisory Opinion illustrates the role that civil society organisations and individuals may play in shaping the international legal order. For example, Vanuatu, the state that initiated the Advisory Opinion, was counselled by NGOs and students. And even though the Court formally stuck to its procedural rules and the formal boundaries of standing, allowing only States and international organisations to present written or oral statements, the proceedings show how civil society and individuals indirectly partook in the interpretation of legal vocabulary and standards.[39] In this context, the significance of narrated stories is revealed. Viewed through a narratological lens the ICJ's Advisory Opinion and its proceedings have acted as an archive of narrated microhistories which records the lived experiences of those most affected by climate change and which might compensate the absence of a factual *in concreto* assessment by the Court.[40]

IV. The Integration of Science into Law

International law has increasingly been called upon to regulate complex factual scenarios and uncertain risks, a development closely linked to the emergence of what has been described as a global risk society.[41] Scientific expertise has thus become a central component of international risk regulation.[42] International climate change governance is *the* paradigmatic example of this development. The Court devotes a considerable part of its

38 For an overarching account, see Jan Sändig, Jochen von Bernstorff, Andreas Hasenclever (eds,), *Affectedness and Participation in International Institutions* (Routlegde, 2020).

39 Lillian Robb and Vishal Prasad, 'Both a "Global" and an "International" Court of Justice', in this volume.

40 Rashmi Dharia, '"Vanishing Yams", A Food Microhistory in the Climate Change Advisory Opinion', in this volume.

41 Ulrich Beck, *Risikogesellschaft* (Suhrkamp, 1986); Ulrich Beck, *Weltrisikogesellschaft* (Suhrkamp, 2008).

42 Jacqueline Peel, *Science and Risk Regulation in International Law* (Cambridge University Press, 2010); Monika Ambrus, Rosemary Rayfuse and Wouter Werner (eds), *Risk and the Regulation of Uncertainty in International Law* (Oxford University Press, 2017).

Advisory Opinion to climate science. It addresses the epistemic authority of science in international law with a view to the temperature target that constitutes the normative hook for state obligations under the Paris Agreement. In order to illustrate the centrality of (climate) science for international law's regulatory grip on climate change, the Court begins its Advisory Opinion by telling the (hi)story of the emergence of international environmental and climate law as a reaction to and a product of the solidification of scientific knowledge on environmental degradation.[43]

A substantive part of the Advisory Opinion then deals with establishing the scientific consensus on climate change.[44] For this, the ICJ relies 'primarily on the IPCC reports, which participants agree'[45] to 'constitute comprehensive and authoritative restatements of the best available science about climate change'[46]. The Court thus reinforces the IPCC's epistemic authority. The establishment of a scientific consensus around the scientific assessments provided by the IPCC is of crucial importance to the reasoning, as the Court assigns a central role to science in the formation and the legitimation of normative benchmarks. In doings so, the Court displays hitherto unknown levels of epistemic deference.[47]

V. Re-negotiation of the postcolonial international legal order

An aspect of international law's struggle to overcome the reverberations of its colonial past manifests itself in the increasingly unsatisfactory legal distinction between 'developed' and 'developing' countries. As international climate law occupies a central place in the ongoing re-negotiation of this distinction,[48] the Court's Advisory Opinion had to also address this fault line. This meant tackling the conflict between the major emitting states and the vulnerable states that have contributed least to climate change, yet bear its most severe consequences , both in terms of the legal duties involved and

43 ICJ, *Obligations of States in Respect of Climate Change* (n. 1), paras. 50–71.
44 ICJ, *Obligations of States in Respect of Climate Change* (n. 1), paras. 72–87.
45 ICJ, *Obligations of States in Respect of Climate Change* (n. 1), para. 74.
46 ICJ, *Obligations of States in Respect of Climate Change* (n. 1), para. 284.
47 Katalyn Sulyok, 'On the Science-Coloured Glasses of the ICJ: Harmfulness, Wrongfulness, and Climate Accountability', in this volume.
48 Among many, Sigrid Boysen, *Die postkoloniale Konstellation* (Mohr Siebeck, 2021).

the legal consequences arising from those obligations.[49] The participation of numerous small and highly vulnerable states from the Global South — many of whom engaged with the Court for the first time — underscores the significance that these states attributed to the proceedings as part of their broader pursuit of climate justice.[50] The Court acknowledges the significant contribution of industrialised countries to climate change[51] and signals that states refusing to act on climate protection may incur international responsibility.[52] Whether this also extends to historical emissions, however, is left open.

By emphasising equity and the principle of common but differentiated responsibilities and respective capabilities as interpretative principle,[53] the Court makes clear that it is seeking fair and flexible answers to the question of who should bear the cost of climate protection. This flexibility becomes particularly tangible in the Court's pronouncement that

> 'the addition of the phrase "in the light of different national circumstances" [...] does not change the core of the principle of common but differentiated responsibilities and respective capabilities; rather, *it adds nuance* to the principle by recognising that the status of a State as developed or developing is not static. It depends on an assessment of the current circumstances of the State concerned.'[54]

Thus, the Court follows the steps already taken by the Paris Agreement toward a dynamic differentiation capable of reflecting shifting realities.[55]

Finally, the Court took note of the potential legal implications of climate change for the right to self-determination. However, it refrained from elaborating on them, notwithstanding their demonstrated significance in

49 Lovleen Bhullar, 'The Advisory Opinion on Climate Justice and the "Global North-South Divide"', in this volume.
50 Robb and Prasad (n. 39), in this volume.
51 ICJ, *Obligations of States in Respect of Climate Change* (n. 1), para. 150.
52 ICJ, *Obligations of States in Respect of Climate Change* (n. 1), para. 421.
53 ICJ, *Obligations of States in Respect of Climate Change* (n. 1), para. 151.
54 ICJ, *Obligations of States in Respect of Climate Change* (n. 1), para. 225. [emphasis added].
55 Christina Voigt and Felipe Ferreira, '"Dynamic Differentiation": The Principles of CBDR-RC, Progression and Highest Possible Ambition in the Paris Agreement' TEL 5 (2016), 285–303.

the ILC Study Group's recent report on sea-level rise in relation to international law.[56]

VI. Conclusion

As mentioned above, this edited volume transforms a blogpost symposium into a more structured collection of early assessments of the ICJ's Advisory Opinion on the obligations of States in respect of climate change. Instead of an isolated focus on the Advisory Opinion's significance for international law's role in the struggle of climate change, it aims to offer a first round of shorter scholarly reflections which, taken together, read the Advisory Opinion as a significant catalyst in the ongoing structural transformation of international law. They also identify a range of technical and systemic gaps as well as silences in the Court's reasoning. These 'shortcomings' of the Advisory Opinion on the one hand indicate avenues for further scientific engagement and contestation. They point to the critical pressure points in the Court's systemic construction, aspects which find themselves still at the contested fringes of the ongoing structural transformation of international law. The contributions demonstrate a variety of approaches – ranging from doctrinal, to normative and more critical perspectives.

In light of the contributions of this collection, it seems to us editors that the Court has understood its task—at least in part—as one of ordering international law: offering a structural framework capable of coherently *managing* global climate governance. As we elaborate in greater detail in the conclusion, this vision conceives international law primarily as a regulatory architecture for the cooperative and future-oriented governance of the global commons. International law emerges as an order of shared, future-oriented responsibility. Conversely, one aspect that we believe remains at the contested frontier of this structural transformation, is the question of whether this regulatory architecture will also provide practically viable avenues for redistribution, individual state liability, and compensation or whether it will instead solidify around its managerial function in enforcing states' collective obligations towards the international community of present and future generations.

56 Dave-Inder Comar, 'The ICJ's Historic Nod to Self-Determination and Climate Change Impacts', in this volume.

Part I:
Recalibrating the Sovereignty/Community Interest Divide

1. The Advisory Opinion and the Systemic Integration of International Law through Climate Change

Rising to the Occasion:

The World Court as Architect of a Harmonious International Climate Law Framework

Andrej Lang[*] and Denise Koecke[**]

I. Introduction

Climate change litigation has, at last, reached the World Court, with the International Court of Justice ('ICJ') issuing its highly anticipated Advisory Opinion on the Obligations of States in respect of Climate Change ('AO').[1] The Court held, in a nutshell, that States have binding legal obligations under both treaty and customary international law to prevent, reduce and control greenhouse-gas emissions[2]) and 'failure... to take appropriate action to protect the climate system ... may constitute an internationally wrongful act'.[3]

To evaluate the ruling, this chapter takes an institutional perspective and asks which legal and political challenges the issue of climate change poses for the ICJ and how the Court responded to this challenge. It traces the distinctive institutional role for the ICJ in conversation with the initial voices articulated in the international legal blogosphere in response to the AO.

* Professor of Public Law and Public Economic Law at Chemnitz University of Technology.

** Research Assistant at Chemnitz University of Technology and Law Student at European University Viadrina, Germany.

1 ICJ, *Obligations of States in respect of Climate Change*, Advisory Opinion of of 23 July 2025.

2 ICJ, *Obligations of States in Respect of Climate Change* (n. 1), para. 347.

3 ICJ, *Obligations of States in Respect of Climate Change* (n. 1), para. 427; cf. also 221.

More specifically, the chapter identifies and responds to three distinctive positions among those varied voices.

First, skeptics had, prior to the AO, raised concerns about the merits of addressing climate change through the ICJ, pointing to the multiple pitfalls and political minefields of an advisory opinion.[4] In the aftermath of the AO, Bodansky and Biniaz have expressed concern that the opinion may 'have unintended chilling effects on the conduct of global climate diplomacy' and undermine the positive and important advancement of the Paris Agreement.[5] Although this stream of scholarship brings a keen sense of legal realism to the broader debate and points to important legitimacy-related constraints of international courts confronted with the climate crisis as well as the uncertain political consequences of climate rulings, it seems doubtful that the most urgent challenge of our time is the one issue in which we should forego the contributions of courts in clarifying what the law is. Put differently, the ICJ can and did, in fact, make a valuable contribution to addressing climate change; at the same time, it is true that defining a proper role requires taking into account the limits of the judicial function and its interaction with the political process.

Second, on the other side of the spectrum, many legal scholars expected a bolder and more activist role of the ICJ given the urgency of the climate crisis and criticized the Court for not going far enough. Prost, for example, describes the AO as 'a weak opinion' that is 'riddled with omissions, inconsistencies and banalities' and laments the inability of legal scholarship 'to distinguish genuine progress from mediocrity'.[6] This critique, however, tends to overlook that the necessary legal adaptations to the climate challenge need to be reconciled with legal stability and continuity, and cannot overcome the consensual structure of international law.

Third, the AO has been celebrated as a pivotal moment or turning point in climate governance that represents 'a watershed moment in the global

---

4 See, e.g., Daniel Bodansky, 'Advisory Opinions on Climate Change: Some Preliminary Questions', RECIEL 32 (2023), 185; Jianping Guo, Wanqiang Li and Haoyu Tian, 'The climate advisory opinion: A medicine with side-effects?', Marine Policy 156 (2023), Article 105817; Maria Antonia Tigre and Armando Rocha, 'Competing Perspectives and Dialogue in Climate Change Advisory Opinions', AJIL Unbound 117 (2023), 287.

5 Daniel Bodansky and Susan Biniaz, 'The ICJ's Advisory Opinion on Climate Change: Does It Throw a Wrench into the Negotiator's Toolbox of Diplomatic Problem-Solving Techniques?', EJIL:Talk!, 23 September 2025.

6 Mario Prost, 'Disaster Passing as Miracle? A Critical Take on the ICJ's Climate Advisory Opinion', EJIL:Talk!, 14 August 2025.

struggle for climate justice',[7] 'the start of a new era of climate accountability at a global level',[8] or a 'historic legal victory for small States'.[9] While this portrayal of the AO as a substantial victory for the cause of climate justice may be useful as part of a climate mobilization strategy, it overstates the limited role and impact that an advisory opinion of the ICJ can have for the broader struggle against climate change.

This chapter contends instead that properly assessing the AO requires, at the outset, to temper our expectations and to appreciate the delicate legal and political balance the ICJ was required to strike between the magnitude of the climate crisis as an existential global threat and the judicial prudence required of the World Court that remains dependent on state consent and legitimacy. It sets forth the argument that the ICJ has largely risen to the occasion not by providing 'a complete solution to the climate change problem',[10] but by defining its role as architect of systemic integration in international climate law, forging a harmonious international legal framework on climate change that integrates the diverse sources of international law and prior rulings of international courts and tribunals into a coherent legal architecture (III.). In doing so, the Court lived up to its role as a global public forum in the climate change advisory proceedings (II.). In addition, the Court managed to navigate its institutional limits and the political sensitivities of international climate change adjudication by establishing general climate change obligations, while avoiding controversial determinations on the responsibilities of specific States, and by relying on pre-existing legal notions and well-established principles such as the duties of due diligence and cooperation (IV.). One caveat is the Court's ambiguous treatment of the right to a clean, healthy and sustainable environment, likely reflecting a formulaic compromise between judicial ambition and restraint (V.).

7 Margaretha Wewerinke-Singh, 'ICJ Advisory Opinion and the Future of Climate Responsibility', IISD-SDG Knowledge Hub, 11 September 2024.

8 Katie Kouchakji, 'Climate crisis: ICJ's historic opinion sets the tone for future litigation', IBA Environment Correspondent, 1 August 2025, citing Danilo Garrido, legal counsel at NGO Greenpeace International.

9 Natricia Duncan, 'Caribbean leaders hail ICJ climate ruling as 'historic' win for small island States', The Guardian, 25 July 2025, citing Ralph Gonsalves, the prime minister of St Vincent and the Grenadines.

10 Declaration of Judge Tladi, *Obligations of States in Respect of Climate Change*, Advisory Opinion of 23 July 2025, para. 38.

II. The ICJ and the Advisory Process as a Global Public Forum

The ICJ is institutionally and procedurally well-positioned to fulfill an architectural role. As opposed to other international courts adjudicating specific bodies of international law such as the United Nations Convention on the Law of the Sea ('UNCLOS'), in the case of ITLOS, or regional human rights treaties, in the case of the Inter-American Court of Human Rights ('IACtHR') and the European Court of Human Rights ('ECtHR'), the ICJ covers international law generally. The ICJ was, accordingly, tasked with comprehensively laying down the obligations of States with respect to climate change under public international law by the General Assembly ('GA'). For this purpose, the procedural build-up to advisory opinions in general – and to the climate change proceedings in particular – confers valuable 'process-based legitimacy' on the ICJ.[11]

The GA's request seeking the Opinion was bolstered with the authority of a majority vote, being co-sponsored by 132 States [12]. In total, 96 States delivered oral statements during the widely covered public hearings before the ICJ in December 2024 – the broadest participation in the Court's history. Moreover, civil society actors have extensively participated in the proceedings – from initiating the General Assembly's Request, over campaigning among States, to issuing written and oral statements.[13] Finally, the Court furthered the authoritative nature of its opinion by adopting it unanimously – as only the fifth of all 29 advisory opinions delivered by the ICJ so far.

The broad participation of the community of States in these advisory proceedings 'unlike any that have previously come before the Court'[14] and its institutional character as 'the principal judicial organ of the United Nations' (Art. 92 UN Charter) vested the Court with distinct authority and legitimacy. Against this background, the Court was predestined to act as a global public forum on the climate change obligations of States and to establish a coherent legal framework integrating diverse state perspectives ranging from historically high-emitting States to particularly vulnerable

---

11 Daniel Bodansky (n. 4), 191.

12 See UNGA Res 77/276 of 29 March 2023; ICJ, *Obligations of States in Respect of Climate Change* (n. 1), para. 47.

13 Lillian Robb and Vishal Prasad, 'Both a "Global" and an "International" Court of Justice', in this volume.

14 ICJ, *Obligations of States in Respect of Climate Change* (n. 1), para. 456.

small island nations.[15] An added advantage of the advisory process was that its legally non-binding outcome spared the Court from the higher stakes and jurisdictional hurdles of legally binding contentious proceedings.

III. Building a Harmonious International Climate Law Framework

As indicated at the outset, the Opinion outlines the contours of a harmonious international legal framework on climate change that integrates the diverse sources of international law and prior rulings of international courts and tribunals into a coherent legal architecture.

1. Systemic Integration

The main interpretive tool utilized by the ICJ was the principle of systemic integration – though not explicitly referred to as such. With its help, the Court did not only systematically integrate the climate treaties into the workings of the international legal order, thus maintaining its coherence and integrity, it also rejected the argument of big emitters, such as the US, Japan, and Russia, that the climate change treaties would constitute *leges speciales* and therefore displace other rules of international law.[16]

The Court noted based on the findings of the International Law Commission that the application of the *lex specialis* principle requires either 'some actual inconsistency' between the international treaty obligations and customary principles or 'a discernable intention that one provision is to exclude the other'.[17] The Court could not ascertain either.[18] Neither did

15 For the proposition that International courts provide a forum for 'public debate about ideas, public norms, and societal values', see Emilie Hafner-Burton, Sergio Puig and David Victor, 'Against Secrecy: The Social Cost of International Dispute Settlement', Yale J. Int'l L. 42 (2017), 279 (288); see also Rozemarijn Roland Holst, 'Taking the Current when It Serves: Prospects and Challenges for an ITLOS Advisory Opinion on Oceans and Climate Change', RECIEL 32 (2023), 1 (4): advisory proceedings could 'go some way towards accommodating the diversity and multilateral character of interests involved'.

16 See United States of America, Written Statement (ICJ, Obligations of States in Respect of Climate Change, 22 March 2024), para. 4.1; Japan, Written Statement (ICJ, Obligations of States in Respect of Climate Change, 22 March 2024), paras. 14–18.

17 ICJ, *Obligations of States in Respect of Climate Change* (n. 1), para. 167.

18 ICJ, *Obligations of States in Respect of Climate Change* (n. 1), paras. 168-170.

'the object and purpose of the climate change treaties [...] contradict other rules or principles of international law' nor did these treaties intend to 'replace such other rules or principles',[19] considering that 'the preambles of the UNFCCC and the Paris Agreement themselves contain references to other rules and principles'.[20] By rejecting the *lex specialis* argument ,[21] the Court simultaneously dismissed a conception of international law as a conglomerate of self-contained regimes. Rather than entrenching an atomistic fragmentation between specialized climate change law and general international law, the Court's reasoning reflects a shift towards the systemic integration of international law.[22]

Instead, the Court noted 'that it is a generally recognized principle that, when several rules bear on a single issue, they should, to the extent possible, be interpreted so as to give rise to a single set of compatible obligations',[23] thereby utilizing harmonious interpretation to present treaty law and custom as a complimentary skein.[24] Hence, climate change treaties and general customary principles, or international human rights law for that matter, are not so different as to displace one another; they are rather so similar, as to invite harmonious rapprochement.[25]

The systemic integration between the different international legal rules operates in both directions: '[T]he obligations arising from the climate change treaties, as interpreted herein, and State practice in implementing them inform the general customary obligations, just as the general customary obligations provide guidance for the interpretation of the climate change treaties'.[26] Similarly, 'international human rights law, the climate

19 ICJ, *Obligations of States in Respect of Climate Change* (n. 1), para. 169.

20 ICJ, *Obligations of States in Respect of Climate Change* (n. 1), para. 169.

21 ICJ, *Obligations of States in Respect of Climate Change* (n. 1), para. 171. See also Joint Declaration of Judges Charlesworth, Brant, Cleveland, and Aurescu, *Obligations of States in Respect of Climate Change*, Advisory Opinion of 23 July 2025, para. 2.

22 Angela Wewerinke-Singh, 'Harmonizing Sources, Hardening Duties', Verfassungsblog, 11 August 2025.

23 ICJ, *Obligations of States in Respect of Climate Change* (n. 1), para. 165.

24 Joint Declaration of Judges Charlesworth, Brant, Cleveland and Aurescu (n. 21), para. 9.

25 On the relationship between climate change treaties and custom, see Julian Arato and Justina Uriburu, 'Treaty and Custom in the ICJ's Climate Change Opinion', EJIL:Talk!, 24 July 2025; on the relationship with international human law, see Corina Heri, 'Human Rights in the ICJ's Climate Opinion', Verfassungsblog, 1 August 2025.

26 ICJ, *Obligations of States in Respect of Climate Change* (n. 1), para. 313.

change treaties and other relevant environmental treaties [...] inform each other'.[27]

A manifestation of the mutual interaction between treaty and custom is, according to the Court, that a 'compliance in full and in good faith by a State with the climate change treaties [...] suggests that this State substantially complies with the general customary duties'.[28] Put differently: Compliance with the Paris Agreement creates a rebuttable presumption of compliance with the general customary duties to prevent significant environmental harm and to co-operate.[29]

This approach has been criticized as reading like '*lex specialis* by another name',[30] allegedly downgrading 'the autonomous force of customary law'.[31] There is, however, a substantial difference between using *lex specialis* as a rule to resolve a conflict of norms and pursuing a harmonious integration of different sources of law. Whereas the former formalistically results in one legal source displacing the other, the latter operates more flexibly through a rebuttable presumption that 'gives room for nuance and complexity.'[32] More specifically, it enables 'treaty and customary obligations to enrich one another', making both 'more robust'.[33] On the one hand, climate change treaties may, for example, enrich the customary principle of due diligence by providing more specific 'standards that may enable or facilitate the identification and application of the diligence that is due in specific instances [under customary international law]'.[34] On the other hand, embedding the rather weak Paris Agreement, with its sweeping deferral to state discretion and its lack of formal enforcement mechanisms, into the more robust structures of general customary law may give 'more teeth' to its obligations. Overall, the Court's holistic integration of treaty and custom as well as of international human rights and environmental law in the Opinion, is likely to produce significant legal consequences yet to be discerned in legal discourse and in contentious proceedings in the following months and years.

27 ICJ, *Obligations of States in Respect of Climate Change* (n. 1), para. 404.
28 ICJ, *Obligations of States in Respect of Climate Change* (n. 1), para. 314.
29 Arato and Uriburu (n. 25).
30 Mario Prost (n. 6).
31 Mario Prost (n. 6).
32 Declaration of Judge Nolte, *Obligations of States in Respect of Climate Change*, Advisory Opinion of 23 July 2025, para. 13.
33 Arato and Uriburu (n. 25).
34 ICJ, *Obligations of States in Respect of Climate Change* (n. 1), para. 313.

2. Global Minimum Baseline

The ICJ's approach towards the rulings of other international adjudicatory bodies – such as the UN Human Rights Committee, ECtHR, ITLOS, IACtHR – on the matters of climate change further exemplifies the architectural role the Court assumed. The ICJ was in a challenging position, risking to contradict previous international rulings and thereby creating 'confusion and undermine the credibility and authority of international courts and tribunals'.[35] Seemingly aware of this risk, the Court carefully steered clear of contradictory pronouncements. It did so by drawing generously on the climate change jurisprudence of ITLOS, as well as selectively on regional human rights courts, and the Human Rights Committee. Aiming 'to achieve the necessary clarity and the essential consistency of international law, as well as legal security',[36] the ICJ notably departed from its usual restraint in referencing other international bodies.[37] This judicial cross-fertilization arguably enriches the coherence of the international legal order.

While stating not to be bound by the ITLOS' interpretations, the Court transposed the Tribunal's notion of 'stringent due diligence' from the narrower context of maritime pollution to the broader field of climate change law, applying it, for instance, to the obligations under the Paris Agreement.[38] It not only reaffirmed the findings of this previous ruling but also universalized its contents for non-members of the UNCLOS, productively cross-fertilizing the law of the sea and the international climate law regime.

For example, the Court recognized the IACtHR's Advisory Opinion No. 32,[39] issued only a few weeks prior to the ICJ's ruling, albeit without engaging with its substance. Although some of the Inter-American Court's findings – *inter alia* irreversible harm to the environment being a *ius cogens* crime[40] or the expansion of extraterritorial jurisdiction for transboundary human rights violations[41] – are notably more progressive than those of the Court, the latter neither reasserted nor negated them in substance.

35 Laurence Boisson de Chazournes, 'The Advisory Function of the International Court of Justice: Various Facets', ASIL Proceedings (2024), 192 (194).
36 ICJ, *Obligations of States in Respect of Climate Change* (n. 1), para. 338.
37 Andreas Kulick, 'Great Expectations', in this volume.
38 ICJ, *Obligations of States in Respect of Climate Change* (n. 1), para. 252.
39 IACtHR, *Climate Emergency and Human Rights*, Advisory Opinion of May 29, 2025, AO No. 32/25.
40 IACtHR, *Climate Emergency and Human Rights* (n. 39), para. 293.
41 IACtHR, *Climate Emergency and Human Rights* (n. 39), para. 278.

It contended itself with 'legitimizing the rights-based approach to climate change',[42] providing an authoritative back-up and encouragement for human rights bodies such as the IACtHR, but also the ECtHR or the Human Rights Committee, to develop their climate change jurisprudence.

In the end, the ICJ was conscious that it is not – and cannot be – a human rights court.[43] This explains, for example, why the AO did not, aside from generally asserting that States' human rights obligations under universal human rights treaties may apply extraterritorially depending on the specific circumstances[44], delve into matters of extraterritorial jurisdiction for human rights violations arising from greenhouse gas emissions, thereby safeguarding the human rights courts' room to maneuver. Whereas the IACtHR is very forward in recognizing that persons outside the territory of the respondent State may be under the American Convention's jurisdiction if the harm emanates from within that State's territory,[45] the ECtHR has outwardly dismissed arguments in this direction.[46] The ICJ can impossibly provide a universal answer to questions of extraterritoriality; any substantial involvement would have simultaneously over- and underscored what human rights bodies have established in their jurisprudence.

The ICJ consequently opted for a global minimum baseline approach that avoided pronouncements on the precise scope of regional or specialized treaty commitments. This approach acknowledges the distinct normative space occupied by regional and specialized regimes, while integrating them into a broader global framework of climate obligations. Since the Court kept the door open to regional groups of States – such as the those of the American Convention – to adopt a higher standard of climate protection, the diverging approaches of those Courts present an opportunity, rather than a threat to the uniformity of international law.[47]

---

42 Corina Heri (n. 25).
43 Corina Heri (n. 25).
44 ICJ, *Obligations of States in Respect of Climate Change* (n. 1), paras. 394-402.
45 Corina Heri (n. 25).
46 ECtHR, Duarte Agostinho and Others v. Portugal and Others, Application No. 39371/20.
47 Helen Keller, 'A Right to a Clean, Healthy and Sustainable Environment – or perhaps not (yet)?', in this volume.

IV. A Middle Ground Between Backlash-provoking Specificity and Issue-skirting Generality and Between 'Making' and 'Applying' the Law

One of the challenges for the ICJ was to thread the needle between overly specific, highly ambitious and innovative duties, and cautious general holdings that fail to advance the legal landscape.[48] It did so by establishing concrete and robust climate change obligations without controversially venturing into how States ought to specifically design their climate change policies.

More specifically, the Court affirmed in a reasoned manner that violations of climate protection obligations compel States to provide reparations,[49] despite some States arguing that the diffuse nature of climate change would preclude the general application of the rules of reparation.[50] At the same time, the ICJ confined itself to establishing the general framework of state responsibility in relation to climate change, while reserving an '*in concreto* assessment' of the responsibility of individual or groups of States to a 'case-by-case' analysis to be undertaken in future contentious litigation .[51] It wisely refrained from imposing more specific state obligations, such as enumerating concrete measures to reduce greenhouse gas emissions as part of States' nationally determined contributions (NDCs) or spelling out how damages from floodings in small-island States are to be calculated.

This does not, of course, imply that emitting States should escape international responsibility. But establishing such responsibility presupposes a concrete dispute between specific parties that meets jurisdictional requirements, rigorous fact-finding through formal evidentiary mechanisms, and detailed legal analysis refined through adversarial engagement – all hallmarks of contentious proceedings, and not the advisory process. Or, in Cass Sunstein's words, *one case at a time.*[52]

In addition, the Court succeeded, at least for the most part, in making legal adjustments necessitated by climate change in an evolutive and measured way. It did so by basing the international climate change framework on pre-existing and generally accepted legal principles such as the duty

48 Daniel Bodansky (n. 4), 192; Aref Shams, 'Tempering Great Expectations: The Legitimacy Constraints and the Conflict Function of International Courts in International Climate Litigation', RECIEL 32 (2023), 193 (201).

49 ICJ, *Obligations of States in Respect of Climate Change* (n. 1), paras. 449-450.

50 ICJ, *Obligations of States in Respect of Climate Change* (n. 1), para. 434.

51 ICJ, *Obligations of States in Respect of Climate Change* (n. 1), para. 161.

52 For this judicial approach, see Cass Sunstein, *One Case at a Time: Judicial Minimalism on the Supreme Court* (Harvard University Press 1999).

to prevent or the duty to cooperate rather than introducing new and avant-gardist notions exclusively tailored to the specifics of climate change. For example, the ICJ expanded the customary rule to prevent significant (transboundary) harm to the environment. Some States indeed submitted that this duty remains limited to situations of direct cross-border harm.[53] The Court, however, broadened its scope, holding that the customary duty to prevent significant harm to the environment also applies with respect to the climate system and other parts of the environment'.[54]

Although the phenomenon of climate change requires profound modifications of 'our habits, comforts and current way of life',[55] it is doubtful that a bold act of judicial disruption by the ICJ would have served the global climate movement well. It would have likely provoked strong backlash by high-emitting States and stretched the legal and legitimacy-related limits of the World Court. Instead, its judicial role is better served by reconciling the legal adjustments necessitated by climate change with the need for legal stability and continuity. In the final paragraph of its Opinion, the Court reflects its institutional constraints accordingly, noting 'the limits of its judicial function' and the 'important but ultimately limited role [of international law] in resolving this [climate change] problem'.[56]

V. Right to a Clean, Healthy and Sustainable Environment

In order to specify with a concrete example how to strike – or not to strike – the fine line between overly ambitious lawmaking and progressive development of the law, this final section analyzes the Court's pronouncement on the right to a clean, healthy and sustainable environment. Although the ICJ has mostly done well to maneuver between these two poles, its holdings on the matter of the proposed right to a clean, healthy and sustainable environment are less convincing.

The Court derives the right from its recognition in human rights instruments ,[57] domestic systems,[58] and a General Assembly Resolution.[59]

---

53 ICJ, *Obligations of States in Respect of Climate Change* (n. 1), para. 133.
54 ICJ, *Obligations of States in Respect of Climate Change* (n. 1), para. 134.
55 ICJ, *Obligations of States in Respect of Climate Change* (n. 1), para. 456.
56 ICJ, *Obligations of States in Respect of Climate Change* (n. 1), para. 456.
57 ICJ, *Obligations of States in Respect of Climate Change* (n. 1), para. 390.
58 ICJ, *Obligations of States in Respect of Climate Change* (n. 1), para. 390.
59 ICJ, *Obligations of States in Respect of Climate Change* (n. 1), para. 392.

While the Opinion starts out to describe something resembling *opinio iuris* among the international community, the ICJ stopped short of expressly denoting an autonomous right to a clean, healthy and sustainable environment as customary international law. It stressed instead its close interrelationship with other human rights 'such as the right to life, the right to health and the right to an adequate standard of living, including access to water, food and housing', holding that it was 'a precondition for', 'inherent in' or 'essential for the enjoyment of other human rights'.[60]

What this ultimately means is already subject to debate in international legal scholarship. It appears that almost any position conceivable on the right to a clean, healthy and sustainable environment can be read into the Advisory Opinion: the right being custom, emerging custom (which is arguably most aligned with the holdings of the Court), a human right on its own, an accessory (horizontal) principle within the human rights domain, authoritative soft law, possibly even less than that. This ambivalence in the Court's reasoning is likely a reflection of a formulaic compromise between the majority and the more ambitious minority of judges. Judge Bhandari, for example, asserts that a right to a clean, healthy and sustainable environment exists under customary international law and criticizes the Court for failing to 'ultimately affirm[]' its existence or to 'clarify its normative status'.[61]

Without entering into a detailed analysis of existing state practice, there are good reasons for the ICJ, from a holistic perspective, not to recognize a new customary right to a healthy environment at the current stage of legal development.[62] Although the Court plays an important role in identifying customary international law – what it recognizes as custom 'is often regarded as determinative'[63] – it needs to exercise this delicate judicial authority judiciously so as not to undermine it. In the process of developing customary law, the ICJ should not stand at the forefront of international

60 ICJ, *Obligations of States in Respect of Climate Change* (n. 1), para. 393.

61 Separate Opinion of Judge Bhandari, *Obligations of States in Respect of Climate Change*, Advisory Opinion of 23 July 2025, para. 3; see also Separate Opinion of Judge Aurescu, *Obligations of States in Respect of Climate Change*, Advisory Opinion of 23 July 2025, paras. 27–46; Declaration of Judge Tladi (n. 10), paras. 24–33.

62 It's a different matter – on which we take no position – to argue that a right to a healthy environment should be created on the global international stage through treaty or state practice.

63 Gleider Hernández, 'International Judicial Law-Making', in: Catherine Brölmann and Yannick Radi (eds.), *Research Handbook on the Theory and Practice of International Lawmaking* (Edward Elgar Publishing 2016), 200 (207).

legal innovations but serve as a 'consolidating force'[64] that ratifies a broad and sufficiently robust consensus. The fact that the IACtHR – a regional human rights court – has affirmed the right to a healthy environment as an autonomous right does not mean that the ICJ – a global inter-state court – ought to do the same.[65] The inescapable reality is that the ICJ crucially depends on – and cannot substitute for – a broad political consensus among states.

Once the ICJ chose not to take that route, it would have arguably been more prudent to engage less – or perhaps not at all – with the right to a clean, healthy and sustainable environment. While it appears the Court sought, with its elaboration, to bolster the emerging custom given its 'importance',[66] the passages on the right are arguably the most aspirational and least doctrinally grounded in the entire Opinion.[67] The Court's scarce and repetitive pronouncements neither contribute to a substantial resolution of the issues surrounding substantive and procedural status of the right, nor do they add much legal clarity. It is not surprising that numerous commentators and individual judges have criticized that neither the current status of this right under international law, nor whether it is a self-standing norm is clarified.

VI. Conclusion

In sum, the ICJ has – for the most part – demonstrated the necessary self-awareness of its institutional role and limits. Its emphasis on setting up a harmonious international climate law framework is doctrinally sound, yet sufficiently bold. In so doing, the Court has reaffirmed its role as an architect of an integrated legal order capable of confronting the 'ongoing climate crisis'.[68]

---

64 Gleider Hernández (n. 63), 207.

65 But see Corina Heri (n. 25).

66 ICJ, *Obligations of States in Respect of Climate Change* (n. 1), para. 391.

67 Critical Andreas Kulick, 'Great Expectations', in this volume.

68 ICJ, *Obligations of States in Respect of Climate Change* (n. 1), para. 456.

Strengthening International Climate Obligations Beyond Paris: Situating the ICJ's Opinion within a Comparative Legal Context

Phillip Paiement and Corina Heri***

I. Introduction

The ICJ's Advisory Opinion on the Obligations of States in respect of Climate Change[1] concludes a 15-month period of rapid developments in the crystallization of international law as it pertains to the climate emergency. Beginning with the first climate rulings of the European Court of Human Rights (ECtHR) – most notably, the *KlimaSeniorinnen* judgment[2] – in April 2024, later the 2024 Advisory Opinion of the International Tribunal of the Law of the Sea (ITLOS)[3] and then the Advisory Opinion of the Inter-American Court of Human Rights (IACtHR)[4] just two months ago, considerable clarity has been achieved as to the obligations arising from diverse subfields of international law. In the present post, we explore the ICJ's Advisory Opinion, issued on 23 July 2025. To better understand the Opinion and its innovations, we compare it to the findings of other international courts across three focal areas, namely the consolidation of the 1.5°C maximum warming threshold (II.), production-side obligations (III.) and reparations for climate-related harm (IV.). We show that, in

* Professor of Law & Governance in the Anthropocene at Tilburg Law School at Tilburg University. His research is funded by the ERC 2021 Starting Grant TransLitigate (101039648). The views expressed here are only of the author and do not reflect those of the EU or ERC.

** Assistant Professor of Constitutional and Administrative Law at Tilburg Law School and involved in these proceedings on behalf of the International Union for Conservation of Nature.

1 ICJ, *Obligations of States in Respect of Climate Change*, Advisory Opinion of 23 July 2025, No. 187.

2 ECtHR (Grand Chamber), *Verein KlimaSeniorinnen Schweiz and Others v. Switzerland*, judgement of 9 April 2024, no 53600/20.

3 ITLOS, *Request for an Advisory Opinion Submitted by the Commission of Small Island States on Climate Change and International Law*, Advisory Opinion of 21 May 2024, case no. 31.

4 IACtHR, *Advisory Opinion on Climate Emergency and Human Rights*, 29 May 2025, AO-32/25.

these three areas, the ICJ removed crucial barriers to effective, meaningful international climate obligations – but that more work is certainly needed to hold States accountable for their impacts on the global climate.

II. Consolidating the 1.5°C Maximum Warming Threshold

A first development that transcends recent international climate cases and opinions is the consolidation of the 1.5°C warming threshold as the key benchmark for evaluating States' obligations with respect to climate change mitigation. The Paris Agreement infamously included a dual maximum warming target, with the objective of both '[h]olding the increase in the global average temperature to well below 2°C above pre-industrial levels and pursuing efforts to limit the temperature increase to 1.5°C above pre-industrial levels'.[5]

Domestic courts had struggled to translate the dual objectives into concrete obligations. For example, the Dutch *Urgenda* case imposed a 25 % emissions reduction obligation that favoured the 2°C maximum warming threshold[6] and the German *Neubauer* decision[7] emphasized the awkwardly indeterminate objective enshrined in the Paris Agreement, with its aim of staying 'well below 2°C and preferably 1.5°C'. However, the IPCC's evolving scientific accounts of the harm associated with 1.5°C of warming, combined with the Parties' commitments in the 2021 Glasgow Climate Pact,[8] have since shifted emphasis towards the 1.5°C threshold despite its more aspirational phrasing in the Paris Agreement.

These latter sources informed the ICJ's decision to definitively consolidate the more ambitious warming threshold. The Court stated that it 'considers the 1.5°C threshold to be the parties' agreed primary temperature goal for limiting the global average temperature increase under the Paris Agreement' and that this threshold is associated with the current 'best

5 Paris Agreement, 12 December 2015, 3156 UNTS 79, Art. 2(1)a.

6 For the final judgment in this case, see Dutch Hoge Raad, *The Netherlands v. Stichting Urgenda*, judgement of 13 January 2020, ECLI:NL:HR:2019:2007.

7 German Federal Constitutional Court, Order of 24 March 2021, 1 BvR 2656/18 and others, BVerfGE 157, 30.

8 Conference of the Parties serving as the meeting of the Parties to the Paris Agreement, 'Glasgow Climate Pact', Decision 1/CMA.3, 13 November 2021, as published in FCCC/PA/CMA/2021/10/Add.1, 8 March 2022.

available science'.[9] As such, 1.5°C, and not 2°C, is to be used in evaluating the sufficiency of States' actions with respect to their Paris Agreement obligations. As a reflection of 'best available science', the 1.5°C threshold also strongly informs States' obligation to prevent significant harm to the environment,[10] although the ICJ stopped short of explicitly defining warming beyond 1.5°C to constitute 'significant harm' in terms of the customary no-harm rule clarified elsewhere in the opinion.[11] This consolidation around the 1.5°C maximum warming objective reflects similar conclusions in the IACtHR and ITLOS opinions, as well as the *KlimaSeniorinnen* judgment.[12] The rapid transition from a 2°C to 1.5°C threshold in the past five years is all the more remarkable given that 2024 was the first year above 1.5°C,[13] which, if continued over the coming years, would mark the beginning of the failure to meet the Paris Agreement objective and prevent irreversible, far-reaching harm.

At the same time, the crystallization of the 1.5°C threshold raises questions about the legal consequences of climate-related harms which occur at warming levels *under* 1.5°C. Scholars have already noted how the use of such a threshold can prevent accountability for climate-related harms that are already ongoing, as well as distract from questions of equity associated with the historic, cumulative emissions that have particularly profited a small group of States at the expense of the global climate system.[14] The ICJ did observe that, in general, 'the accumulation of GHG emissions in the atmosphere is causing significant harm to the climate system and other parts of the environment'.[15] It also noted, concerning reparations, that 'what constitutes a wrongful act is not the emissions in and of themselves but actions or omissions causing significant harm to the climate system

9 ICJ, *Obligations of States in Respect of Climate Change* (n. 1), para. 224.

10 ICJ, *Obligations of States in Respect of Climate Change* (n. 1), para. 278.

11 ICJ, *Obligations of States in Respect of Climate Change* (n. 1), especially paras. 272–300.

12 IACtHR, *Advisory Opinion on Climate Emergency and Human Rights* (n. 4), para. 509; ITLOS, *Request for an Advisory Opinion Submitted by the Commission of Small Island States on Climate Change and International Law* (n. 3), para. 243; ECtHR, *KlimaSeniorinnen* (n. 2), para. 436.

13 Emanuele Bevacqua, Carl-Friedrich Schleussner and Jakob Zscheischler, 'A Year Above 1.5 °C Signals that Earth is Most Probably Within the 20-year Period that Will Reach the Paris Agreement Limit', *Nature Climate Change* 15 (2025), 262–265.

14 Juan Auz and Phillip Paiement, 'The Neocolonial Violence of the 1.5°C Threshold', Open Global Rights, 5 October 2023.

15 ICJ, *Obligations of States in Respect of Climate Change* (n. 1), para. 278.

in breach of a State's international obligations'.[16] This suggests that the evaluation of whether a State is committing an internationally unlawful act by failing to act diligently in their effort to prevent significant harm via direct or indirect contributions to GHG emissions remains a question to be evaluated separately from – though informed in part by – the Paris Agreement obligations of pursuing mitigation to remain under 1.5°C. But such a clarification is not explicitly found in the Advisory Opinion.

III. Bringing Attention Towards Production-side Obligations

A second area in which the ICJ's Advisory Opinion marked a stark departure from the text of the Paris Agreement is in the recognition of State obligations related to the production of fossil fuels – a disruptive and controversial but vitally important finding.[17] The Paris Agreement's Art. 4 obligations around Nationally Determined Contributions exclusively focus on States' commitments to achieve 'economy-wide absolute emissions reduction', referring to all sectors of fossil fuel consumption, but with no commitments related to fossil fuel production. While the COP28 outcome document highlighted the need to transition away from fossil fuels and related subsidies,[18] few fossil fuel-producing States focus on reducing fossil fuel production in their most recent NDCs.[19]

Nonetheless, the ICJ remarked unequivocally that the '[f]ailure of a State to take appropriate action to protect the climate system from GHG emissions — including through fossil fuel production, fossil fuel consumption, the granting of fossil fuel exploration licences or the provision of fossil fuel subsidies — may constitute an internationally wrongful act which

16 ICJ, *Obligations of States in Respect of Climate Change* (n. 1), para. 429.

17 Jannika Jahn and Marlene Letsch, 'Progress Through Disruption? What Role for the ICJ in the Advisory Opinion on Climate Change', EJIL:Talk!, 22 January 2025; Andrej Lang and Denise Koecke, 'Rising to the Occasion: The World Court as Architect of a Harmonious International Climate LawFramework', in this volume; Marisa McVey and Annalisa Savaresi, 'The ICJ Advisory Opinion on Climate Change: A Business and Human Rights Perspective', Opinio Juris, 4 August 2025.

18 Conference of the Parties serving as the meeting of the Parties to the Paris Agreement, 'Outcome of the First Global Stocktake', draft decision -/CMA.5, 13 December 2023, FCCC/PA/CMA/2023/L.17, para. 28(d) and (h).

19 Natalie Jones, 'What NDCs 3.0 Are (and Aren't) Saying About Fossil Fuel Production', IISD Insight, 6 June 2025.

is attributable to that State'.[20] It derived this finding based on its own well-established case-law that 'the conduct of any organ of a State must be regarded as an act of that State'.[21] Although not explicitly drawing on a legal comparison, this too, parallels the IACtHR's Advisory Opinion.[22] It is a remarkable development that stands in contrast to a predominant trend in climate litigation, which has tended to focus on consumption-related obligations of States. The ICJ builds on this production-side obligation to further specify that States have an obligation to regulate the activities of private actors engaged in both production and consumption of fossil fuels as part of their 'regulatory due diligence'.[23]

The ICJ's finding on regulatory due diligence obligations is particularly impactful in the context of litigation against influential production-side private actors (for instance, claims against BNP Paribas[24] and TotalEnergies[25] in France, Mercedes-Benz[26] and BMW[27] in Germany, and ING[28] and Royal Dutch Shell[29] in the Netherlands). Oil and gas companies, financial sector actors and other major economic actors who mainly contribute to climate change through the Scope 3 emissions associated with the consumption of their eventual products often face minimal legislative or regulatory frameworks requiring the reduction of their Scope 1, 2 and 3 emissions. Instead, the respective States have chosen to largely use market mechanisms to trigger consumption reductions. The question here is whether the ICJ has laid the groundwork for treating these responses as situations in which States have failed to act diligently to regulate the production-side private actors in

20 ICJ, *Obligations of States in Respect of Climate Change* (n. 1), para. 427.

21 ICJ, *Armed Activities on the Territory of the Congo* (Democratic Republic of the Congo v. Uganda), merits, judgement of 19 December 2005, ICJ Reports 2005, 168, para. 213, citing ICJ, *Difference Relating to Immunity from Legal Process of a Special Rapporteur of the Commission on Human Rights*, Advisory Opinion of 29 April 1999, ICJ Reports 1999 (I) 87, para. 62.

22 IACtHR, *Advisory Opinion on Climate Emergency and Human Rights* (n. 4), para. 353.

23 ICJ, *Obligations of States in Respect of Climate Change* (n. 1), para. 428.

24 Tribunal judiciaire de Paris, *Notre Affaire à Tous, Les Amis de la Terre, and Oxfam France v. BNP Paribas*, summons of 23 February 2023.

25 Paris Court of Appeal, *Greenpeace France and Others v. TotalEnergies SE*, judgment of 18 June 2024, no. RG 23/14348.

26 Landgericht Stuttgart, 13 September 2022, 17 O 789/21 (*Metz et al. v Mercedes-Benz*).

27 Oberlandesgericht München, 12 October 2023, 32 U 936/23 (*Metz et al. v BMW*).

28 *Milieudefensie v. ING Bank and Others*, summons of 16 January 2025.

29 The Hague Court of Appeal, *Milieudefensie and Others v Royal Dutch Shell PLC and Others*, 12 November 2024, ECLI:NL:GHDHA:2024:2100.

their jurisdiction; in other words: a situation of regulatory failure. If so, that would have a tremendous impact on both the legal consequences for those States, as well as for the production-side private actors themselves, who argue that their compliance with existing regulatory frameworks affords them a 'safe haven' from civil liability related to harm resulting indirectly from their actions.

IV. Reparations for Climate-related Harm

A third notable area in which the ICJ's Advisory Opinion expanded on the international climate regime concerns reparations. This issue relates to long-standing debates on compensation and redistribution taking place under the United Nations Framework Convention on Climate Change (UNFCCC) umbrella.[30] For example, the Paris Agreement was adopted in the understanding that its provision on loss and damage, Article 8 of the Agreement, 'does not involve or provide a basis for any liability or compensation'.[31] In recent years, this starting point has been complemented by the operationalization of loss and damage funding mechanisms that operate on a pledge-based (voluntary) basis.[32] As estimates of the economic and non-economic loss and damage associated with climate change continue to mount, these mechanisms remain grossly inadequate to compensate climate-vulnerable States, raising serious equity concerns.[33]

The Court was asked to consider whether the customary rules on State responsibility, which go beyond what is provided for in the Paris Agreement, apply to breaches of climate-related obligations – or whether the application of these rules is instead precluded by the climate treaties, as a *lex specialis.* In considering this, the Court held that, because the relevant provisions of the Paris Agreement do not concern responsibility or the

30 United Nations Framework Convention on Climate Change, 9 May 1992, 1771 UNTS 107.

31 Conference of the Parties to the UNFCCC, 'Adoption of the Paris Agreement', Decision 1/CP.21, 29 January 2016, FCCC/CP/2015/10/Add.1, para. 51.

32 For a discussion of recent developments, see Adrián Martínez Blanco and Patrick Toussaint, 'Addressing Loss and Damage at COP29 and Beyond: Priorities and Uncertainties in the Future of Loss and Damage Finance', Völkerrechtsblog, 13 November 2024.

33 On non-economic loss and damage, see Alejandra Padin-Dujon, 'What is "Non-Economic" Loss and Damage (NELD)?', Grantham Institute Explainers, 20 June 2023.

settling of disputes, they do not exclude the application of customary rules on reparation. The Court went on to clarify issues of attribution (including concerning fossil fuels and private actors, as discussed above) and causation, and held that the main mitigation obligations set forth in the climate change treaties apply *erga omnes*, meaning that any State can bring proceedings against infringements of these collective obligations. It then clarified the legal consequences arising from breaches of climate-related obligations, including duties to perform the obligations breached, to put an end to the wrongful act (including by amending domestic law), and the duty of reparation, which can include obligations of restitution (restoring infrastructure and ecosystems), financial compensation and satisfaction (for example, formal apologies or educating society about climate change).[34]

Here, too, the ICJ's findings are explicitly rooted in the Court's own past case-law, without relying on comparative legal arguments. Situating these findings comparatively shows that the ICJ's Advisory Opinion goes beyond that of the ITLOS – which was not asked to consider responsibility or liability – and also beyond the *KlimaSeniorinnen* judgment of the ECtHR, which awarded only modest costs and expenses. The IACtHR, by contrast, transcended the loss and damage debate, and like the ICJ explored a broad range of measures required to provide reparation. The IACtHR has a strong track-record in this regard, having recognized obligations to provide financial compensation, restitution, rehabilitation, satisfaction and guarantees of non-repetition.[35] Its climate Advisory Opinion highlighted the need to provide victims with effective redress, restore ecosystems, fund conservation, provide adequate medical care, and reduce vulnerability.[36] And, by declaring planetary habitability a norm of *jus cogens*,[37] the IACtHR likewise seems to have recognized that it gives rise to obligations *erga omnes*.

34 Previously, on compensation, see ICJ, *Certain Activities Carried Out by Nicaragua in the Border Area* (Costa Rica v. Nicaragua), compensation, judgement of 16 December 2015, ICJ Reports 2018, 5.

35 For an analysis, see Juan Auz, 'The Political Ecology of Climate Remedies in Latin America and the Caribbean: Comparing Compliance between National and Inter-American Litigation', JHRP 16(1) (2024), 182–207.

36 IACtHR, *Advisory Opinion on Climate Emergency and Human Rights* (n. 4), paras. 556–559.

37 IACtHR, *Advisory Opinion on Climate Emergency and Human Rights* (n. 4), para. 291.

There are, however, some notable differences between the two opinions. First, the IACtHR derived its findings on reparations from the human right to an effective remedy, and not from customary law as the ICJ did.[38] Secondly, as a human rights court, the IACtHR focused on the rights of individuals, communities and nature; the ICJ, although contemplating the possibility of reparations claims for breaches of human rights law in the abstract, was predominantly focused on reparation between States, and left the issue of individual claims to specialized treaty regimes.[39] Thirdly, the IACtHR contemplated the possibility of debt relief for States, something the ICJ was wary of.[40] And last but not least, the IACtHR's opinion takes a contextual and vulnerability-sensitive approach to reparations, mentioning that they must be based on both science and (Indigenous and traditional) knowledge, and must guarantee effective access to justice for the individuals and communities concerned.[41] By contrast, in its remedial considerations, the ICJ not only refused to differentiate among States based on their level of vulnerability to the impacts of climate change,[42] but also did not engage with the barriers to justice facing vulnerable individuals.

This comparison shows that, while throwing the door wide open to reparations claims on the interstate level – subject, of course, to States' acceptance of its jurisdiction[43] – the ICJ retained ambiguity around available remedies for affected peoples and individuals. This highlights the continued value of the work of human rights treaties and courts, as an important complement to interstate proceedings.

V. Conclusion

The ICJ's Advisory Opinion definitively announced a new era of international climate change law, an era in which the UNFCCC, Paris Agreement

38 For a discussion see Juan Auz, 'The Inter-American Court of Human Rights' Advisory Opinion on the Climate Emergency: A Global South Contribution to Climate Governance', EJIL:Talk!, 18 July 2025.

39 ICJ, *Obligations of States in Respect of Climate Change* (n. 1), paras. 111, 433 and 449.

40 Contrast IACtHR, *Advisory Opinion on Climate Emergency and Human Rights* (n. 4), para. 208, with ICJ, *Obligations of States in Respect of Climate Change* (n. 1), para. 262.

41 IACtHR, *Advisory Opinion on Climate Emergency and Human Rights* (n. 4), para. 559.

42 ICJ, *Obligations of States in Respect of Climate Change* (n. 1), paras. 109–110.

43 Article 36 of the ICJ Statute (Statute of the International Court of Justice, 24 October 1945, XV UNCIO 355).

and Kyoto Protocol are but few of many relevant instruments framing the obligations of States with respect to climate change. In doing so, the Court addressed make-or-break issues for international obligations in this context that have emerged in the past two years of international adjudication, including but not limited to the themes addressed here: the consolidation of the 1.5°C maximum warming threshold, the recognition of production-side obligations, and finally, the identification of diverse remedies available when States fail to perform the climate obligations they have *erga omnes*. While the Court does not rely on comparative argumentation in these three contexts, it is nevertheless apparent that the substance of its findings did not emerge in a vacuum. Instead, they consolidate ongoing legal developments and debates, yielding extensive alignment with the findings of other international adjudicators – especially the IACtHR – regarding all three themes explored here. Ultimately, the Court delivered a remarkable opinion that performs a challenging task of maintaining the successful elements of the Paris Agreement while contextualizing them in a much further-reaching set of diverse obligations, the latter of which seriously bring into question the sufficiency of climate and energy policies of developed States around the world.

The ICJ and the UN Climate Regime: Clarifying Mitigation Obligations under the Paris Agreement

Christina Voigt[*]

I. An Opinion by the 'World Court'

The 2-hour reading of the climate change Advisory Opinion by the president of the International Court of Justice (ICJ/the Court), judge Yuji Iwasawa, on 23 July 2025 was a historical moment. The Court put forward its legal view on two fundamental questions of international law concerning an existential threat of planetary proportions that imperils all forms of life and the very health of our planet.[1] Not only had this case attracted the highest level of participation in both the history of the Court and that of its predecessor, the Permanent Court of International Justice;[2] it also concerned a legal issue never before addressed by the Court. In light of this, a commentator aptly noted: 'With this opinion, the ICJ really became the World Court'.

For those of us who were in the Great Hall of Justice that afternoon, this was tangible and audible by the gasps (and even tears) of euphoria and relief by several participants in the audience, especially by those who worked the hardest to get this case to the world´s highest court; who are most affected by the impacts of climate change.

The Court spoke with authority, clarity, consistency and comprehensiveness. By doing so, it left no doubt about the multiple, parallel and mutually supportive legal obligations of States to protect the climate system, stemming from various international treaties as well as customary international rules, based on a stringent due diligence standard – and about the legal consequences if these obligations are breached.

---

* Professor of Law, University of Oslo, Norway. Chair of the IUCN World Commission on Environmental Law, and lead legal counsel for IUCN in the ICJ AO proceedings.

1 ICJ, *Obligations of States in Respect of Climate Change*, Advisory Opinion of 23 July 2025, para. 456.

2 ICJ Press release, 23 July 2025, available at < https://www.icj-cij.org/sites/default/files/case-related/187/187-20250723-pre-01-00-en.pdf>.

II. ICJ as the First International Court to Interpret the Paris Agreement

Much has been and will be written about the findings of the Court. Many aspects deserve deeper analysis.[3] However, in the following, I will focus on one aspect which may have the most immediate impact: the clarification by the Court of the mitigation obligations under the Paris Agreement.

As a court of general competence, the ICJ considered the UN climate treaties, i.e. the UNFCCC, Kyoto Protocol and the Paris Agreement, to be principal legal instruments regulating the international response to the global problem of climate change[4] among the directly relevant applicable

3 These include, for example, the customary obligations of harm prevention and cooperation in the context of climate change (see Jutta Brunnée, 'The Advisory Opinion on *Obligations of States in Respect of Climate Change*: Harm Prevention under Customary International Law', in this volume; Jannika Jahn and Nele Suchantke, 'The ICJ Advisory Opinion on Climate Change: From Carbon Sovereignty to Trusteeship of the Climate Commons', in this volume), the elements for determining strict due diligence (again see Jutta Brunnée, 'The Advisory Opinion on *Obligations of States in Respect of Climate Change*: Harm Prevention under Customary International Law', in this volume), the mutual supportiveness of different treaties (see Andrej Lang and Denise Koecke, 'Rising to the Occasion: The World Court as Architect of a Harmonious International Climate Law Framework', in this volume), human right to a clean, healthy and sustainable environment as a precondition for other human rights (see Hellen Keller, 'A Right to a Clean, Healthy and Sustainable Environment – or Perhaps not (yet)?', in this volume), the legal effects of sea level rise, such as the absence of an obligation of States to update charts of maritime zones (ICJ, *Obligations of States in Respect of Climate Change* (n. 1), paras. 358–362. See Rozemarijn Roland Holst, 'Climate Change Law and the Law of the Sea: Systemic Impacts of the ICJ and ITLOS Advisory Opinions Read Together', in this volume) and the presumption of the continuity of statehood even if constituent elements disappear (ICJ, *Obligations of States in Respect of Climate Change* (n. 1), para. 363. See Dave-Inder Comar, 'The ICJ's Historic Nod to Self-Determination and Climate Change Impacts', in this volume), migration and the role of non-refoulement (ICJ, *Obligations of States in Respect of Climate Change* (n. 1), para. 378. See Malavika Rao'Climate Displacement in the ICJ's Advisory Opinion: Recognised but not Resolved', in this volume), obligations *erga omnes* (see again Jannika Jahn and Nele Suchantke, 'The ICJ Advisory Opinion on Climate Change: From Carbon Sovereignty to Trusteeship of the Climate Commons', in this volume), the implications of non-repetition and cessation of internationally wrongful acts, as well as the consequences of State responsibility (see Phillip Paiement and Corina Heri, 'Strengthening International Climate Obligations Beyond Paris: Situating the ICJ's Opinion within a Comparative Legal Context', in this volume) – and many more.

4 ICJ, *Obligations of States in Respect of Climate Change* (n. 1), para. 116.

law sources.[5] This allowed it to be the first international court to interpret the provisions of the Paris Agreement with a profound level of detail.[6]

This situation was not unexpected. Many participants had during the proceedings pointed to the Paris Agreement in their written and oral statements. The challenge, however, was that the legal weight and views regarding the Agreement differed significantly: from being worth nothing, to being the only game in town, but with only discretionary, voluntary commitments. The Court proved both ends of this spectrum of opinions wrong.

By applying a careful and diligent legal analysis, it interpreted the provisions of the Paris Agreement in light of its the object and purpose and context. In doing so, it established the clear content of the Agreement's climate change mitigation provisions. This is not a small feat, especially given the long and contentious negotiations of the Agreement[7] and its high degree of complexity and ambiguity.[8]

III. The Relationship between UNFCCC and the Paris Agreement

The Court clarified the relationship between the UNFCCC and the Agreement (and the Kyoto Protocol) as both being independent international treaties with their own decision-making bodies – the COP and the CMA (and CMP), respectively. It also reiterated that the Paris Agreement is not a protocol to the UNFCCC.[9] Yet, they complement each other.[10] While the UNFCCC serves a foundational and coordinating purpose for its related

---

5 Which also included the UN Charter, UNCLOS, international human rights treaties, CBD, the Ozone treaties (Vienna Convention and Montreal Protocol), UNCCD, customary norms, i.e. harm prevention and cooperation, and relevant principles.

6 ITLOS and the IACtHR in their respective climate change Advisory Opinions had referred to the Paris Agreement as relevant in the interpretations of the legal treaties under their jurisdiction but did not provide a detailed interpretation of the Agreement.

7 Daniel Klein, Daniel Klein, María Pía Carazo, Meinhard Doelle, Jane Bulmer, Andrew Higham (eds), *The Paris Agreement on Climate Change: Analysis and Commentary* (Oxford University Press 2017); Lavanya Rajamani, 'The 2015 Paris Agreement: Interplay Between Hard, Soft and Non-Obligations', JEL 28 (2016) 337–358.

8 Daniel Bodansky, 'The Legal Character of the Paris Agreement', RECIEL 25 (2016), 142–150.

9 ICJ, *Obligations of States in Respect of Climate Change* (n. 1), para. 193.

10 ICJ, *Obligations of States in Respect of Climate Change* (n. 1), para. 120.

legal instruments on climate change, including the Paris Agreement,[11] the Agreement translates the basic principles and general obligations of the UNFCCC into a set of more specific, interrelated obligations.[12]

While the Court recognizes the Paris Agreement as the most recent and most comprehensive universal treaty addressing climate change, it did not consider it to be *lex posterior* nor *lex specialis* to the UNFCCC.[13] The Court based this finding on the absence of any incompatibility between the two treaties. In particular the explicit reference in the chapeau of Art. 2 of the Agreement to 'enhancing the implementation of the Convention, including its objective' considered the Court to indicate that the Paris Agreement furthers the UNFCCC's ultimate objective of 'stabilization of the greenhouse gas concentrations in the atmosphere at a level that would prevent dangerous anthropogenic interference with the climate system' (UNFCCC, Article 2) – and does not conflict with it.[14] It even went so far to consider the UNFCCC's overall objective to constitute the object and purpose of the Paris Agreement, with the temperature goal of the Agreement providing a means for achieving this object and purpose.[15] The Court therefore found that not only are the two treaties not incompatible, but are mutually supportive, with the Paris Agreement providing greater specification to the general obligations contained in the UNFCCC.[16]

In this context, the Court also clarified that while the UN climate treaties are the principal instruments with respect to climate change obligations, they do not constitute *lex specialis* in relation to other rules with respect to climate change – both treaty and customary international law.[17] The Court could not find any actual inconsistencies between the climate change treaties and other relevant ules and principles of international law.[18] Rather, it considered them a single set of compatible obligations;[19] informing and complementing each other in a mutually supportive manner.[20]

---

11 ICJ, *Obligations of States in Respect of Climate Change* (n. 1), para. 117.
12 ICJ, *Obligations of States in Respect of Climate Change* (n. 1), paras. 120, 195.
13 ICJ, *Obligations of States in Respect of Climate Change* (n. 1), para. 223.
14 ICJ, *Obligations of States in Respect of Climate Change* (n. 1), para. 194.
15 ICJ, *Obligations of States in Respect of Climate Change* (n. 1), para. 225.
16 ICJ, *Obligations of States in Respect of Climate Change* (n. 1), para. 195.
17 ICJ, *Obligations of States in Respect of Climate Change* (n. 1), para. 163.
18 ICJ, *Obligations of States in Respect of Climate Change* (n. 1), para. 168.
19 ICJ, *Obligations of States in Respect of Climate Change* (n. 1), para 165.
20 ICJ, *Obligations of States in Respect of Climate Change* (n. 1), paras. 324, 329, 334. See Andrej Lang and Denise Koecke (n. 3), in this volume.

IV. The 1.5°C Temperature Goal

One of the most surprising elements in the interpretation of the Paris Agreement is the Court´s dealing with the temperature goal. The Court first established that the Agreement´s aim of 'holding the increase in the global average temperature to well below 2°C above pre-industrial levels' and pursuing efforts 'to limit the temperature increase to 1.5°C above pre-industrial levels' in Art. 2.1(a) represents an 'important concretization',[21] and 'specification and quantification'[22] of the UNFCCCs overall objective of preventing dangerous interference with the climate system.

Yet, Art. 2.1(a) mentions two goals: 'well below 2°C' and '1.5°C'. Here, the Court clarified that 1.5°C has become the 'scientifically based consensus target under the Paris Agreement' and is the 'primary temperature goal'.[23] It bases its finding on decisions by the CMA after the Agreement was adopted, especially the Glasgow Climate Pact (Decision 1/CMA.3) and the Outcome of the First Global Stocktake (Decision 1/CMA.5), which, in the Court's view, express agreement in substance between the parties regarding the interpretation of Articles 2 and 4 of the Paris Agreement, and thus constitute subsequent agreements in relation to the interpretation of the Paris Agreement within the meaning of Article 31.3(a) of the Vienna Convention on the Law of Treaties. This finding in the context of the temperature goal provides helpful guidance on the relative importance of the temperature goals to each other and on the question of to which goal to adhere.

This finding by the Court may have relevant implications in future negotiations under the CMA. It puts considerable legal weight on CMA decisions. While this can be a positive development, it may also complicate further the process of reaching consensus, if parties expect that their consensus expressed in, from the outset non-binding, CMA decisions can be interpreted as binding subsequent agreements.

V. Mitigation Obligations in the Paris Agreement

In the Advisory Opinion in general, and in the analysis of the Paris Agreement in particular, the Court put significant focus on mitigation

21 ICJ, *Obligations of States in Respect of Climate Change* (n. 1), para. 223.
22 ICJ, *Obligations of States in Respect of Climate Change* (n. 1), para. 270.
23 ICJ, *Obligations of States in Respect of Climate Change* (n. 1), para. 224.

obligations as those are most directly linked to 'protecting the climate system'. The Court therefore set out to clarify the mitigation obligations in the Paris Agreement, which are found in art. 4.[24] It distinguished them in obligations of result and obligations of conduct, although admitting that these categories are not always clear cut and are mutually supportive.[25] In interpreting the provisions in art. 4, the Court took into account the temperature goal contained in Article 2 and referenced in Article 4, paragraph 1, which constitutes, in addition to the object and purpose of the Agreement, the 'context' relevant for the interpretation of obligations in the Paris Agreement.[26]

1. Obligations of Result

With respect to mitigation, the Court identified several obligations of result: Art. 4.2 (to prepare, communicate and maintain successive NDCs), Art. 4.9 (every 5 years), Art. 4.13 (accounting) and Art. 4.12 (registration in public registry).[27] Although these are obligations of result (and procedural in nature), the Court noted that the 'mere formal preparation, communication and maintenance of successive NDCs is not sufficient to comply with the obligations under Article 4'.[28] It explained that 'an obligation of result, such as, for example, an obligation to "adopt national policies and take corresponding measures on the mitigation of climate change", cannot be met merely by the adoption of any policies and the taking of corresponding measures. To comply with this obligation of result, the policies so adopted, and the measures so taken must be such that they are able to achieve the required goal. In other words, the adoption of a policy, and the taking

24 ICJ, *Obligations of States in Respect of Climate Change* (n. 1), para. 230.

25 ICJ, *Obligations of States in Respect of Climate Change* (n. 1), para. 228.

26 ICJ, *Obligations of States in Respect of Climate Change* (n. 1), para. 231.

27 ICJ, *Obligations of States in Respect of Climate Change* (n. 1), para. 235. Other obligations of result, such as to submit Biennial Transparency Reports under Art. 13.7 PA, to participate in the Facilitative Multilateral Consideration of progress under Art. 13.11 PA, and the communication of biennial information under Art. 9.5 PA (see for these obligations: Decision 20/CMA.1, para 22.1(a)) were not considered by the Court.

28 ICJ, *Obligations of States in Respect of Climate Change* (n. 1), para. 236.

of related measures, as a mere formality is not sufficient to discharge the obligation of result.'[29]

This led the Court to consider obligations with respect to the *content* of NDCs.

2. Obligations of Conduct

a) Content of NDCs

The legal status of NDCs, especially regarding their content, was one of the most contentious issues during the negotiations of the Paris Agreement. Several parties wanted NDCs to be legally binding, for example by being annexed to the Paris Agreement. Other Parties were of the view that the 'pledge and review' concept which emerged from the Copenhagen Accord was the appropriate way forward, where submitting NDCs would be merely a procedural obligation, but their content, and especially their achievement, would not fall within the legally-binding scope of the Agreement. The compromise was the formulation in Art. 4.2, which is silent on the content of NDCs, and the ambiguous formulation in Art. 4.2, second sentence, on the aim to achieve NDC. Ever since the adoption of the Agreement, it was therefore often (misleadingly) characterised as 'bottom-up' and NDCs as voluntary and discretionary.

The ICJ smashed this characterisation by clearly confirming that both the content and the implementation and achievement of NDCs are obligations of conduct, based on a stringent due diligence standard.

It explained that States do not enjoy unfettered discretion when preparing NDCs.[30] Rather, their discretion is limited.[31] As an obligation of conduct, parties are obliged to exercise due diligence when putting forward their NDC. Accordingly, NDCs must satisfy certain expectations and standards under the Paris Agreement that apply to parties in preparing their NDCs, as set out in Art. 4.3.[32]

---

29 ICJ, *Obligations of States in Respect of Climate Change* (n. 1), para. 208.
30 ICJ, *Obligations of States in Respect of Climate Change* (n. 1), para. 270.
31 ICJ, *Obligations of States in Respect of Climate Change* (n. 1), para. 245.
32 ICJ, *Obligations of States in Respect of Climate Change* (n. 1), para. 249.

The Court clarified that Art. 4.3 is not a merely voluntary expectation. It stated that:

> 'While Article 4, paragraph 3, uses the term "will", rather than the prescriptive term "shall" in relation to the content of NDCs, the Court considers that the provision is not to be read as merely hortatory, as suggested by some participants. Rather, the term "will" is used here in a prescriptive sense, reflecting the expectation that "successive nationally determined contributions will represent a progression" and "reflect [a party's] highest possible ambition", without prescribing precisely what constitutes a progression, or what reflects a party's highest possible ambition. In these proceedings, it falls on the Court to shed light on the meaning and scope of the terms contained in Article 4, paragraph 3, thereby clarifying for parties their obligations relating to the content of their NDCs.'[33]

These standards require, first, that NDCs need to represent a progression, which the Court interpreted as a legal obligation of due diligence that 'a party's NDCs must become more demanding over time'.[34]

Second, the Court stated that, as a requirement of exercising due diligence, a party's NDCs must reflect highest possible ambition, to which many parties had referred to in their oral statements. It stated:

> 'While this term is not defined in the Paris Agreement, the Court considers that the level of ambition to be reflected in a party's NDCs has not been left entirely to the discretion of the parties. The provision [...] reveals that the content of a party's NDCs must, in fulfilment of its obligations under the Paris Agreement, be capable of making an adequate contribution to the achievement of the temperature goal. In the present instance, the relevant context is to be found, inter alia, in Article 3, which sets the expectation that parties are to "undertake and communicate ambitious efforts as defined in Articles 4, 7, 9, 10, 11 and 13 with the view to achieving the purpose of this Agreement as set out in Article 2. This provision reveals the necessity for the ambition contained in a party's NDC to relate to the object and purpose of the Agreement set out in

33 ICJ, *Obligations of States in Respect of Climate Change* (n. 1), para. 240.
34 ICJ, *Obligations of States in Respect of Climate Change* (n. 1), para. 241.

Article 2, i.e. to hold the increase in the global average temperature to below 1.5°C.'[35]

Literature had long pointed to such obligations of conduct contained in the Paris Agreement[36] and has recently provided more detail on the contours of 'highest possible ambition' in Art. 4.3.[37] It is suggested there that in the preparation of NDCs a State must do the best it can – its utmost – when preparing each successive NDC. The preparation of the NDC needs to be based on a comprehensive assessment of all mitigation options in all relevant sectors. Parties should deploy all political, legal, socio-economic, financial and institutional capacities and possibilities in defining their NDC objectives. Moreover, parties are expected to align their level of ambition with their respective responsibilities and capabilities, considering national circumstances. Parties also need to plan their climate strategies holistically and within a long-term period. In this context, it is important to align NDCs with long-term low greenhouse gas emission development strategies.

Third, parties must be informed by the outcomes of the Global Stocktake in the preparation of their NDCs, according to Arts. 14.3 and 4.9., and when communicating their NDCs must provide the information necessary for clarity, transparency and understanding, according to Art. 4.8.

All these elements determine the obligation of conduct to be exercised by parties when preparing the content of their NDC.

The standard applicable to this obligation of conduct is due diligence, which varies depending on a range of factors such as the risk of harm and the urgency involved, the need to take appropriate and, if necessary, precautionary measures, which take account of scientific and technological information, as well as relevant rules and international standards, and which vary depending on each State's respective capabilities, undertaking risk assessments and notifying and consulting other States, as appropriate.[38]

---

35 ICJ, *Obligations of States in Respect of Climate Change* (n. 1), para. 242.

36 Voigt, Christina, 'The Paris Agreement: What is the standard of conduct for Parties?', QIL 26 (2016), 17–28; Christina Voigt, 'The Power of the Paris Agreement in International Climate Litigation', RECIEL 32 (2023), 237 -249; Benoit Mayer, 'The 'Highest Possible Ambition' on Climate Change Mitigation as a Legal Standard' ICLQ 73 (2024), 285–317.

37 Voigt, Christina; Sauter, Philipp; Guerreiro Teixeira Rita; Rogelj, Joeri; Schleussner, Carl and Sulyok, Katalin, 'The Legal Power of Highest Possible Ambition – Setting Legal and Scientific Benchmarks to Assess Highest Possible Ambition under Article 4(3) of the Paris Agreement', CLLA 15 (2025), 1–24.

38 ICJ, *Obligations of States in Respect of Climate Change* (n. 1), para. 134.

Because of the seriousness of the threat posed by climate change, the Court considered that the standard of due diligence is stringent when preparing each party´s successive NDC.[39] According to the Court, this means that 'each party has to do its utmost to ensure that the NDCs it puts forward represent its highest possible ambition in order to realize the objectives of the Agreement'.[40]

NDCs must satisfy these standards under the Paris Agreement. A breach of this obligation of conduct would constitute an internationally wrongful act which can give rise to State responsibility.

b) Implementation and Achievement of NDCs

Further, not only the content of NDCs, but also their national implementation and achievement are obligations of conduct and are not voluntary. The Court noted that the obligation that parties 'shall pursue domestic mitigation measures' in Art. 4.2 (second sentence) is substantive in nature and creates an individual obligation of conduct for each party to the Agreement.[41]

This does not mean that parties are obligated to achieve their NDC targets, but rather that they must make best efforts, based on stringent due diligence to obtain such a result.[42] The Court considered that the obligation to 'pursue domestic mitigation measures' that aim to achieve the objectives of their NDCs requires States to be proactive and pursue domestic measures that are reasonably capable of achieving the NDCs set by them, including in relation to activities carried out by private actors.[43] These measures may include putting in place a national system, including legislation, administrative procedures and an enforcement mechanism, and exercising adequate vigilance to make such a system function effectively, with a view to achieving the objectives in their NDCs.'[44]

39 ICJ, *Obligations of States in Respect of Climate Change* (n. 1), para. 246.

40 ICJ, *Obligations of States in Respect of Climate Change* (n. 1), paras. 246, 270.

41 ICJ, *Obligations of States in Respect of Climate Change* (n. 1), para. 251.

42 ICJ, *Obligations of States in Respect of Climate Change* (n. 1), para. 254. See also Jutta Brunnée (n. 3), in this volume.

43 ICJ, *Obligations of States in Respect of Climate Change* (n. 1), para. 252. See Harro van Asselt, 'The Private Life of the ICJ Advisory Opinion on Climate Change', in this volume.

44 ICJ, *Obligations of States in Respect of Climate Change* (n. 1), para. 253.

VI. The Role of Common but Differentiated Responsibilities and Respective Capabilities (CBDR-RC), In the Light of Different National Circumstances

The obligation of conduct to do the utmost when preparing NDCs that progressively represent highest possible ambition, and the obligation of conduct to deploy best efforts when pursuing domestic measures to implement and achieve the NDCs apply to all parties. However, consistent with the principle of common but differentiated responsibilities and respective capabilities, the standard varies.[45] The Court noted that CBDR reflects the need to distribute equitably the burdens of the obligations in respect of climate change.

The Court observed that CBDR does not categorically place different burdens on whether a State is a developed or developing country. Rather, in the view of the Court, the principle calls for taking into account the circumstances of the State in question, such as historical and current contributions to cumulative GHG emissions, and their different current capabilities and national circumstances, including their economic and social level of development and other national circumstances.[46] The Court also observed that this principle has been formulated in the Paris Agreement by the addition of the phrase 'in the light of different national circumstances' which adds nuance to the principle by recognising that the status of a State as developed or developing is not static.[47]

Importantly, in this dynamic context, the Court notes that:

> 'on one end of the spectrum are the most developed States which have contributed significantly to the overall amount of GHG emissions since the Industrial Revolution, and which have resources and the technical capacity to implement wide-ranging emission reductions. On the other end are those least developed States that have contributed only minimally to

45 ICJ, *Obligations of States in Respect of Climate Change* (n. 1), para. 247.

46 ICJ, *Obligations of States in Respect of Climate Change* (n. 1), para. 148. See Lovleen Buhllar, 'The Advisory Opinion on Climate Justice and the "Global North-South Divide"', in this volume.

47 ICJ, *Obligations of States in Respect of Climate Change* (n. 1), para. 226. See on the nuanced and dynamic nature of CBDR, Christina Voigt and Felipe Ferreira, '"Dynamic Differentiation": The Principles of CBDR-RC, Progression and Highest Possible Ambition in the Paris Agreement' TEL 5 (2016), 285–303.

> historical emissions and have only a limited capacity to transform their economies. In between are States that have progressed considerably in their development since the conclusion of the UNFCCC in 1992, in line with that instrument's expectation that "the share of global emissions originating in developing countries will grow to meet their social and development needs" (UNFCCC, third preambular paragraph), and some of which now contribute significantly to global GHG emissions and possess the capacity to engage in meaningful mitigation and adaptation efforts, as well as other States with significant resources and technical capabilities to contribute to addressing global climate change.'[48]

Here, the observations by the Court on CBDR in the context of the customary harm prevention rule are also of relevance. In referring to the International Tribunal of the Law of the Sea climate change Advisory Opinion, the Court noted that CBDR 'requires a State with greater capabilities and sufficient resources to do more than a State not so well placed', but that, based on CBDR, 'implementing the obligation of due diligence requires even the latter State to take all the means at its disposal to protect the climate system in accordance with its capabilities and available resources'.[49] It stated:

> 'The difference between the respective capabilities of States, as one of the factors which determines the diligence required, cannot therefore merely result from a distinction between developed and developing countries, but must also depend on their respective national circumstances. The multifactorial and evolutive character of the due diligence standard entails that, as States develop economically and their capacity increases, so too are the requirements of diligence heightened. Finally, the reference to available means and capabilities cannot justify undue delay or a general exemption from the obligation to exercise due diligence.'[50]

VII. Legal Consequences

The clarification by the Court of the mitigation obligations in the Paris Agreement is crucial. The Agreement, while not the only treaty to contain climate change mitigation obligations, is the most comprehensive and spe-

48 ICJ, *Obligations of States in Respect of Climate Change* (n. 1), para. 150.
49 ICJ, *Obligations of States in Respect of Climate Change* (n. 1), para. 291.
50 ICJ, *Obligations of States in Respect of Climate Change* (n. 1), para. 292.

cific one. It is also the one to which due to the annual meeting of the COP significant political and stake-holder attention is garnered. Moreover, its 5-year cycles are put in place to ensure that Parties consistently and repeatedly review and improve their mitigation ambition. Importantly, the Court showed that the characterisation of the Agreement as voluntary, discretionary or 'bottom-up' was unfounded. Rather, Parties have a set of concrete obligations of result and obligations of conduct which must be exercised with stringent due diligence. Nothing is voluntary!

In the clear words of the Court

> 'to comply with their mitigation obligations, all parties must take measures, in fulfilment of their obligations under the Paris Agreement, that make an adequate contribution to achieving the collective temperature goal; these measures must be reflected in parties' NDCs which must be adjusted to be more demanding every five years; and these NDCs must, when taken together, be capable of achieving the temperature goal and the purposes of the Agreement. While the scope and content of measures contained in the NDCs may vary in accordance with the means available to parties and their capabilities, parties do not enjoy unfettered discretion in the preparation of their NDCs. Each party has a due diligence obligation to do its utmost to ensure that the NDCs it puts forward represent its highest possible ambition in order to realise the objectives of the Agreement (Article 4, paragraph 2). Consequently, parties have an obligation to undertake best efforts to achieve the content of their NDCs.'[51]

The interpretation of the preparation of NDCs as an obligation of conduct with Art. 4.3 establishing due diligence requirements in this regard had already been put forward right after the adoption of the Paris Agreement.[52] Yet, it took years before it was taken up in academic writing more broadly.[53] It is, thus, an important development in the discourse on the Paris Agreement, that the ICJ embraced the same understanding and clearly reject the perception of NDCs falling entirely in the discretion of States. This finding

51 ICJ, *Obligations of States in Respect of Climate Change* (n. 1), para. 270.
52 Christina Voigt (n. 36); Voigt and Ferreira (n. 47).
53 Mayer (n. 36); Lavanya Rajamani, 'Due Diligence in International Climate Change Law' in Anne Peters, Heike Krieger and Leonhard Kreuzer (eds), *Due Diligence in the International Legal Order* (Oxford University Press 2020), 163–180.

by the ICJ sent a powerful, timely and important signal to Parties in the preparation of the NDCs not only in 2025 – but every 5 years thereafter.

Finally, the clarification of the legal obligations regarding NDC may have immediate impact in domestic climate litigation. The interpretation of article 4 that says that every State must do its utmost in adopting – and then use its best efforts when implementing – an NDC of its highest possible ambition will be useful in domestic legal proceedings where Courts are asked to review the effectiveness and legality of their countries' climate plans and their implementation. States must use their regulatory power to be proactive and pursue measures that are reasonably capable of achieving the NDCs. This might be the push needed to close the ambition and implementation gap in NDCs.

However, if states do not follow suit, the ICJ clearly stated the consequences:

> 'Failure of a State to take appropriate action to protect the climate system from GHG emissions — including through fossil fuel production, fossil fuel consumption, the granting of fossil fuel exploration licences or the provision of fossil fuel subsidies — may constitute an internationally wrongful act which is attributable to that State. The Court also emphasizes that the internationally wrongful act in question is not the emission of GHGs per se, but the breach of conventional and customary obligations identified under question (a) pertaining to the protection of the climate system from significant harm resulting from anthropogenic emissions of such gases.'[54]

This includes the mitigation obligations under the Paris Agreement.

VIII. Conclusions

In the, so far, 10 years of its existence, the Paris Agreement has often been dismissively characterised as 'soft', 'weak' or 'voluntary'. The Court set an end to such misleading characterisation.

When it comes to mitigation, there is no voluntarism.

All parties to the Paris Agreement have an obligation of result to prepare, communicate and maintain successive and progressive NDC, and a sub-

54 ICJ, *Obligations of States in Respect of Climate Change* (n. 1), para. 427.

stantive obligation of conduct to act with stringent due diligence in putting forward increasingly demanding NDCs at the level of their highest possible ambition, that make an adequate contribution to achieving the 1.5°C goal, in accordance with their common but differentiated responsibilities and respective capabilities. They also must pursue, as a matter of obligation of conduct based on stringent due diligence, domestic mitigation measures capable of achieving the objectives set out in their NDCs.

While the ICJ Advisory Opinion contains many important, far-reaching findings. This one might have the most direct and immediate impact.

Climate Change Law and the Law of the Sea: Systemic Impacts of the ICJ and ITLOS Advisory Opinions Read Together

*Rozemarijn Roland Holst**

I. Introduction

From among the rich pickings of the International Court of Justice's ('ICJ') unanimous Advisory Opinion on climate change, this contribution focusses specifically on the relationship between international climate change law and the law of the sea. In doing so, it will reflect on the systemic impacts of the ICJ Advisory Opinion read together with the Advisory Opinion on climate change handed down by the International Tribunal for the Law of the Sea ('ITLOS') on 21 May 2024.[1]

The relationship between these parallel proceedings, both requested under the leadership of Small Island Developing States ('SIDS'), has been one of complementarity from the outset.[2] With both opinions now handed down, we can conclude that this complementarity and mutual supportiveness is reflected in their substantive findings too. It bears emphasis that the ICJ and ITLOS had different mandates and a different jurisdictional scope within which to answer the questions put to them. As a court of general jurisdiction, the ICJ has a broad mandate to interpret obligations of States in respect of climate change arising under any area of international law, with particular regard to those mentioned in the UN General Assembly's request,[3] including the Charter of the United Nations, the UN Convention on the Law of the Sea ('UNCLOS'), international human rights law, the

---

* Lecturer in International Environmental Law at the University of Edinburgh Law School.

1 ITLOS, *Request for an Advisory Opinion Submitted by the Commission of Small Island States on Climate Change and International Law,* Advisory Opinion of 21 May 2024, case no. 31.

2 Payam Akhavan and Rozemarijn Roland Holst, 'What Are the Legally Binding Obligations of States in Respect of Climate Change?' *IISD SDG Knowledge Hub*, 14 August 2024.

3 UNGA Res. 77/276 of 29 March 2023, 'Request for an Advisory Opinion of the International Court of Justice on the Obligations of States in Respect of Climate Change.

UN Framework Convention on Climate Change ('UNFCCC'), the Paris Agreement, and customary international environmental law. ITLOS' mandate is limited to interpreting UNCLOS, and the questions submitted to it concerned the obligations of States to protect and preserve the marine environment under Part XII of UNCLOS.[4] That said, both requests invited the ICJ and ITLOS respectively to clarify the relationship between international climate change law and the law of the sea, as indeed they did.

II. Issues Common to Both Requests

While the questions put to the ICJ were broader than those put to ITLOS, the Court recognises that there are issues common to the two requests.[5] It explains that '[a]lthough the Court is not obliged, in the exercise of its judicial functions, to model its own interpretation of UNCLOS on that of ITLOS, it considers that, in so far as it is called upon to interpret the Convention, it should ascribe great weight to the interpretation adopted by the Tribunal'.[6]

The ICJ proceeds to affirm ITLOS' main substantive findings, including: that anthropocentric GHG emissions fall under the definition of 'pollution of the marine environment' under UNCLOS Article 1(1)(4); that obligations under Part XII of UNCLOS to prevent, reduce and control pollution of the marine environment are thus applicable;[7] and that the obligation under UNCLOS Article 192 consists of a positive obligation to take measures to protect and preserve the marine environment and a negative obligation

4 COSIS, Request for an Advisory Opinion of 12 December 2022. See for a discussion i.a. Benoit Mayer, 'Request for an Advisory Opinion Submitted by the Commission of Small Island States on Climate Change and International Law' AJIL 119 (2025) 153-160; Joshua Paine, 'The ITLOS Advisory Opinion on Climate Change: Selected Issues of Treaty Interpretation', EJIL: Talk!, 3 June 2024; Diane Desierto, '"Stringent Due Diligence", Duties of Cooperation and Assistance to Climate Vulnerable States, and the Selective Integration of External Rules in the ITLOS Advisory Opinion on Climate Change and International Law', EJIL: Talk!, 3 June 2024.

5 ICJ, *Obligations of States in Respect of Climate Change*, Advisory Opinion of 23 July 2025, para. 337.

6 ICJ, *Obligations of States in Respect of Climate Change* (n. 5), para. 338.

7 ICJ, *Obligations of States in Respect of Climate Change* (n. 5), paras. 339–340; ITLOS, *Request for an Advisory Opinion Submitted by the Commission of Small Island States on Climate Change and International Law* (n. 1), paras. 161–179.

not to degrade it.[8] The ICJ also followed ITLOS in stressing that the standard of due diligence required in implementing these obligations under UNCLOS articles 192 and 194 is 'stringent' given the high risk of harm, and more severe for the riskier activities, while taking States' different capabilities into account.[9]

On the relationship between these obligations under UNCLOS and obligations under the climate change treaties, ITLOS – as the first international tribunal to rule on this matter – laid down several important foundations. First of all, ITLOS clarified that while the UNFCCC and Paris Agreement are 'relevant in interpreting and applying the Convention with respect to marine pollution from anthropogenic GHG emissions', the Tribunal does not consider that obligations under UNCLOS 'would be satisfied simply by complying with the obligations and commitments under the Paris Agreement'.[10] Secondly, it categorically rejected the argument put forward by some participants that the Paris Agreement constitutes a *lex specialis* to UNCLOS and that the latter therefore cannot impose more stringent requirements in relation to climate change than those contained in the Paris Agreement.[11] The Tribunal stressed that the 'Convention and the Paris Agreement are separate agreements, with separate sets of obligations' and that while the Paris Agreements complements UNCLOS, it 'does not supersede the latter'.[12]

The ICJ echoes this approach and applies it more broadly to the relationship between the climate change treaties and other rules of international law.[13] The ICJ also categorically rejected a variety of *lex specialis*-based arguments to the effect that the climate change regime would exclude the application of other rules of international law.[14] The Court further specified

8 ICJ, *Obligations in Respect of Climate Change* (n. 5), para. 342; ITLOS, *Request for an Advisory Opinion Submitted by the Commission of Small Island States on Climate Change and International Law* (n. 1), paras. 385, 387.

9 ICJ, *Obligations in Respect of Climate Change* (n. 5), paras. 343, 347; ITLOS, *Request for an Advisory Opinion Submitted by the Commission of Small Island States on Climate Change and International Law* (n. 1), paras. 239, 241.

10 ITLOS, *Request for an Advisory Opinion Submitted by the Commission of Small Island States on Climate Change and International Law* (n. 1), para. 223.

11 ITLOS, *Request for an Advisory Opinion Submitted by the Commission of Small Island States on Climate Change and International Law* (n. 1), paras. 220–221, 224.

12 ITLOS, *Request for an Advisory Opinion Submitted by the Commission of Small Island States on Climate Change and International Law* (n. 1), para. 223.

13 ICJ, *Obligations in Respect of Climate Change* (n. 5), paras. 309–315; 354.

14 ICJ, *Obligations in Respect of Climate Change* (n. 5), paras. 162–171.

that treaty obligations do not constitute *lex specialis* in relation to rules of customary international law, and that customary obligations are not fulfilled simply by States complying with their obligations under the climate change treaties.[15]

III. Issues on Which the ICJ Went Further

There are several points on which the ICJ could go further than ITLOS in spelling out the relationship between the law of the sea and climate change law, given its broader mandate to interpret for example the Paris Agreement in its own right, and not solely for the purposes of interpreting obligations under UNCLOS. For example, ITLOS – noting broad scientific agreement on the need to keep global warming below 1.5°C – identified this lower end of the temperature goal formulated in Article 2(1)(a) of the Paris Agreement as one relevant factor that States need to take into account in adopting the necessary measures to comply with obligations under UNCLOS.[16] The ICJ dealt with this point more elaborately and systematically, identifying not just scientific consensus on the 1.5°C target but also a series of COP decisions that, according to the Court, reflect subsequent agreement of the parties in relation to the interpretation of the Paris Agreement within the meaning of Article 31(3)(a) of the Vienna Convention on the Law of Treaties.[17]

Similarly, on the legal nature of States' nationally determined contributions ('NDCs') under the Paris Agreement, ITLOS observed briefly that the Paris Agreement 'does not require the Parties to reduce GHG emissions to any specific level according to a mandatory timeline but leaves each Party to determine its own national contributions in this regard'.[18] This

15 ICJ, *Obligations in Respect of Climate Change* (n. 5), para. 314. See also, Joint Declaration of Judges Charlesworth, Brant, Cleveland, and Aurescu as well as Declaration of Judge Nolte, *Obligations of States in Respect of Climate Change*, Advisory Opinion of 23 July 2025, para. 13; and for a discussion Julian Arato and Justina Uriburu, 'Treaty and Custom in the ICJ's Climate Change Opinion', EJIL: Talk!, 24 July 2025.

16 ITLOS, *Request for an Advisory Opinion Submitted by the Commission of Small Island States on Climate Change and International Law* (n. 1), para. 243.

17 ICJ, *Obligations in Respect of Climate Change* (n. 5), para. 224; and Declaration by Judge Tladi, *Obligations of States in Respect of Climate Change*, Advisory Opinion of 23 July 2025, paras. 9–13.

18 ITLOS, *Request for an Advisory Opinion Submitted by the Commission of Small Island States on Climate Change and International Law* (n. 1), para. 22.

could be read to imply that States enjoy an almost unfettered discretion in determining the content of their NDCs, as many participants in the ICJ proceedings have indeed argued.[19] Based on a detailed interpretation of Article 4 of the Paris Agreement in its context and in light of the object and purpose of the Agreement, the ICJ concluded that the discretion of parties in the preparation of their NDCs is limited, that NDCs must satisfy certain standards under the Paris Agreement and are thus open to scrutiny. Notably States must exercise due diligence and ensure that, when taken together, NDCs are actually capable of achieving the 1.5°C temperature goal.[20]

The ICJ also took the opportunity to interpret a number of obligations under UNCLOS in relation to sea level rise and related issues, which the ITLOS opinion has not dealt with. While several participants in the ITLOS proceedings spoke to issues concerning the impacts of sea level rise on existing maritime entitlements, this was not part of the questions put to the Tribunal and thus, according to the Tribunal, outside the scope of the request.[21] Many participants raised these issues again in the ICJ proceedings, and the Court opted to explicitly address them. Drawing on state practice and with reference to the work of the International Law Commission,[22] the ICJ confirms that UNCLOS does not require States to update existing charts showing baselines and outer limits of their maritime zones when these are impacted by sea level rise.[23] The Court also touched on the question of statehood and the loss of territory as a result of sea-level rise and confirmed, for the first time, that 'once a State is established the disappearance of one of its constituent elements would not necessarily entail the loss of its statehood'.[24] It stressed that the duty of States to co-operate in the context of sea level rise is a matter of legal obligation that 'assumes particular significance in this context'.[25]

19 See on this point also ICJ, Declaration by Judge Tladi (n. 17), paras. 15–16.

20 ICJ, *Obligations in Respect of Climate Change* (n. 5), paras. 237–249.

21 ITLOS, *Request for an Advisory Opinion Submitted by the Commission of Small Island States on Climate Change and International Law* (n. 1), paras. 149–150.

22 Final Report of the Study Group on sea level rise in relation to international law, Official Records of the General Assembly, Eightieth Session, Supplement No. 10 (UN doc. A/80/10, Annex I), Report of the International Law Commission on its work at its Seventy-sixth Session.

23 ICJ, *Obligations in Respect of Climate Change* (n. 5), paras. 355–362.

24 ICJ, *Obligations in Respect of Climate Change* (n. 5), para. 363.

25 ICJ, *Obligations in Respect of Climate Change* (n. 5), para. 364.

Finally, where the ITLOS opinion only made cursory references to the intersections of climate change, the law of the sea, and obligations arising under other areas of international law, including human rights,[26] and other multilateral environmental agreements such as the Convention on Biodiversity,[27] the ICJ opinion interprets obligations arising under these regimes in the context of climate change in a more systemic manner, repeatedly stressing how such obligations 'contribute to ensuring the protection of the climate system as a whole' and are thus mutually supportive.[28] The commitment to systemic integration and harmonious interpretation reflected throughout the opinion provides reference points on which state practice and further normative developments can, and hopefully will, build.

IV. Concluding Remarks

The ocean-climate nexus is integral to the health of our global climate system. In legal terms, it is only one, but a very crucial aspect on which both ICJ and ITLOS opinions have had complementary and mutually supportive impacts in terms of recognition, clarification, and systemic integration of obligations arising under different regimes that historically lack coordination. It is also an aspect of particular significance to the SIDS who led both campaigns, and testament to their concerted efforts to seek clarification of existing obligations under international law that correspond to their fundamental demands for justice.

26 ITLOS, *Request for an Advisory Opinion Submitted by the Commission of Small Island States on Climate Change and International Law* (n. 1), para. 66; and Declaration of Judge Infante Caffi, *Request for an Advisory Opinion Submitted by The Commission of Small Island States on Climate Change and International Law*, Advisory Opinion of 21 May 2024, case no. 31. See for a discussion also Khaled Elmahmoud, 'The ITLOS Advisory Opinion: Human Rights as a Withered Branch of International Law?', *EJIL: Talk!*, 24 June 2024.

27 ITLOS, *Request for an Advisory Opinion Submitted by The Commission of Small Island States on Climate Change and International Law* (n. 1), paras. 388, 439.

28 ICJ, *Obligations in Respect of Climate Change* (n. 5), paras. 316–330; 369–404.

A Right to a Clean, Healthy and Sustainable Environment – or perhaps not (yet)?

Helen Keller[*]

I. Introduction

In the lead up to the Advisory Opinion on climate change[1] by the International Court of Justice (ICJ) there were high expectations of a groundbreaking intervention that clears any doubt about the content of legal obligations in relation to climate change and the consequences of their breach. At first glance, these expectations appear to have been met. However, upon closer examination, it becomes clear that various statements made by the ICJ pertaining to the intersection between climate change and human rights law remain vague. This chapter will highlight the relevant findings and then provide an overall assessment. First, the Court's response to the *lex specialis* argument will be considered and then its doctrinal findings as to the content and scope of human rights obligations related to climate change will be laid out. This will be followed by a brief assessment of the Advisory Opinion for its contribution towards settling the debate on difficult legal topics. Despite missed opportunities and the lack of clarity in the Advisory Opinion, its potential impact needs to be appreciated, as going forward, national and international courts will have no choice but to adopt the tone and commitment of this Advisory Opinion when dealing with issues of climate law.

II. Harmonizing Approach and Rejection of the lex specialis Argument

Having read the ICJ's opinion on climate change, readers may well ask themselves whether the Court recognized a right to a healthy, clean and

---

* Professor of Public Law and European and Public International Law at the University of Zurich.

1 ICJ, *Obligations of States in Respect of Climate Change*, Advisory Opinion of 23 July 2025.

sustainable environment. The answer is not straightforward. The ICJ approached a possible response in several steps. First, the ICJ recognized the relationship between the climate protection regime and human rights. The long list of legal regimes that form part of the 'most directly relevant applicable law' for the purpose of this Advisory Opinion in the climate context also includes international human rights guarantees, albeit only in second-to-last place.[2] With this finding, the ICJ is aligning with a discernible trend in international law that recognizes climate change as a matter of human rights concern. This seemingly obvious statement is important because of controversy over the extent to which climate issues should be viewed through the lens of human rights, particularly in the wake of the *KlimaSeniorinnen v. Switzerland* ruling.[3] The ECtHR was heavily criticised for establishing a link between Article 8 of the ECHR and the climate regime.[4] This approach, however, has now been fully confirmed by the ICJ. The ICJ emphasized 'that international human rights law, the climate change treaties and other relevant environmental treaties [...] inform each other. States must therefore take their obligations under international human rights law into account when implementing their obligation under the climate change treaties [...]'.[5] This statement is important in three respects: Firstly, it opens legal avenues to human rights bodies and courts. Because we do not have a central body for enforcing climate-related concerns,[6] this legal recourse is of paramount importance. Secondly, this statement is crucial for interpreting the obligations under the Paris Agreement. Finally, it is also of great practical relevance for the implementation of judgments by human rights bodies and courts (for example, in the case of the *KlimaSeniorinnen*[7]).

At this point, the ICJ could have stopped. However, the Court went further, engaging in a second step by recognizing a right to a clean, healthy

2 ICJ, *Obligations of States in Respect of Climate Change* (n. 1), paras. 145 and 172.

3 ECtHR (Grand Chamber), *Verein KlimaSeniorinnen and Others v. Switzerland*, judgement of 9 April 2024, no 53600/20.

4 Most prominently: Alexander Zahar, 'With *Swiss Seniors* the Climate-Litigation Movement Chalks up Another Hollow Victory', CLLA 14 (2024), 285–316.

5 ICJ, *Obligations of States in Respect of Climate Change* (n. 1), para. 404.

6 See for a deeper discussion Helen Keller, Viktoriya Gurash and Corina Heri, 'Do We Need an International Climate Court', HJIL 85(3) (2025), 725–756..

7 Committee of Ministers, 1537th meeting, 15–17 September 2025 (DH), 1537th meeting, 15–17 September 2025 (DH), *Verein KlimaSeniorinnen Schweiz and Others v. Switzerland* (Appl. No. 53600/20), CM/Notes/1537/H46-37.

and sustainable environment, presenting it as 'inherent in', a 'precondition' to or 'essential' for the effective enjoyment of other human rights.[8] The Court, however, does not say whether it recognizes this as a self-standing right. The statements in several separate opinions make it clear that there was no consensus among the judges as to whether this right has achieved the character of an international customary law norm.[9] The content of a right to a healthy, clean and sustainable environment is not fleshed out in the Advisory Opinion. Judge Charlesworth gives a possible description of the procedural and substantive aspects of this right[10] and links it to the mitigation and adaptation obligation in the climate context.[11] It seems obvious that the judges had differing opinions on the content of such a right.

III. Non-refoulment for Climate Migrants

The debate surrounding a possible human right to a healthy environment should not distract observers from another important finding. The ICJ has declared the principle of non-refoulement applicable in the context of climate change.[12] Here, too, the ICJ can point to prominent statements in this regard, most notably from the Human Rights Committee.[13] From now on, asylum authorities will have to consider non-refoulement when examining asylum applications from climate migrants. However, the ICJ fails to explain to the reader what this principle, which forms part of *jus cogens*, entails *in concreto*. Judge Aurescu suggests that climate non-refoulement includes positive obligations to take proactive measures for the prevention of refoulement and to ensure that other rights are respected

8 ICJ, *Obligations of States in Respect of Climate Change* (n. 1), para. 393.
9 See Separate Opinion of Judge Aurescu, *Obligations of States in Respect of Climate Change*, Advisory Opinion of 23 July 2025, para. 28; Separate Opinion of Judge Bhandari, *Obligations of States in Respect of Climate Change*, Advisory Opinion of 23 July 2025, para. 3; Separate Opinion of Judge Charlesworth, *Obligations of States in Respect of Climate Change*, Advisory Opinion of 23 July 2025, para. 8; Declaration of Judge Tladi, *Obligations of States in Respect of Climate Change*, Advisory Opinion of 23 July 2025, paras. 24 et seqq.
10 Separate Opinion of Judge Charlesworth (n. 9), para. 9.
11 Separate =pinion of Judge Charlesworth (n. 9), para. 10.
12 ICJ, *Obligations of States in Respect of Climate Change* (n. 1), para. 378.
13 Human Rights Committee, *Teitiota v. New Zealand,* 24 October 2019, doc. CCPR/C/127/D/2728/216.

during the individuals' stay in the State's territory.[14] He mentions *inter alia* a duty to conduct an individualized risk assessment, an obligation to admit those seeking protection and to issues temporary residence permits. At a time when asylum laws are being tightened almost everywhere in the world, these statements are important yet politically controversial. They will require further clarification through case law at both the national and international levels.

IV. Extraterritoriality

In light of the global nature of the climate change problem, do human rights treaties create obligations for a state party towards those residing outside its territory? In this regard, the ICJ very carefully left the door open while summarizing the position under international law.[15] Apart from omitting any discussion of the ECtHR's position in *Duarte Agostinho*,[16] the ICJ ultimately left the question unanswered.[17]

The development of case law on extraterritoriality illustrates how international bodies can interpret international law differently. Rather than being a threat to international law, these differences present an opportunity. Undoubtedly, the ECtHR has the strictest case law in this area. In *Duarte Agostinho*, the ECtHR limited the Convention's applicability to victims of climate-related breaches of ECHR obligations to individuals within the ECHR Member State's territorial jurisdiction and it did not deal with possible issues of extraterritorial jurisdiction, such as those which might arise, for instance, in the context of more localised transboundary environmental harm.[18] The ECtHR then argued that first, the United Nations Framework Convention on Climate Change (UNFCCC) and Articles 1 and 2 of the Draft Articles on Prevention of Transboundary Harm from Hazardous Activities[19]

14 Separate Opinion of Judge Aurescu (n. 9), para. 25 *in fine.*

15 ICJ, *Obligations of States in Respect of Climate Change* (n. 1), paras. 395 et seqq.

16 ECtHR (Grand Chamber), *Duarte Agostinho and Others v. Portugal and 32 Others,* decision of 9 April 2024, no. 39371/20.

17 ICJ, *Obligations of States in Respect of Climate Change* (n. 1), para. 402.

18 ECtHR, *Duarte Agostinho* (n. 16), para. 167.

19 ILC, 'Draft Articles on Prevention of Transboundary Harm from Hazardous Activities', YILCB (2001), Vol. II, Part Two.

> 'are *documents of a fundamentally different nature* than the Convention [...]. Secondly, the former are primarily designed to govern the relationships between States, while the Convention comprises more than mere reciprocal engagements between Contracting States and rather creates, over and above a network of mutual, bilateral undertakings, a system of objective human rights obligations [...]. Lastly, while the above-mentioned documents refer to the issue of "damage" or "harm" occurring outside the borders of a State, they do not seem to suggest that such "damage" or "harm" would bring any impacted individuals under the jurisdiction of the State from which the damage or harm originated. In fact, these instruments clearly differentiate between the activity causing the damage or harm, which emanates from the jurisdiction of one State, and their effects, which fall within the jurisdiction of another State.'[20]

While the ICJ generally attempts to harmonise the various areas of law in its Advisory Opinion, the ECtHR in *Duarte Agostinho* makes a strict distinction between the ECHR and the U.N. climate regime for questions of jurisdiction. Only time will tell which approach is more convincing.

V. Wanted: Accuracy, Boldness, and Clarity!

The text of the opinion is unclear in many regards. While it is understandable that the ICJ cannot settle every issue in an opinion down to the last detail, many passages remain vague. Even those involved in the adoption of this opinion complain about the deliberately open wording in some places. Judge Aurescu laments that this Opinion is excessively and unnecessarily cautious and minimalist.[21] Judge Nolte likens the Opinion to a Delphic Oracle[22] and Judge Yusuf states that he is reminded of Alice in Wonderland where Humpty Dumpty says 'when I use a word, it means just what I choose it to mean – neither more nor less.'[23]

---

20 ECtHR, *Duarte Agostinho* (n. 16), para. 212, all references omitted, emphasis in the original.

21 Separate Opinion of Judge Aurescu (n. 9), para. 1.

22 Declaration of Judge Nolte, *Obligations of States in Respect of Climate Change*, Advisory Opinion of 23 July 2025, para. 34.

23 Separate Opinion of Judge Yusuf, *Obligations of States in Respect of Climate Change*, Advisory Opinion of 23 July 2025, para. 6.

Needless to say, we would have liked to see more clarity regarding the role of human rights in the climate context. This applies not only to the content of a possible fundamental right to a clean, healthy and sustainable environment, but also to the principle of non-refoulement under climate law. The ICJ says little about active and passive legal standing in human rights proceedings. Although it refers to future generations on several occasions,[24] it does not address how their interests can be asserted in a complaint procedure. The same applies to the vulnerability of certain groups or States. Future proceedings in climate litigation will need to provide clarification at the national and international levels.

The list of things that the ICJ could clarify may seem long. This is certainly due to the high expectations placed on the ICJ in advance. While certain aspects of the Advisory Opinion remain vague, from an overall perspective, expectations have largely been met. This must be stressed at this point. It is a remarkable achievement that the ICJ adopted the Advisory Opinion unanimously – 'a rarity in the history of the Court's advisory jurisprudence'.[25] Although the Advisory Opinion is not strictly binding, it will undoubtedly influence future legal developments significantly. It sets a tone of commitment, responsibility and alertness for the discussion on the further development in climate law.

24 ICJ, *Obligations of States in Respect of Climate Change* (n. 1), paras. 157, 273, 313, 373, 377.

25 Declaration of Judge Tladi (n. 9), para. 2.

Climate Displacement in the ICJ's Advisory Opinion: Recognised but not Resolved

Malavika Rao[*]

I. Introduction: How the ICJ Addressed Climate Displacement

The ICJ's Advisory Opinion of 23 July 2025 is momentous, confirming that States owe binding obligations in respect of climate change under customary international law and treaty law, across environmental, human rights, and UNCLOS frameworks.[1] These duties apply individually, and collectively through cooperation, with particular regard to States especially affected by climate change, such as Small Island Developing States (SIDS) facing sea-level rise.[2] That said, as this chapter contends, the Court's treatment is limited and peripheral when it comes to addressing legal obligations for displacement arising from climate impacts.[3]

The Court recognises that sea-level rise threatens the territorial integrity of SIDS and low-lying coastal States, implicating their permanent sovereignty over natural resources and loss of territory.[4] The Court further notes that forced displacement, both internal and cross-border, is among the adverse impacts of climate change in this context. Here, the Court references the *Ioane Teitiota* case, acknowledging in principle that displacement may trigger the principle of non-refoulement under Article 6 of the International Covenant on Civil and Political Rights (ICCPR), where return would expose an individual to a real risk of irreparable harm to the right to

* Postdoctoral Research Fellow at the Cambridge Centre for Environment, Energy and Natural Resource Governance (C-EENRG) at the University of Cambridge. This research was supported by the Swiss National Science Foundation (SNSF).

1 ICJ, *Obligations of States in respect of Climate Change*, Advisory Opinion of 23 July 2025, (hereinafter, the 'ICJ Opinion').

2 A full list of SIDS can be found here: https://www.un.org/ohrlls/content/list-sids.

3 See also, Lena Riemer, 'A Single Paragraph's Promise: The ICJ's Advisory Opinion on Climate Change and the Understated Question of Human Displacement', Verfassungsblog, 26 July 2025.

4 ICJ, *Obligations of States in respect of Climate Change* (n. 1), paras. 357, 363.

life, signalling the relevance of human rights norms in addressing climate displacement.[5]

However, beyond this brief recognition, the Court does not specify the legal consequences for countries of origin and host States in relation to displacement. While the Court addresses other duties such as the duty to cooperate, aspects of state responsibility and loss and damage in relation to climate change elsewhere in the opinion, these are not explicitly connected to the need to prevent or respond to displacement arising in such contexts, which might have been relevant. As a result, climate displacement as a *systemic*, *foreseeable*, and *politically urgent* phenomenon remains unresolved and underdeveloped in the Court's reasoning. In this regard, Judge Aurescu, in his Separate Opinion, characterises the Court's analysis of non-refoulement as 'incomplete', suggesting that it could have been strengthened by addressing the positive obligations of States to take proactive measures to prevent refoulement and to ensure that the rights of displaced persons in host countries are protected and fulfilled.[6]

Empirically, displacement is integral to the climate conversation. The IOM notes climate-related migration is an autonomous and spontaneous adaptation tool for communities confronting slow-onset and sudden-onset climatic hazards compounded by food insecurity.[7] The IDMC also notes how climate change has driven more frequent hazards causing displacement, while also observing that more than three-quarters of people internally displaced by conflict and violence at the end of 2024 were living in countries with high or very high vulnerability to climate change.[8]

Against this background, this chapter focuses on how climate displacement fits within the ICJ Opinion's scope and what the ICJ Opinion leaves open. As the IPCC observes, climate displacement will disproportionately

---

5 ICJ, *Obligations of States in respect of Climate Change* (n. 1), para. 378.

6 Separate Opinion of Judge Aurescu, *Obligations of States in Respect of Climate Change*, Advisory Opinion of 23 July 2025, paras. 25–26.

7 Pablo Escribano and Diego Pons Gandini, 'Climate change, food insecurity and human mobility: Interlinkages, evidence and action' in: Marie McAuliffe and Linda Adhiambo Oucho (eds), *World Migration Report 2024* (International Organization for Migration 2024), 198–219 (207), available at: https://publications.iom.int/books/world-migration-report-2024.

8 Internal Displacement Monitoring Centre (IDMC), *Global Report on Internal Displacement 2025 (GRID)* (Geneva: IDMC, 13 May 2025), 13.

affect Pacific SIDS,[9] as displacement would be an unavoidable consequence of sea-level rise causing the loss of habitable land, flooding, crop destruction, and salt water encroachment.[10] The following sections offer some initial reflections on key areas relevant for cross-border climate displacement that merit deeper engagement.

II. Displacement Framed as Peripheral

The Court frames displacement, primarily, as a consequence of the adverse effects of climate change, including extreme weather events, sea-level rise, land degradation, coastal erosion, ocean acidification, and glacial retreat.[11] As recorded by the Court, these impacts are leading to displacement of affected persons and further threatening food insecurity, water scarcity, loss of livelihoods, and hindering efforts toward poverty eradication and sustainable development. In the context of SIDS and low-lying coastal States, the Court links sea-level rise to both internal and cross-border displacement, alongside the erosion of territorial integrity and permanent sovereignty over natural resources.[12]

While the Court establishes a nexus between displacement and climate change, it does not recognise climate displacement as a distinct legal phenomenon situated within the broader ecosystem of international migration law, comprising various bodies of laws, principles and norms that together regulate migration.[13] As one of many drivers of internal and cross-border movement, climate change raises complex questions of legal status and entitlement to international protection, requiring engagement with multiple legal regimes. These include the 1951 Refugee Convention and its 1967 Protocol, which addresses refugee protection to people fleeing a well-founded fear of persecution arising from one of the five specific grounds of race,

9 Intergovernmental Panel on Climate Change (IPCC), 'Summary for Policymakers' in: Valérie Masson-Delmotte et al. (eds), *Climate Change 2021: The Physical Science Basis. Contribution of Working Group I to the Sixth Assessment Report of the IPCC* (Cambridge University Press 2021), 3–32 (sec. A.1.5); Solomon Islands, Written Statement, in: ICJ, Obligations of States in respect of Climate Change (Request for Advisory Opinion), 22 March 2024, Doc. 187–20240322-WRI-30–00-EN, para. 218.

10 IPCC (n. 9)

11 ICJ, *Obligations of States in respect of Climate Change* (n. 1), preambular para. 7.

12 ICJ, *Obligations of States in respect of Climate Change* (n. 1), para. 357.

13 International Organization for Migration (IOM), Glossary on Migration (International Migration Law No. 34), (Geneva: IOM 2019), 113.

religion, nationality, membership of social group, or political opinion.[14] Climate impacts, by themselves, generally do not satisfy this definition unless there is a nexus to persecution on one of the above grounds.[15] Protection rooted in international human rights law, also referred to as complementary or subsidiary protection frameworks, can prohibit return when there is a real risk of irreparable harm, engaging instruments such as the ICCPR,[16] CAT,[17] and CRC[18] for child-specific assessments.

Regional instruments such as the OAU Convention, 1969 and the Cartagena Declaration, 1984 extend protection beyond the 1951 Refugee Convention.[19] The OAU Convention, in Article I(2), covers persons compelled to leave owing to 'events seriously disturbing public order', which has been interpreted as potentially including situations arising from natural disasters or environmental degradation.[20] Similarly, the Cartagena Declaration recommends a broader regional definition encompassing those whose lives, safety, or freedom are threatened by generalized violence, massive violations of human rights, or 'other circumstances which have seriously disturbed public order'.[21] In practice, several Latin American States have

14 *Convention relating to the Status of Refugees,* 28 July 1951, 189 UNTS 137, (entered into force 22 April 1954), Art. 1A(2).

15 David Cantor, Bruce Burson, Brian Aycock, Nikolas Feith Tan, Thekli Anastasiou, Emily Arnold-Fernandez, Carla Field, Cleo Hansen-Lohrey, Walter Kälin, Gillian Kane, Steve Miron, Malavika Rao, Beatriz Sánchez Mojica, Chiara Scissa, Sanjula Weerasinghe and Tamara Wood, 'International Protection, Disasters and Climate Change', IJRL 36 (2024), 176–197.

16 *International Covenant on Civil and Political Rights (ICCPR),* 16 December 1966, 999 UNTS 171 (entered into force 23 March 1976), Arts. 6 and 7.

17 *Convention against Torture and Other Cruel, Inhuman or Degrading Treatment or Punishment (CAT),* 10 December 1984, 1465 UNTS 85 (entered into force 26 June 1987), Art. 3.

18 *Convention on the Rights of the Child (CRC),* 20 November 1989, 1577 UNTS 3 (entered into force 2 September 1990), Arts. 6 and 3.

19 UNHCR Executive Committee, *Persons covered by the OAU Convention Governing the Specific Aspects of Refugee Problems in Africa and by the Cartagena Declaration on Refugees* (Submitted by the African Group and the Latin American Group), EC/1992/SCP/CRP.6, 6 April 1992.

20 *Convention Governing the Specific Aspects of Refugee Problems in Africa (OAU Refugee Convention),* 10 September 1969, 1001 UNTS 45, (entered into force 20 June 1974).

21 *Cartagena Declaration on Refugees,* adopted by the Colloquium on the International Protection of Refugees in Central America, Mexico and Panama, Cartagena de Indias, Colombia, 22 November 1984, reprinted in Annual Report of the Inter-American Commission on Human Rights 1984–1985, OEA/Ser.L/V/II.66, doc. 10, rev. 1, 190–193; available at: OAS PDF and UNHCR.

applied this Cartagena formula in disaster contexts, for example in relation to displacement following the 2010 Haiti earthquake.[22] While soft law instruments such as the Nansen Initiative[23] or initiatives such as the Platform on Disaster Displacement[24] are not binding, they nonetheless influence practice by guiding the admission, stay, planned relocation, and cooperation in cross-border displacement in disaster and climate contexts.

Therefore, determining legal protection for persons fleeing contexts involving climate change as a driver requires a nuanced legal analysis that considers causation and risk in individual cases and interpretation of the above instruments in light of such harm. In its absence, the treatment of displacement, such as in the ICJ's Opinion, remains peripheral.

III. States' Claims pertaining to Climate Displacement before the ICJ

Several States, in their written and oral submissions to the ICJ, presented climate displacement as a pressing and multifaceted issue, a context that frames the background against which the ICJ Opinion was delivered. Vanuatu argued that reparations include not only monetary compensation but also restitution and non-monetary forms of redress for displacement-related harms.[25] Kiribati highlighted that there need to be remedies and redress for loss and damage specifically in relation to climate-induced mobility,[26] also noting the gendered dimensions of climate displacement, noting that nearly 80 % of those displaced are women and children.[27] Tuvalu, in its submission, drew attention to the destruction of coastal infrastructure

---

22 David James Cantor, *Cross-border Displacement, Climate Change and Disasters: Latin America and the Caribbean* (UNHCR 2018), 18.

23 *The Nansen Initiative, Agenda for the Protection of Cross-Border Displaced Persons in the Context of Disasters and Climate Change*, Volume I: Protection Agenda (2015), available at: https://disasterdisplacement.org/wp-content/uploads/2014/08/EN_Protection_Agenda_Volume_I_-low_res.pdf.

24 *Platform on Disaster Displacement (PDD), Strategy 2024–2030* (14 December 2023).

25 Vanuatu, Written Statement, in: ICJ, Obligations of States in respect of Climate Change (Request for Advisory Opinion), 21 March 2024, Doc. 187–20240321-WRI-06–00-EN, para. 8.

26 Kiribati, Written Comments, in: ICJ, Obligations of States in respect of Climate Change (Request for Advisory Opinion), 22 March 2024, Doc. 187–20240815-WRI-04–00-EN, para.21.

27 Kiribati, Written Statement, in: ICJ, Obligations of States in respect of Climate Change (Request for Advisory Opinion), 22 March 2024, Doc. 187–20240322-WRI-13–00-EN, para. 81.

caused by extreme weather events, referencing Tropical Cyclone Pam in 2015, which displaced nearly half its population.[28] Likewise, for Bangladesh, climate displacement poses an incremental threat of loss and damage, placing strain on its capacity to finance adaptation measures.[29]

In its written statement and during the oral hearings, Solomon Islands stressed that five of its islands were already lost due to sea-level rise, while also noting that relocation threatens its customary land ownership system and risks social strife and conflict in the country.[30] It urged the Court to read the questions through the entire corpus of international law, including States' obligations under the Paris Agreement, human rights law and refugee law, and the CBDR principle.[31] On cross-border climate displacement, it urged the Court that the principle of non-refoulement ought to be read in relation to persons fleeing climate change, especially in line with the regional standard of 'disruption of public order' contained in the Cartagena Declaration on Refugees, 1984.[32] The submission also situated these claims in the lived experiences of the displaced i-Kiribati people living on Vaghen (Wagina) Island in Choiseul Province of Solomon Islands since the 1930s, who are currently facing further threats of displacement from sea-level rise. Solomon Islands also submitted that the Court must interpret the obligations under UNCLOS to protect the marine environment as taking measures to mitigate pollution of the marine environment, including protecting coastal communities reliant on the habitat and ocean ecosystems for their livelihoods.[33]

In the above submissions, displacement has been portrayed beyond the aspect of physical relocation, as a profound loss of place, property, identity, and culture, exacerbating socio-economic deprivations and disrupting

---

28 Tuvalu, Written Statement, in: ICJ, Obligations of States in respect of Climate Change (Request for Advisory Opinion), 22 March 2024, Doc. 187–20240322-WRI-05–00-EN, para. 42.

29 Bangladesh, Written Statement, in: ICJ, Obligations of States in respect of Climate Change (Request for Advisory Opinion), 25 March 2024, Doc. 187–20240325-WRI-01–00-EN, para. 69.

30 Earth Negotiations Bulletin, 'Summary of the International Court of Justice Hearings on States' Obligations in Respect of Climate Change: 2–13 December 2024' (16 December 2024), p. 13, available at: https://enb.iisd.org/sites/default/files/2024-12/icj10e.pdf.

31 Earth Negotiations Bulletin (n. 30).

32 Earth Negotiations Bulletin (n. 30).

33 Solomon Islands, Written Statement (n. 9), paras. 220–224.

access to basic resources such as food, housing, etc.[34] Yet, the Court's reasoning fails to capture the full gravity of climate displacement as a systemic and existential threat warranting legal protections, particularly for the most vulnerable States.

IV. Teitiota and the Limits of Non-Refoulement

With its reference to *Ioane Teitiota v New Zealand*, the Court reiterates the UN Human Rights Committee's finding on the application of the principle of non-refoulement, recognising that the effects of climate change may, in certain circumstances, trigger obligations under Article 6 of the ICCPR.[35] The *Teitiota* case concerned a Kiribati national who sought asylum in New Zealand, asserting that he faced an imminent risk to life from climate change and sea-level rise, which had forced him to migrate to New Zealand. After the New Zealand courts denied his claim, Mr. Teitiota filed a communication with the UN Human Rights Committee.[36] The HRC dismissed the communication on its merits, however noting that, given that the risk of an entire country becoming submerged under water is such an extreme risk, the conditions of life in such a country may become incompatible with the right to life with dignity before the risk is realised.[37] While referencing *Teitiota*, the ICJ could have engaged more fully with the legal uncertainties that *Teitiota* has generated, particularly the contested question of whether the applicable standard for protection requires a risk that is 'imminent.' As Foster and McAdam have argued, while the threshold remains one of 'real risk,' the framing in *Teitiota* has led to confusion and inconsistent interpretations of the standard over time.[38] This clarification could be especially critical for SIDS, where climate impacts such as sea-level rise and the degradation of arable land unfold gradually but are nonetheless serious

34 For example, Solomon Islands, Written Statement (n. 9), para. 225.

35 ICJ, *Obligations of States in respect of Climate Change* (n. 1), para 378.

36 High Court: *Teitiota v Chief Executive of the Ministry of Business, Innovation and Employment*, [2013] NZHC 3125 (26 Nov 2013); Court of Appeal: *Teitiota v Chief Executive of the Ministry of Business, Innovation and Employment*, [2014] NZCA 173 (8 May 2014); *IPT: AF (Kiribati)*, [2013] NZIPT 800413 (25 June 2013).

37 UN Human Rights Committee, *Ioane Teitiota v New Zealand*, Views adopted 24 Oct 2019 (pub. 7 Jan 2020), CCPR/C/127/D/2728/2016, para. 9.11.

38 Michelle Foster and Jane McAdam, 'Analysis of "Imminence" in International Protection Claims: *Teitiota v New Zealand* and Beyond', ICLQ 71 (2022), 975–982.

and foreseeable. In alignment, the HRC General Comment 36 recognised that foreseeable threats and life-threatening situations can engage Article 6 without requiring imminence or actual loss of life.[39]

More broadly, the principle of non-refoulement, while integral to international protection, is only one step among a range of protections in addressing climate displacement. As an individualised and reactive safeguard, it applies at the point of return and offers no durable solutions or preventive protection for communities at risk. Judge Aurescu observes some of the other aspects of protection in his Separate Opinion, stating that the Court might have clarified how the principle of non-refoulement could be complemented by obligations such as the duty to conduct individualised risk assessments, obligation of admission, issuance of temporary visas, planned relocation, etc.[40] Thus, the ICJ Opinion leaves open key questions about how persons facing cross-border displacement can be protected under international law.

V. Missing Connections to Displacement: Statelessness, International Cooperation and Loss and Damage

The ICJ Opinion affirms a range of obligations on States to protect the climate system and to uphold the rights of present and future generations. However, it does not engage directly with how these obligations apply to the issue of displacement. There are at least three areas, such as statelessness, international cooperation, and loss and damage, where such a connection is relevant but insufficiently addressed.

1. Statelessness

The Court rightly affirms that the disappearance of territory due to sea-level rise does not necessarily lead to the loss of statehood, thereby supporting the continuity of statehood and maritime entitlements.[41] However, the Court does not address the fate of displaced populations from such territo-

39 UN Human Rights Committee, 'General comment No. 36, Article 6 (Right to Life)', CCPR/C/GC/36, 3 September 2019, para. 7.

40 Separate Opinion of Judge Aurescu (n. 6), para. 26.

41 ICJ, *Obligations of States in respect of Climate Change* (n. 1), paras 355–365.

ries, who may no longer reside within the physical territory of their State. This is an important gap, particularly for some SIDS, where the risk of entire communities being forced to relocate raises urgent questions regarding nationality, how they might access their rights, and the prevention of statelessness. While the Court acknowledges the link between sea-level rise and the right of self-determination, it does not clarify how this right will be realised for persons who might be territorially detached from their State. A useful example here is the Australia-Tuvalu Falepili Union Treaty, which both recognises Tuvalu's continuing statehood and sovereignty notwithstanding the impact of sea-level rise, and creates a special human mobility pathway enabling citizens of Tuvalu to live, study and work in Australia with access to Australian education, health, income and family support on arrival, thus linking preservation of statehood to pathways of residency.[42]

2. International Cooperation

Likewise, the Court affirms that the duty to cooperate is a self-standing rule of customary international law, grounded in the United Nations Charter and widely reflected in treaties and declarations.[43] It upholds the importance of coordinated international action to prevent significant harm and to protect the global environment. In the context of climate change, this responsibility is further informed by the principle of common but differentiated responsibilities and respective capabilities, which highlight how burdens to prevent, finance and technically assist affected countries are allocated. Yet the ICJ Opinion does not indicate how this duty might function in response to climate displacement. By contrast, instruments such as the New York Declaration for Refugees and Migrants, 2016[44] and the Global Compact for Migration, 2018[45] stress that international cooperation,

42 Government of Australia and Government of Tuvalu, *Australia-Tuvalu Falepili Union* (Rarotonga, 9 November 2023; in force 28 August 2024), [2024] ATS 10, Art. 2 para. 2 lit. (b) and Art. 3.

43 ICJ, *Obligations of States in respect of Climate Change* (n. 1), paras. 140–142.

44 UN General Assembly, *New York Declaration for Refugees and Migrants*, UN Doc A/RES/71/1 (3 Oct 2016) paras. 7, 11, 24, 28, 38, 40, 58, 62, 68.

45 UN General Assembly, *Global Compact for Safe, Orderly and Regular Migration*, GA Res 73/195 (19 December 2018), UN Doc A/RES/73/195, Annex paras. 7, 8, 11, 15 (Guiding principles: 'International cooperation'), 42–43; Objective 23 (chapeau para. 39).

through capacity-building, financial support and responsibility-sharing, is essential in responding to migration.

3. Loss and Damage

In relation to loss and damage, the Court confirms that Article 8 of the Paris Agreement provides a basis for cooperative support, while noting that it does not establish liability or compensation.[46] This interpretation aligns with the approach taken in previous COP decisions, but leaves unresolved the question of how displacement is to be addressed. Displacement is increasingly recognised as a form of non-economic loss within the loss and damage framework by the UNFCCC, linking it to the loss of habitability from a lack of security, livelihood, health and well-being, triggered by climate change.[47] Moreover, the Warsaw International Mechanism for Loss and Damage includes a dedicated Task Force on Displacement to enhance cooperation and facilitation in relation to human mobility, migration and planned relocation.[48] Nonetheless, the Court offers limited guidance on how this framework might evolve to address the irreversible consequences of climate displacement.

VI. The IACtHR on Climate Displacement: A Comparison

By comparison, the Advisory Opinion of the Inter-American Court on Human Rights (IACtHR) of May 2025 on the climate emergency and human rights treats climate-related human mobility as an independent rights question under Article 22 of the American Convention on Human Rights, which addresses freedom of movement and residence.[49] It articulates duties

46 ICJ, *Obligations of States in respect of Climate Change* (n. 1), paras. 414–420.

47 United Nations Framework Convention on Climate Change (UNFCCC), *Non-Economic Losses – Featuring loss of territory and habitability, ecosystem services and biodiversity, and cultural heritage* (Technical paper, 2024), 13, available at: https://unfccc.int/sites/default/files/resource/nels_paper_2024.pdf.

48 International Organization for Migration (IOM), Environmental Migration Portal, 'Task Force on Displacement', available at: https://environmentalmigration.iom.int/task-force-displacement.

49 IACtHR, *Advisory Opinion on Climate Emergency and Human Rights*, 29 May 2025, AO-32/25, paras. 414–417.

of States in this regard, including on family unity and specific safeguards for children,[50] to legislate and govern planned relocations through adequate human rights framework that assigns institutional responsibilities and provides comprehensive reparations for affected persons,[51] to enable safe and regular cross-border mobility,[52] to create admission categories such as humanitarian visas, temporary residence, or refugee-analogous protection, to secure non-refoulement,[53] and to provide consular and humanitarian assistance within a cooperation mandate. Importantly, the IACtHR situates human mobility within its broader remedial and cooperation framework, referencing loss and damage financing and urging dedicated funds to manage climate mobility[54]. It reviews Article 8 of the Paris Agreement, the Warsaw International Mechanism and the new Loss and Damage Fund,[55] and urges the operationalisation of international funds so vulnerable countries can cope with human mobility generated by climate change.[56] Thus, the IACtHR goes further in developing a rights-based blueprint for climate displacement that States can implement, both to prevent and as long-term solutions.[57] However, like the ICJ's Opinion, the IACtHR does not substantially elaborate beyond the non-refoulement standard in *Ioane Teitiota*, which it cites in this context.[58]

50 IACtHR, *Advisory Opinion on Climate Emergency and Human Rights* (n. 49), paras. 428, 434.

51 IACtHR, *Advisory Opinion on Climate Emergency and Human Rights* (n. 49), paras. 428, 434.
IACtHR, *Advisory Opinion on Climate Emergency and Human Rights* (n. 49), paras. 425–429.

52 IACtHR, *Advisory Opinion on Climate Emergency and Human Rights* (n. 49), para. 432.

53 IACtHR, *Advisory Opinion on Climate Emergency and Human Rights* (n. 49), para. 433.

54 IACtHR, *Advisory Opinion on Climate Emergency and Human Rights* (n. 49), para. 432.

55 IACtHR, *Advisory Opinion on Climate Emergency and Human Rights* (n. 49), paras. 199–201.

56 IACtHR, *Advisory Opinion on Climate Emergency and Human Rights* (n. 49), para. 431.

57 IACtHR, *Advisory Opinion on Climate Emergency and Human Rights* (n. 49), para. 433.

58 IACtHR, *Advisory Opinion on Climate Emergency and Human Rights* (n. 49), para. 433, fn. 734.

VII. Conclusion

It is no doubt that the ICJ's Opinion on climate change clearly marks a landmark development in clarifying the legal obligations of States and the legal consequences arising from climate change under international law. While displacement was not the sole focus of the Opinion, the reasons outlined above demonstrate how a closer engagement with this issue would have strengthened the Court's contribution to shaping a comprehensive legal response that better protects the rights of persons displaced by climate change. Moreover, as legal protections for such persons are being progressively developed, clarifying the law at this juncture would have been especially valuable. At the same time, the Court's recognition of human rights dimensions of climate change may also be read as a judicial opening, one that implicitly invites international and regional human rights treaty bodies and national courts to interpret and apply existing protections more expansively in response to climate displacement.

Great Expectations

*Andreas Kulick**

I. Introduction

General media as well as experts' assessment seem to be unanimous that the 23 July 2025 Advisory Opinion of the International Court of Justice ('ICJ' or 'Court') on Obligations of States in respect of Climate Change[1] is a historic, 'land-mark opinion'[2]. Indeed, expectations were high before its delivery and remain so in its aftermath. However, a glance at the Court's own *jurisprudence constante* seems to pour cold water on any expected relevant impact of this, as in fact any, advisory opinion. Since 1950, the Court consistently underlines that 'as such, [an advisory opinion] has no binding force'[3]. Accordingly, when the Special Chamber of the International Tribunal for the Law of the Sea ('ITLOS') in *Mauritius v. Maldives* recently sought to grant the ICJ's *Chagos* opinion[4] *de facto res judicata* effect,[5] this received wide-spread criticism.[6]

---

*Professor of Public International Law and Public Law at Johannes Gutenberg University of Mainz.

1 ICJ, *Obligations of States in respect of Climate Change*, Advisory Opinion of 23 July 2025.

2 'Nations who fail to curb fossil fuels could be ordered to pay reparations, top UN court rules', The Guardian, 23 July 2025, available at https://www.theguardian.com/environment/2025/jul/23/healthy-environment-is-a-human-right-top-un-court-rules, last accessed 20 September 2025.

3 ICJ, *Interpretation of Peace Treaties with Bulgaria, Hungary and Romania*, Advisory Opinion of 30 March 1950, ICJ Rep. 65, 71.

4 ICJ, *Legal Consequences of the Separation of the Chagos Archipelago from Mauritius in 1965*, Advisory Opinion of 25 February 2019, ICJ Rep. 95.

5 ITLOS (Special Chamber), *Dispute Concerning Delimitation of the Maritime Boundary between Mauritius and Maldives in the Indian Ocean (Mauritius v. Maldives)*, Judgement of 28 January 2021, paras. 202–205.

6 *E.g.* Fabian Simon Eichberger, 'The Legal Effect of ICJ Advisory Opinions Redefined? The Mauritius/Maldives Delimitation Case – Judgment on Preliminary Objections', MJIL 22 (2021), 383, 398–399 (noting also that the ICJ rejected a similar argument introduced by Portugal in *East Timor (Portugal v. Australia)*, Judgement of 30 June 1995, ICJ Rep. 90, 103–104, paras. 30–31).

Yet, when invoking prior 'case-law' as persuasive international precedent, the Court and other international judicial bodies refer to advisory opinions and decisions in contentious proceedings in an indiscriminate fashion, as the International Law Commission ('ILC') recently noted.[7] So, where does such legal impact come from and how should we assess the impact of this 'landmark' opinion? I submit that the lasting legal impact and influence of the Advisory Opinion of 23 July – like that of any of the Court's opinions – depends to a considerable degree on how well the Court succeeds in managing and responding to expectations held prior to its delivery. This harkens back, and pertains to, the World Court's judicial function, no less.[8]

II. Expectations

In a recent article, I argue that stakeholders pursue advisory opinions before the ICJ with one or several of a total of six different expectations in mind, ranging from 'advice as advice' to 'advice as miracle'.[9] Their 'persuasiveness'[10] and thus their relevance and impact regarding future case law depends to a considerable degree on how well the Court succeeds in managing these expectations in its Opinion.[11] With respect to the Climate Change Advisory Opinion, two of these expectations are of particular interest.

---

7 International Law Commission, First report on subsidiary means for the determination of rules of international law, 74th session, Geneva, 24 April-2 June and 3 July-4 August 2023, by Charles Chernor Jalloh, Special Rapporteur, p. 93, para. 278, available at https://digitallibrary.un.org/record/4010690?v=pdf, last accessed 20 September 2025.

8 See on the latter, seminally, Gleider I. Hernández, *The International Court of Justice and the Judicial Function* (Oxford University Press 2014).

9 Andreas Kulick, 'Between Advice and Miracle: Expectations and Persuasiveness of ICJ Advisory Opinions' ICLR 27 (2025), 33, 37–51.

10 I distinguish this term both from 'authority', which is content-independent (see e.g. Frederick Schauer, 'Authority and Authorities', Va. L. Rev. 94 (2008), 1931, 1940–1944; Ingo Venzke, *How Interpretation Makes International Law* (Oxford University Press 2012), 63; Ingo Venzke, 'Between Power and Persuasion: On International Institutions' Authority in Making Law', TLT 4 (2013), 354, 370) and from persuasion, which is content-dependent (e.g. Frederick Schauer, 'Authority and Authorities', Va. L. Rev. 94 (2008), 1931 (1940). 'Persuasiveness' inheres both content-independent and content-dependent elements, see Kulick (n. 9), 56–60.

11 See Kulick (n. 9), 56–60.

(1) Stakeholders may seek an advisory opinion to have the Court ascertain and develop the law on abstract and general legal questions. It was expected that the ICJ would provide 'advice as law-development' pertaining to a whole panoply of complex doctrinal issues, including: the relationship of the United Nations Framework Convention on Climate Change ('UNFCCC') and the Paris Agreement ('PA') as well as of climate change treaties and customary international law; the elements and scope of due diligence standards; the potential existence of a human right to a clean and healthy environment; as well as various matters of state responsibility, causation and compensation among them.

(2) In addition, advice may be sought from the Court to resolve a grand societal debate: 'Advice as miracle'. Arguably, some expectations attached to the present Opinion concerned its potential to single-handedly transform worldwide climate policy. I submit that only once before has the Court been confronted with expectations of a similar magnitude – and fared rather badly in handling them: In its *Nuclear Weapons* Advisory Opinion[12] it had no clear answer to the fundamental societal question whether nuclear weapons and their use were to be banned by international law *tout court*.

III. Expectation Management and the Court's Judicial Function

When discussing admissibility, the Court underlined its 'judicial function', citing *Nuclear Weapons*[13] to stress that, when issuing an advisory opinion, it 'states the existing law and does not legislate'[14]. It echoes a similar point later, quoting from *Fisheries Jurisdiction* that 'the Court, as a court of law, cannot render judgments *sub specie legis ferendae*.'[15] This pertains to both expectations at play regarding the Opinion of 23 July 2025.

---

12 See ICJ, *Legality of the Threat or Use of Nuclear Weapons*, Advisory Opinion of 8 July 1996, ICJ Rep. 226, para. 105.

13 ICJ, *Legality of the Threat or Use of Nuclear Weapons* (n. 12), para. 18.

14 ICJ, *Legality of the Threat or Use of Nuclear Weapons* (n. 12), para. 48.

15 ICJ, *Fisheries Jurisdiction (United Kingdom of Great Britain and Northern Ireland v. Iceland)*, Judgement of 25 July 1974, ICJ Rep. 3, para. 53.

With respect to the 'advice as miracle' expectation, the Opinion and the Judges' separate opinions and declarations[16] evince unequivocally how much the Court and its Members were aware of the high hopes attached to these proceedings and their outcome. This much becomes apparent not only in the frequent references to the Court's judicial function.[17] The ICJ, further, felt compelled to add a very last paragraph before the *dispositif*. Here, it addresses the enormity of the challenges posed by climate change thus implicitly accounting for the enormous expectations held *vis-à-vis* the Court's Advisory Opinion: '[T]he questions posed … represent more than a legal question: they concern an existential problem of planetary proportions.'.[18] The Court, so it underlines, can only make a modest contribution to the solution: 'The Court, as a court of law, can do no more than address the questions put to it' with respect to 'international law', which 'has an important but ultimately limited role in resolving this problem.'[19] Here, the spectre of *Nuclear Weapons* seems to loom.[20]

Focusing in the following on expectations pertaining to 'advice as law-development', among the almost infinite number and variety of legal issues potentially to be addressed and clarified regarding States' obligations in respect of climate change, the Court arguably did not shy away from tackling many of the most pertinent matters. Some of the most important contributions to the development of international climate change law are doubtless to be found in its analysis of the climate change treaties as well as their interrelationship and their interaction with customary international law. The Court emphasizes that the PA is neither *lex specialis* regarding the UNFCCC nor are the climate treaties *leges speciales vis-à-vis* customary standards such as the principles of prevention or co-operation.[21] Similarly, the ICJ clarifies that 'discretion' regarding the PA Contracting Parties' NDCs under Art. 4(2) is not unlimited but rather guided by a requirement

16 *E.g.* Declaration of Judge Nolte, *Obligations of States in respect of Climate Change*, Advisory Opinion of 23 July 2025, para. 1.

17 *E.g.* ICJ, *Obligations of States in respect of Climate Change* (n. 1), paras. 45, 48, 100, 338 and 456.

18 ICJ, *Obligations of States in respect of Climate Change* (n. 1), para. 456.

19 ICJ, *Obligations of States in respect of Climate Change* (n. 1), para. 456. See also the Declaration of Judge Tladi, *Obligations of States in respect of Climate Change*, Advisory Opinion of 23 July 2025, para. 38.

20 Note the frequent references to the 1996 opinion in the text: ICJ, *Obligations of States in respect of Climate Change* (n. 1), paras. 48, 98, 114, 134, 141, 155, 272, 373.

21 ICJ, *Obligations of States in respect of Climate Change* (n. 1), paras. 162–171, 187–195 and 309–315.

of progression and the obligation of a 1.5° Celsius threshold,[22] the latter deriving from the interpretation of Art. 2(1) PA.[23] Moreover, it engages in a detailed and differentiated discussion of the contours and conditions of the due diligence standards in both the PA[24] and especially under the customary prevention principle.[25] Overall, these sections, as most parts of the Advisory Opinion, are exceptionally well-reasoned, displaying an impressive attention to doctrinal precision and detail.[26]

Nonetheless, as is almost inevitable in such a long opinion addressing a wide range of matters, there are some passages less convincingly argued than others. Among those, the Court's identification of a 'human right to a clear, healthy and sustainable environment' stands out as probably most wanting: it remains rather opaque whether the Court regards it as a self-standing right or rather accessory to other treaty provisions and it is equally unclear whether the opinion asserts this right as a rule of custom[27] or rather derives it from necessary implication[28] or functionality.[29]

Similarly, the distinction between customary principles[30] and 'other principles'[31] merely 'guiding ... the interpretation and application of the most directly relevant legal rules'[32] will probably raise more questions than it answers: Are they 'general principles of law' or rather 'general principles of law formed within the international legal system', in the parlance of the ILC[33] – or are they rather interpretative maxims similar to *effet utile* or *contra proferentem*, but special to the climate law regime (exclusively or also

22 ICJ, *Obligations of States in respect of Climate Change* (n. 1), paras. 237 et seq.

23 ICJ, *Obligations of States in respect of Climate Change* (n. 1), paras. 222 et seq.

24 E.g. ICJ, *Obligations of States in respect of Climate Change* (n. 1), paras. 246, 258.

25 ICJ, *Obligations of States in respect of Climate Change* (n. 1), paras. 280–300.

26 See also, with similar assessment, Julian Arato and Justina Uriburu, 'Treaty and Custom in the ICJ's Climate Change Opinion', EJIL Talk!, 24 July 2025.

27 Separate Opinion of Judge Aurescu, *Obligations of States in respect of Climate Change*, Advisory Opinion of 23 July 2025, paras. 28 et seq.; and Declaration of Judge Tladi (n.19),, paraparas. 29 et seq.

28 ICJ, *Obligations of States in respect of Climate Change* (n. 1), para. 393: 'precondition', 'inherent'.

29 ICJ, *Obligations of States in respect of Climate Change* (n. 1), paras. 391 and 393: 'importance', 'essential'.

30 ICJ, *Obligations of States in respect of Climate Change* (n. 1), paras. 131–142.

31 ICJ, *Obligations of States in respect of Climate Change* (n. 1), paras. 146–161.

32 ICJ, *Obligations of States in respect of Climate Change* (n. 1), para. 161.

33 See International Law Commission, Fourth report on general principles of law, Seventy-sixth session, Geneva, 14 April-30 May and 30 June-31 July 2025, by Marcelo Vázquez-Bermúdez, Special Rapporteur, pp. 26 et seq.

beyond? Only regarding treaty interpretation or custom interpretation as well?)? I could go on).

Finally, the Court is most curt where the highest potential for litigation lies: While the discussion of Question *(b)* contains many important doctrinal pronouncements, I agree with Judge Nolte[34] in his assessment that the comparatively short statements on reparation, especially compensation,[35] leave a lot of room for interpretation and thus will likely entail[36] considerable contentious litigation – whereas I do not share his opinion that such litigation may necessarily be 'counterproductive'.[37]

IV. Conclusions

The lasting effect of this Advisory Opinion will remain in its response to the expectation of and thereby its contribution to law-development. The proof is in the pudding of the 'persuasiveness'[38] of the Court's argumentation regarding the individual legal pronouncements. While the Court and the individual Judges, for good political reasons, need to emphasize that the ICJ can only state, analyse and apply, but never create the law, the Court undoubtedly attains a law-developing function – however, within the confines of thorough legal argumentation.

Through what arguably falls squarely within its judicial function, the Opinion of 23 July 2025 has indeed made an important contribution to the climate change debate, not least because it relied for the most part on robust legal reasoning. Even most of the more progressive and innovative findings are thoroughly reasoned and backed up by doctrine, especially by extensive references to case law. It is of note here that this Court, which usually is rather sparse in citing other international courts and other adjudicatory bodies, in this Opinion summons an impressive amount of other judicial authorities – from ITLOS to regional human rights courts or the

34 Declaration of Judge Nolte (n. 16), , paras. 18 et seq.

35 ICJ, *Obligations of States in respect of Climate Change* (n. 1), paras. 449–455.

36 See 'Australia warned it could face legal action over 'wrongful' fossil fuel actions after landmark climate ruling from world's top court', The Guardian of 24 July 2025, available at https://www.theguardian.com/environment/2025/jul/24/australia-warned-it-could-face-legal-action-over-fossil-fuels-after-icj-landmark-climate-ruling, last accessed 20 September 2025.

37 Declaration of Judge Nolte (n. 16), para. 34.

38 Kulick (n. 9), 56 et seq.

Human Rights Committee – to corroborate its legal analysis. ITLOS alone is cited no less than 28 times in the Opinion.

The potentially high relevance of the Court's pronouncements on central legal questions pertaining to States' obligations in respect of climate change, finally, results from its careful expectation management. The ICJ emphasises its important but limited role in a debate that eventually can only find resolution through 'human will and wisdom'[39]: law-development: yes; miracle-working: no. This is not at all to say that litigation and arbitration based on many of the Court's doctrinal pronouncements could not and should not be pursued by claimants. Especially the findings on Art. 2(1) and 4(2) PA as well as the customary requirements of the prevention principle and its due diligence standards, particularly *vis-à-vis* fossil fuel exploration, production and consumption,[40] provide avenues for contentious proceedings before the ICJ and beyond. The Court exercised its judicial function precisely with the view to future law application, including through adjudication. Nonetheless, it makes clear that eventually, it is the political process that needs to find the final responses to the grand societal debate on, as the Court puts it, this 'existential problem of planetary proportions'.[41] In Judge Tladi's words: 'It requires those in decision-making positions to make the right choices for the sake of the future of our planet.'[42] Hopefully, they will be guided by the legal requirements, standards and guidelines so aptly clarified in this 'landmark opinion' – and maybe also by future case law inspired by and building upon it.

39 ICJ, *Obligations of States in respect of Climate Change* (n. 1), para. 456.
40 See ICJ, *Obligations of States in respect of Climate Change* (n. 1), para. 427.
41 ICJ, *Obligations of States in respect of Climate Change* (n. 1), para. 456.
42 Declaration of Judge Tladi (19), para. para. 38.

One Climate, Many Courts:

The ICJ Advisory Opinion on Climate Change, Systemic Integration, Cross-Judicial Law-Making, and Interjudicialism

*Khaled El Mahmoud**

I. Introduction

On 23 July 2025, the International Court of Justice ('ICJ' or 'Court') issued its Advisory Opinion on the *Obligations of States in respect of Climate Change*, marking a significant moment in the evolving landscape of international climate change law.[1] Notably, the ICJ engaged in sustained and explicit dialogue with the 2024 Advisory Opinion of the International Tribunal for the Law of the Sea ('ITLOS' or 'Tribunal'), alongside recent pronouncements by regional human rights courts, such as the European Court of Human Rights and the Inter-American Court of Human Rights, as well as quasi-judicial institutions, such as the Human Rights Committee. These cross-references evidence a maturing judicial practice of cross-institutional engagement.[2]

Yet, this chapter focuses specifically on ITLOS, examining how its 2024 Advisory Opinion informed, shaped, and, in some respects, structured the ICJ's own legal reasoning. It analyses the manner in which the Tribunal's interpretations were integrated into the ICJ's opinion to support a more coherent and cross-regime legal framework for addressing climate change. In doing so, it reflects on the broader implications of this judicial convergence for an emerging phenomenon, which may be termed *'cross-judicial law-making'*.

---

* Law Clerk at the Higher Regional Court of Berlin.

1 ICJ, *Obligations of States in respect of Climate Change*, Advisory Opinion of 23 July 2025.

2 Shotaro Hamamoto, 'Judicial Cross-Referencing', in: Hélène Ruiz Fabri (ed), *Max Planck Encyclopedia of International Procedural Law* (2022).

II. The ICJ's Engagement with ITLOS' Advisory Opinion

The ICJ's reliance on ITLOS' reasoning can be broadly categorised into two dimensions: first, the application of rules, principles, and standards of general international law, and second, the interpretation of specific obligations under UNCLOS. This convergence reflects a broader pattern of mutual judicial engagement. While the ICJ has drawn extensively on ITLOS' interpretations, ITLOS has likewise relied on the jurisprudence of the ICJ in its 2024 Advisory Opinion, most notably in relation to environmental impact assessments ('EIAs').[3] These reciprocal references underscore the growing convergence between the two courts, contributing to a coherent body of international jurisprudence. While reference to the ICJ as the *principal judicial organ* of the UN is to be expected given its preeminent position in the international legal order, the ICJ's reliance on ITLOS marks a more notable development, signalling an increasing normative authority accorded to its judicial determinations.[4]

1. Rules, Principles, and Standards of General International Law

The ICJ expressly endorsed the ITribunal's articulation of *due diligence* as a core element of States' obligations of conduct.[5] The Court affirmed that due diligence is not a fixed or uniform standard but one that varies in light of contextual factors, including the gravity of the threat posed, in this case, by climate change conduct.[6] In particular, the ICJ emphasised that the standard of due diligence applicable to the preparation of nationally determined contributions must be stringent, reflecting the severity and urgency of the climate crisis.[7] The ICJ, echoing ITLOS' reasoning, underscored that due

3 ITLOS, *Request for an Advisory Opinion submitted by the Commission of Small Island States on Climate Change and International Law*, Advisory Opinion of 21 May 2024, paras. 356, 363, 398.

4 Cf. Lan Ngoc Nguyen, 'The Public Authority of the International Tribunal for the Law of the Sea', in: Hélène Ruiz Fabri and others (eds), *International Judicial Legitimacy* (Nomos 2020).

5 ICJ, *Obligations of States in respect of Climate Change* (n. 1), paras. 251–2; ITLOS, *Request for an Advisory Opinion submitted by the Commission of Small Island States on Climate Change and International Law* (n. 3), paras. 233, 239–40.

6 ICJ, *Obligations of States in respect of Climate Change* (n 1), para. 254.

7 ICJ, *Obligations of States in respect of Climate Change* (n. 1), para. 246.

diligence assumes particular significance where the relevant activities are predominantly undertaken by non-State entities.[8]

Furthermore, the ICJ clarified that the determination of what due diligence requires in a given case must be guided by *current standards.* Such standards may derive not only from binding sources (*e.g.*, treaties and customary international law) but also from non-binding instruments, including relevant decisions adopted by the Conferences of the Parties ('COPs') to the climate change treaties and recommended technical norms and practices, where appropriate.[9] In this regard, the Court reinforced the ITLOS' view that the due diligence standard is inherently 'variable', shaped by developments in both, law and practice.[10] Accordingly, States are expected to adapt their conduct in line with emerging scientific knowledge, policy frameworks, and evolving expectations of responsible environmental governance.

With respect to scientific knowledge, both the ICJ and ITLOS acknowledged the work of the Intergovernmental Panel on Climate Change ('IPCC') as representing the best available science, going so far as to recognise its reports as authoritative assessments of the state of scientific knowledge on climate change.[11] Both courts grounded their judicial determinations in this science, adopting a common approach that climate change obligations cannot be divorced from climate change science.[12] In this context, the ICJ further reinforced States' obligations by holding that they must 'use their best efforts, in line with the best available science' and went beyond the ITLOS by expressly linking the concept of 'best efforts' to 'best available practice'.[13] At the same time, ITLOS qualified the weight of science in determining State obligations, stating that '[h]owever, this

---

8 ICJ, *Obligations of States in respect of Climate Change* (n. 1), para. 252.

9 ICJ, *Obligations of States in respect of Climate Change* (n. 1), para. 300. Cf. ITLOS, *Request for an Advisory Opinion submitted by the Commission of Small Island States on Climate Change and International Law* (n. 3), para. 239.

10 ICJ, *Obligations of States in respect of Climate Change* (n. 1), para. 300..

11 ICJ, *Obligations of States in respect of Climate Change* (n. 1), para. 74. Cf. ITLOS, *Request for an Advisory Opinion submitted by the Commission of Small Island States on Climate Change and International Law* (n. 3), para. 208. See also Sulyok, 'On the Science-Coloured Glasses of the ICJ: Harmfulness, Wrongfulness, and Climate Accountability', in this volume.

12 ICJ, *Obligations of States in respect of Climate Change* (n. 1), para. 284. Cf. ITLOS, *Request for an Advisory Opinion submitted by the Commission of Small Island States on Climate Change and International Law* (n. 3), para. 208.

13 ICJ, *Obligations of States in respect of Climate Change* (n. 1), para. 258.

does not mean that the science alone should determine the content of necessary measures', thereby tempering the otherwise broad effect of recognising IPCC reports as both authoritative and reflective of best available practice.[14]

Moreover, the ICJ aligned itself with the ITLOS in endorsing the view that the scope of a State's due diligence obligation is contingent on its capabilities and resources.[15] In doing so, both courts effectively wove the principle of common but differentiated responsibilities and respective capabilities into the fabric of the due diligence standard, thereby recognising that differentiation in obligations must reflect disparities in capacity. While both concluded that developed States are subject to a more exacting standard of conduct, the ICJ introduced a more nuanced understanding by stressing that capacity-based differentiation must be assessed on a case-by-case basis, rather than through a simplistic developed/developing State binary.[16] In addition, both tribunals affirmed that limitations in available means cannot excuse inaction or justify undue delay in implementing necessary measures.[17]

With respect to EIAs, the ICJ reaffirmed and aligned its reasoning with that of ITLOS, particularly regarding the standard and scope of risk evaluation. In doing so, the ICJ drew on its own established jurisprudence, while simultaneously adding to it by incorporating the reasoning developed by ITLOS. As articulated by ITLOS and endorsed by the ICJ, such an assessment must integrate 'both the probability or foreseeability of harm and its severity or magnitude'.[18] The ICJ underscored that due diligence requires consideration not only of immediate risks but also of those that may manifest over the long term, thereby reflecting the temporal dimension of environmental harm in climate-related contexts.[19] The ICJ further recog-

14 ITLOS, *Request for an Advisory Opinion submitted by the Commission of Small Island States on Climate Change and International Law* (n. 3), para. 212.

15 ICJ, *Obligations of States in respect of Climate Change* (n. 1), para. 291. Cf. ITLOS, *Request for an Advisory Opinion submitted by the Commission of Small Island States on Climate Change and International Law* (n. 3), para. 241.

16 ICJ, *Obligations of States in respect of Climate Change* (n. 1), para. 292.

17 ICJ, *Obligations of States in respect of Climate Change* (n. 1), para. 268. Cf. ITLOS, *Request for an Advisory Opinion submitted by the Commission of Small Island States on Climate Change and International Law* (n. 3),para. 229.

18 ICJ, *Obligations of States in respect of Climate Change* (n. 1), para. 275. Cf. ITLOS, *Request for an Advisory Opinion submitted by the Commission of Small Island States on Climate Change and International Law* (n. 3), paras. 239, 397.

19 ICJ, *Obligations of States in respect of Climate Change* (n. 1), para. 274.

nised that a risk of significant harm may also result from the cumulative effects of multiple activities.[20] In this regard, it echoed ITLOS' position that activities which appear environmentally negligible in isolation may, in combination, produce substantial adverse effects.[21] Consequently, States are under a duty to assess not only the individual environmental implications of activities within their jurisdiction, but also their aggregate and interactive effects, taking into account broader systemic impacts.

The ICJ built upon ITLOS' recognition of the duty to cooperate as a fundamental principle of international environmental law, affirming its status as a rule of customary international law.[22] Notably, the ICJ clarified, again echoing ITLOS, that the duty to cooperate is not exhausted by the mere conclusion or implementation of treaty commitments; rather, it imposes a continuing obligation to pursue cooperative action in good faith, both within and beyond formal legal frameworks.[23]

The ICJ, aligning with ITLOS, acknowledged the complex interplay between treaty obligations under the climate change regime and customary international law.[24] Recognising the difficulty of determining in the abstract the precise extent to which climate treaties and their implementation inform the content and application of customary obligations, the Court held that full and good faith compliance with treaty commitments, '*as interpreted by the Court*', is a strong indicator that a State is substantially fulfilling its general customary duties to prevent significant environmental harm and to cooperate.[25] However, consistent with ITLOS' findings, the ICJ was careful to affirm that such compliance does not, in and of itself, exhaust

---

20 ICJ, *Obligations of States in respect of Climate Change* (n. 1), para. 276.

21 ICJ, *Obligations of States in respect of Climate Change* (n. 1), para 276; Cf. ITLOS, *Request for an Advisory Opinion submitted by the Commission of Small Island States on Climate Change and International Law* (n. 3), para. 365.

22 ICJ, *Obligations of States in respect of Climate Change* (n. 1), para. 140. Cf. ITLOS, *Request for an Advisory Opinion submitted by the Commission of Small Island States on Climate Change and International Law* (n. 3), para. 296.

23 ICJ, *Obligations of States in respect of Climate Change* (n. 1), para. 304. Cf. ITLOS, *Request for an Advisory Opinion submitted by the Commission of Small Island States on Climate Change and International Law* (n. 3), para. 223.

24 ICJ, *Obligations of States in respect of Climate Change* (n. 1), paras. 313–4. Cf. ITLOS, *Request for an Advisory Opinion submitted by the Commission of Small Island States on Climate Change and International Law* (n. 3), paras. 223, 297–99.

25 ICJ, *Obligations of States in respect of Climate Change* (n. 1), paras. 314.

or discharge the distinct obligations imposed by customary international law.[26]

2. Specific Obligations under UNCLOS

In its Advisory Opinion on climate change, the ICJ explicitly and implicitly acknowledged the relevance of ITLOS' prior interpretation of UNCLOS. The ICJ stated that while it 'is not obliged, in the exercise of its judicial functions, to model its own interpretation of UNCLOS on that of ITLOS, it considers that, in so far as it is called upon to interpret the Convention, it should ascribe great weight to the interpretation adopted by the Tribunal [,] [...] "[...] [in order] to achieve the necessary clarity and the essential consistency of international law, as well as legal security"' [ICJ, para. 338].[27] This formulation reflects a nuanced form of judicial deference, grounded in the *institutional authority* of ITLOS as a specialised tribunal.[28] It also discloses a broader methodological choice that permeates the Advisory Opinion: the ICJ seeks to anchor its reasoning in existing jurisprudence and to weave together the various strands of international obligations into a coherent tapestry, thereby promoting systemic integration and enhancing the consistency of the international legal order.

This broader methodological alignment is reflected in the ICJ's subsequent identification of 'the *most relevant* obligations of States under UNCLOS', a formulation that implies that the list it provides is not exhaustive.[29] This phrasing may be understood as an implicit reference to the ITLOS Advisory Opinion, which undertook a more comprehensive and systematic examination of climate change-related obligations under UNCLOS. While the ICJ does not expressly cite ITLOS at this point in the text, the selective manner in which it addressed specific UNCLOS obligations closely mirrors the structure and analytical framework of the ITLOS'

26 ICJ, *Obligations of States in respect of Climate Change* (n. 1), para. 113. Cf. ITLOS, *Request for an Advisory Opinion submitted by the Commission of Small Island States on Climate Change and International Law* (n. 3),paras. 297–99.

27 ICJ, *Obligations of States in respect of Climate Change* (n. 1), paras. 338.

28 *Cf.* Ingo Venzke, 'Understanding the Authority of International Courts and Tribunals: On Delegation and Discursive Construction', Theor Inq L14 (2013), 381-409. .

29 ICJ, *Obligations of States in respect of Climate Change* (n. 1), para. 341.

advisory opinion.[30] The ICJ's statement thus appears to acknowledge the existence of a broader legal analysis already conducted by ITLOS, effectively positioning its own discussion as a targeted elaboration rather than a full exposition. In this sense, the ICJ both defers to and builds upon the Tribunal's more detailed treatment, implicitly reinforcing ITLOS' Advisory Opinion as *the* key interpretative reference point for understanding the application of UNCLOS in the climate context.

Consequently, the ICJ reproduced the reasoning and legal findings of ITLOS through *verbatim* citations and detailed incorporations of ITLOS' interpretation of key provisions, such as Articles 1(1)(4), 192, 193, 194(1) and (2), 197, and 206 UNCLOS.[31] Most notably, the ICJ followed ITLOS' view that anthropogenic GHG emissions qualify as 'pollution of the marine environment' under Article 1(1)(4), thus bringing climate change squarely within the protective scope of Part XII of the Convention.[32] The ICJ also reiterated ITLOS' conclusion that Article 192 entails both positive and negative obligations, and that Article 194 imposes a stringent obligation of conduct requiring States to take all necessary measures.[33] The Court likewise echoed ITLOS' finding that the sovereign rights recognised under Article 193 are circumscribed by environmental duties, and that Article 197 imposes an ongoing obligation of international cooperation that extends beyond treaty participation.[34]

30 ICJ, *Obligations of States in respect of Climate Change* (n. 1), para. 340. Cf. ITLOS, *Request for an Advisory Opinion submitted by the Commission of Small Island States on Climate Change and International Law* (n. 3), paras. 161–79.

31 ICJ, *Obligations of States in respect of Climate Change* (n. 1), paras. 339–54.

32 ICJ, *Obligations of States in respect of Climate Change* (n. 1), para. 340. Cf. ITLOS, *Request for an Advisory Opinion submitted by the Commission of Small Island States on Climate Change and International Law* (n. 3), paras. 161–79.

33 ICJ, *Obligations of States in respect of Climate Change* (n. 1), paras. 342–3. Cf. ITLOS, *Request for an Advisory Opinion submitted by the Commission of Small Island States on Climate Change and International Law* (n. 3), paras. 385, 387, 399.

34 ICJ, *Obligations of States in respect of Climate Change* (n. 1), paras. 344–5. Cf. ITLOS, *Request for an Advisory Opinion submitted by the Commission of Small Island States on Climate Change and International Law* (n. 3), paras. 187, 206–7, 241, 380.

II. Advisory Jurisdiction as a Site of Systemic Integration and 'Cross-Judicial Law-Making'

In light of this substantive cross-institutional engagement evident in the ICJ's Advisory Opinion, particularly its incorporation of legal reasoning from other international judicial bodies, one may discern the gradual emergence of a more coherent body of international climate change law. This development raises a pertinent and hitherto underexplored question concerning the functions of the advisory jurisdiction of international courts. Beyond its traditionally recognised roles, namely, the settlement of disputes, the facilitation of international governance, and the progressive development of international law,[35] might the advisory function also serve a further purpose, namely that of *systemic integration*[36]?

1. Systemic Integration

Such an integrative function, though not prominently addressed in international legal scholarship, merits closer examination in light of the complex nature of contemporary global challenges such as climate change, which inherently traverse multiple and often fragmented legal regimes. While mutual referencing and converging jurisprudential approaches among international courts and tribunals may, at first glance, appear as isolated instances of judicial dialogue, this evolving pattern of cross-referencing between international judicial bodies, such as the ICJ and ITLOS, reveals a more systemic process.[37] Unlike sporadic or context-specific exchanges, this form of engagement is recurrent, substantive, and directed toward the articulation of consistent principles, rules, and standards across fora and legal regimes. In building upon each other's reasoning to develop shared rules, principles, and standards, the courts move beyond dialogue and toward what may be conceptualised as *'cross-judicial lawmaking'*.

35 Andreas Kulick, 'Between Advice and Miracle: Expectations and Persuasiveness of ICJ Advisory Opinions', ICLR 27 (2025), 33-61.

36 Campbell Mclachlan, 'The Principle of Systemic Integration and Article 31(3)(c) of the Vienna Convention', ICLQ, 54 (2005), 279-320.

37 Susan Ann Samuel and Jorge Alejandro Carrillo Bañuelos, 'The Role of Advisory Opinions in International Law in the Context of the Climate Crisis: The Dialogue between the ICJ, the ITLOS, the IACtHR, and the AfCtHPR', in: Maria Antonia Tigre and Armando Rocha (eds), *The Role of Advisory Opinions in International Law in the Context of the Climate Crisis* (Brill 2025), 122–128.

The term *'cross-judicial law-making'* thus refers to a process by which multiple international judicial bodies contribute to the development, clarification, and integration of legal norms in response to a shared regulatory gap or an underdeveloped normative field. Cross-judicial law-making may arise in relation to cross-sectoral challenges, such as climate change, which cut across the traditional boundaries of discrete legal regimes (*e.g.*, environmental law, human rights law, the law of the sea, investment law) and expose *lacunae* or fragmentation within the existing governance architecture.[38] In such cases, some branches of international law may already provide partial legal frameworks, while others, though normatively relevant, may not yet have engaged with the issue, thereby creating a normative deficit. This fragmented legal landscape invites judicial engagement from multiple institutions with varying institutional mandates, jurisdictions, and expertise.

Significantly, cross-judicial law-making does not require that international courts be seized with identical legal questions, nor does it presuppose concurrent advisory proceedings or formal coordination.[39] Rather, it may emerge organically as different courts, when called upon to issue Advisory Opinions, respond to overlapping normative dimensions of the same underlying global problem. Through mutual referencing, convergent reasoning, or the transposition of rules, principles, and standards across legal regimes, courts contribute incrementally to the construction of a coherent legal response. In this regard, both, the ICJ and ITLOS, have emphasised that 'when several rules bear on a single issue, they should, to the extent possible, be interpreted so as to give rise to a single set of compatible obligations'.[40]

In that sense, cross-judicial law-making represents a form of judicially mediated norm development.[41] Drawing conceptually on the notion of *'transjudicialism'*, which describes horizontal dialogue among domestic

---

38 Rita Guerreiro Teixeira and Patrícia Galvão Teles, 'Advisory Opinions and the Development of International Law: An Opportunity for Climate Change Law?', in: Maria Antonia Tigre and Armando Rocha (eds), *The Role of Advisory Opinions in International Law in the Context of the Climate Crisis* (Brill 2025), 47–52.

39 Samuel and Bañuelos (n. 37) 121.

40 ICJ, *Obligations of States in respect of Climate Change* (n. 1), para. 165. Cf. ITLOS, *Request for an Advisory Opinion submitted by the Commission of Small Island States on Climate Change and International Law* (n. 3), para. 136.

41 Cf. Robert Howse and Ruti Teitel, 'Cross-Judging Revisited', N.Y.U. J. Int'l L. & Pol. 46 (2014), 867-874.

courts, this emerging phenomenon among international judicial bodies may be termed *'interjudicialism'*.[42]

2. International Courts as Reactants in the Catalysis of Systemic Integration

However, any catalytic process depends on the presence of reactants, and in the evolving field of international climate change law, the principal reactants have been international judicial institutions themselves. Rather than operating as passive fora for legal interpretation, courts, such as the ICJ, have taken an active role in sustaining processes of systemic integration. While advisory proceedings before the ICJ or ITLOS can only be initiated by certain entities – and behind such initiatives regularly lie the political decisions of States and, in some cases, the influence of civil society – once seized, courts retain discretion as to whether, and to what extent, they engage with the jurisprudence of other judicial bodies.[43] By choosing to cross-reference and align their reasoning, the ICJ and ITLOS deliberately contributed to the consolidation of a coherent legal framework across fragmented regimes, thereby giving practical effect to the principle of systemic integration. Thus, through their advisory jurisdictions, these courts have not only clarified the content of States' legal obligations across distinct legal regimes but have also begun to articulate a convergent legal grammar for addressing the cross-sectoral challenges posed by climate change.[44]

---

42 Cf. Anne-Marie Slaughter, 'A Typology of Transjudicial Communication', U. Rich. L. Rev., 29 (1994), 99-137.

43 Maria Antonia Tigre and Armando Rocha, 'Symposium on the Contours and Limits of Advisory Opinions: Competing Perspectives and Dialogue in Climate Change Advisory Opinions', AJIL UNBOUND 117 (2023), 287 (289). It appears to be broadly accepted in scholarly literature that systemic integration does not constitute a binding legal obligation upon international courts and tribunals. Rather, it is more appropriately understood as an ethical responsibility, guiding judges from different fora to engage in dialogue, consider each other's reasoning, and, where appropriate, align their interpretative approaches in the interest of fostering coherence within the international legal order.

44 See Lang and Köcke, 'Rising to the Occasion: The World Court as Architect of a Harmonious International Climate Law Framework', in this volume.

III. Conclusion

The ICJ's willingness to incorporate ITLOS' reasoning into its own analysis reveals a pragmatic and cooperative judicial posture, one that recognises that normative coherence and legal certainty across regimes are strengthened by acknowledging the interpretative authority of specialised adjudicatory bodies. This approach does not signify institutional subordination, nor does it compromise the ICJ's interpretative autonomy. Rather, it reflects a broader *cooperative epistemology* in international adjudication, one in which judicial bodies, while maintaining their distinct mandates, engage in a process of mutual reinforcement to promote systemic integration.

The Legal Consequences of Climate Harm: Complementarity Between the Advisory Opinions of the International Court of Justice and the Inter-American Court of Human Rights

Juan Auz[*]

I. Introduction

The Advisory Opinions recently issued by the International Court of Justice (ICJ) and the Inter-American Court of Human Rights (IACtHR) offer significant legal guidance on States' climate-related obligations and the consequences of their breach.[1] Both opinions rely on a plethora of international legal sources, from international legal custom as codified by the International Law Commission (ILC) Draft Articles on State Responsibility, which outline key principles such as attribution, causation, and remedies,[2] to soft law like the UN Guiding Principles on Business and Human Rights.[3] They also incorporate foundational principles of international environmental law—prevention, precaution, sustainable development, and common but differentiated responsibilities and capabilities (CBDR-RC)—as set out in treaties such as the UNFCCC and the Paris Agreement.[4]

While both courts diverge in their approach to answering the questions posed by their respective request, mainly due to the legal frameworks delimiting their mandate, the horizontal and vertical logic of their dispute settlement distinctions, and the nature of the legal proceedings, their inter-

---

* Postdoctoral Researcher at Tilburg Law School. His research is funded by the ERC 2021 Starting Grant TransLitigate(101039648). The views expressed here are only of the author and do not reflect those of the EU or ERC.

1 ICJ, *Obligations of States in Respect of Climate Change*, Advisory Opinion of 23 July 2025.; IACtHR, *Advisory Opinion on Climate Emergency and Human Rights*, 29 May 2025, AO-32/25.

2 ILC, 'Articles on the Responsibility of States for Internationally Wrongful Acts with Commentaries', (2001) ILCYB, Vol. II, Part Two, 31, Arts. 31–33.

3 UN Guiding Principles on Business and Human Rights, UN Doc. HR/PUB/11/04 (2011).

4 UN Framework Convention on Climate Change (UNFCCC), 1771 UNTS 107; UN, Paris Agreement to the UNFCCC, 3156 UNTS No. 54113.

pretative outputs can be mutually complemented for climate protection and the benefits derived from it. This post, therefore, focuses on how these courts complement each other in examining questions of attribution, causation, and remedies, which are arguably the main legal consequences used to determine state responsibility in the context of potential climate harm.[5] By analysing and comparing their respective reasoning across these key issues, the post reflects on the broader implications for international climate law.

II. Framing of Questions: Shaping Judicial Responses

The ICJ was asked by the UN General Assembly to address the legal consequences of States' acts and omissions causing significant harm to the climate system.[6] Its task was therefore grounded in international state responsibility. The ICJ was called to interpret existing obligations under international, climate, environmental and human rights law, and to assess how breaches by States can be addressed under international law. This required not only a doctrinal engagement with the ILC's Articles on State Responsibility but also a contextual interpretation of environmental treaty regimes. The ICJ's mandate also required it to evaluate how climate-related harm engages obligations under customary international law.

In contrast, the IACtHR received a request from Chile and Colombia concerning climate change in relation to the Inter-American human rights framework.[7] The IACtHR reformulated the questions to focus on States' obligations to respect, protect, and fulfil the rights of people threatened by climate change, especially vulnerable groups.[8] As a result, the IACtHR did not address doctrinal issues related to state responsibility as outlined by the ILC's Draft Articles and further elaborated by the ICJ in the context of climate change, thereby avoiding discussion of the legal consequences of breaches. Instead, given the scope of the questions and its role as an interpreter of human rights law, it identified the relevant human rights

5 IACtHR, *Advisory Opinion on Climate Emergency and Human Rights* (n. 1), paras. 358–363.
6 ICJ, *Obligations of States in Respect of Climate Change* (n. 1), para. 88.
7 Juan Auz and Thalía Viveros-Uehara, 'Another Advisory Opinion on the Climate Emergency? The Added Value of the Inter-American Court of Human Rights', EJIL:Talk!, 02 March 2023.
8 IACtHR, *Advisory Opinion on Climate Emergency and Human Rights* (n. 1), para. 28.

obligations and examined their application in relation to the climate emergency. Despite this core distinction, the IACtHR outlined procedural rights options for future claimants to seek redress for violations of human rights duties, thus aligning, to a certain extent, with the law of state responsibility.

III. Attribution: Identifying Responsible Actors

Attribution determines whether conduct can be legally imputed to a State.[9] The ICJ provided a detailed, doctrinal analysis based on the ILC Articles. It distinguished scientific attribution (assessing causal contributions to climate change) from legal attribution (imputing conduct to States).[10] The Court reaffirmed the principle that states are responsible for the acts of their organs and for private conduct they fail to regulate with due diligence.[11] Notably, the ICJ highlighted that failure to regulate emissions-intensive activities, including fossil fuel production, subsidisation, and licensing, could give rise to state responsibility.[12] This suggests a broader reading of primary obligations to prevent significant environmental harm.

The IACtHR, while not engaging in a formal doctrinal discussion of attribution under the ILC Articles, reinforced accountability through a human rights lens. Drawing on its earlier jurisprudence, including the *La Oroya* and *Lhaka Honhat* judgments, the Court reiterated that States must prevent foreseeable harm that could infringe protected rights.[13] In this context, the IACtHR considers the failure to regulate environmental risks as a breach of the State's duty to respect, protect, and fulfil rights.[14] Although the Court did not treat attribution as a technical legal concept,

9 Petra Minnerop, 'Climate Causality: From Causation to Attribution' in: Margaretha Wewerinke-Singh and Sarah Mead (eds.), *The Cambridge Handbook on Climate Litigation* (Cambridge University Press 2025) 415–44.

10 ICJ, *Obligations of States in Respect of Climate Change* (n. 1), para. 425.

11 ICJ, *Obligations of States in Respect of Climate Change* (n. 1), paras. 427–428.

12 ICJ, *Obligations of States in Respect of Climate Change* (n. 1), para. 427; Joint Declaration of Judges Bhandari and Cleveland, *Obligations of States in Respect of Climate Change*, Advisory Opinion of 23 July 2025.

13 *IACtHR, Inhabitants of La Oroya v Peru (Preliminary Exceptions, Merits, Reparations and Costs)* judgement of 2023, Series C No. 511; IACtHR, *Caso Comunidades Indígenas Miembros de la Asociación Lhaka Honhat (Nuestra Tierra) v Argentina*, Judgement of 2020, Serie C No. 400.

14 IACtHR, *Advisory Opinion on Climate Emergency and Human Rights* (n. 1), paras. 552–554.

it implicitly held that regulatory omissions were attributable to the State. This interpretation of attribution based on the lack of effective preventive measures in place is consistent with both Courts' understanding of the standards of due diligence, which must be 'enhanced' for the IACtHR and 'stringent' for the ICJ.[15] In both opinions, therefore, attribution might be inferred when a State fails to demonstrate a heightened degree of vigilance and prevention vis-à-vis the risks arising from carbon-intensive activities.

On corporate responsibility, the IACtHR emphasised that States have differentiated obligations based on corporate actors' historical and ongoing contributions to climate change. The IACtHR urged States to regulate transnational corporations and parent companies to ensure accountability for the emissions of their subsidiaries, particularly in fossil fuel-related sectors.[16] The IACtHR, by fleshing out the polluter-pays principle, stressed that certain corporate actors whose operations entail greater risks to the climate shall have stringent obligations, including addressing loss and damage. Contrariwise, the ICJ dismissed the polluter-pays principle altogether as a source for interpretation and therefore did not directly address corporate actors.[17] However, it reaffirmed the duty to regulate private entities,[18] thereby complementing the IACtHR's position, especially in jurisdictions where corporate emissions are significant.

Both Courts also acknowledged the problem of diffuse responsibility. The ICJ stressed that the cumulative nature of emissions does not preclude responsibility. Rather, the ICJ insisted on the scientific and legal feasibility of quantifying each State's contribution to global emissions and of apportioning legal responsibility accordingly.[19] The Court recognised the principle that an injured State may invoke responsibility against any State whose conduct contributed to the harm.[20] The IACtHR, by recognising the right to a safe climate as a derivative of the right to a healthy environment, established that the collective interests of present and future generations and other species in preserving an adequate climate system shall be protect-

---

15 IACtHR, *Advisory Opinion on Climate Emergency and Human Rights* (n. 1), para. 236; ICJ, *Obligations of States in Respect of Climate Change* (n. 1), para. 138.

16 IACtHR, *Advisory Opinion on Climate Emergency and Human Rights* (n. 1), para. 350.

17 ICJ, *Obligations of States in Respect of Climate Change* (n. 1), paras. 159–160.

18 ICJ, *Obligations of States in Respect of Climate Change* (n. 1), para. 428.

19 ICJ, *Obligations of States in Respect of Climate Change* (n. 1), paras. 429–432.

20 ICJ, *Obligations of States in Respect of Climate Change* (n. 1), paras. 441–442.

ed, and that failing to do so gives rise to state responsibility.[21] This opens the door to multilateral climate litigation and further legal development in areas such as joint and several liability and equitable apportionment of liability.

Taken together, the ICJ and IACtHR opinions present two complementary avenues for attribution: one anchored in the parlance of state responsibility as codified by the ILC and the ICJ's case law and the other framed through the human rights obligations of States in relation to people and nature, emphasising differentiated obligations and the regulation of corporate conduct. Future litigants operating across jurisdictions could leverage both frameworks to establish state and corporate responsibility for climate-related harm.

IV. Causation: Connecting Acts to Climate Harm

Causation, per the ILC Articles, requires a sufficient link between the wrongful act and the harm.[22] In the climate context, establishing this link is challenging due to the global and cumulative nature of emissions. Both Courts acknowledged this complexity.

The IACtHR recalls the transboundary nature of harm caused by a damaged climate system,[23] requiring States to provide redress when a causal link exists between the injury and that State's polluting activities within its territory, jurisdiction, or control. Beyond this general reference to causation in the context of transboundary harm, the IACtHR elaborates its operationalisation through procedural rights related to the environment, rather than the broader framework of causation for an internationally wrongful act as outlined by the ICJ. The IACtHR emphasised the need for evidentiary flexibility to ensure access to justice for victims, recommending the use of scientific presumptions and the precautionary principle when establishing direct causation is difficult.[24] It bases this approach on principles such as *pro persona* (favouring the protection of the person), *pro natura* (favouring ecological integrity), and *pro actione* (ensuring effective access to justice).

21 IACtHR, *Advisory Opinion on Climate Emergency and Human Rights* (n. 1), para. 302.
22 ILC, ARSIWA (n. 2), Art. 31.
23 IACtHR, *Advisory Opinion on Climate Emergency and Human Rights* (n. 1), para. 551.
24 IACtHR, *Advisory Opinion on Climate Emergency and Human Rights* (n. 1), paras. 552–554.

In essence, the IACtHR does not engage with the general rationale of causation in the law of state responsibility as per the ICJ, but instead focuses on the procedural aspect of access to justice as a human right, asserting that causation is an evidentiary matter that requires flexibility in assessing injury and responsibility. This approach to causation, through access to justice, recognises the power imbalances often faced by Indigenous peoples and other marginalised groups in proving harm, aligning with the IACtHR's intersectional interpretation of State obligations.

The ICJ, while adhering to the formal causation requirements under international law, adapted its approach to the unique challenges posed by climate change. In that regard, the ICJ emphasised that there is flexibility in establishing a causal nexus between the wrongful act/omission and the alleged damage.[25] In paragraphs 433 to 438, the ICJ distinguished between the causation required for establishing a breach and that necessary for reparation. It reaffirmed that a 'sufficiently direct and certain causal nexus' is necessary for compensation claims, but recognised that this standard is not fixed and must be adjusted according to the nature of the primary obligation and the specific harm.[26] The Court also differentiated between the scientific attribution of climate change and the legal attribution of harm to State conduct, requiring an *in concreto* assessment based on the best available science.[27] Identifying these two elements paved the way for the ICJ to ultimately dismiss any claim that causation is inherently unprovable in the climate context, but stopped short of declaring that causation will always be established. As attribution science advances and becomes more detailed, it may influence future climate lawsuits by better clarifying the extent of the State's conduct involved in climate-related damage inflicted on a State or an individual.

Taken together, the ICJ's two-stage causation test, the recognition that science can satisfy it, and the increasing sophistication of attribution science suggest that future claimants may indeed be able to demonstrate causation in international climate litigation. While the ICJ's careful wording might reflect internal disagreements, it deliberately refrained from closing the door on causation for States' contribution to climate harm. Perhaps, with a flexible view on causation, cases like *RWE v. Lliuya* could succeed

25 ICJ, *Obligations of States in Respect of Climate Change* (n. 1), para. 436.
26 ICJ, *Obligations of States in Respect of Climate Change* (n. 1), para. 436.
27 ICJ, *Obligations of States in Respect of Climate Change* (n. 1), para. 437.

in the future,[28] especially if they rely on the IACtHR's embrace of presumptions of causation even for transboundary harm.

V. Remedies: A Path Towards Climate Reparations?

The ICJ noted that climate harm attributable to a State's act or omission may give rise to the entire 'panoply of legal consequences under the law of State responsibility'.[29] These include obligations of cessation and non-repetition, which apply regardless of whether harm exists, requiring States to revoke all administrative, legislative, and other measures that constitute an internationally wrongful act and to take necessary steps to cut their GHG emissions to meet their obligations.[30] It also confirmed that States must continue to fulfil their obligations despite the breach.[31]

Additionally, the ICJ elaborated on the consequences requiring full reparation, including restitution, compensation and/or satisfaction.[32] It recognised the difficulties of achieving restitution in environmental cases but proposed ecosystem restoration and infrastructure rehabilitation as potential measures.[33] Compensation may include economic losses, environmental damage per se, and consequential damages, with allowances for flexible valuation methods in the face of evidentiary gaps.[34] Satisfaction may take symbolic forms, including declarations of responsibility or apologies.[35] This comprehensive model supports the development of reparations jurisprudence in the context of transboundary environmental harm, whereby the cessation aspect of a remedy, as seen in the *Whaling* case,[36] meets the compensation reparation as awarded in *Certain Activities*.[37]

---

28 Oberlandesgericht Hamm (Germany), *Lliuya v.* RWE *AG*,I-5 U 15/17 (2025).
29 ICJ, *Obligations of States in Respect of Climate Change* (n. 1), para. 445.
30 ICJ, *Obligations of States in Respect of Climate Change* (n. 1), paras. 447–448.
31 ICJ, *Obligations of States in Respect of Climate Change* (n. 1), para. 446.
32 ICJ, *Obligations of States in Respect of Climate Change* (n. 1), paras. 449–445.
33 ICJ, *Obligations of States in Respect of Climate Change* (n. 1), para. 451.
34 ICJ, *Obligations of States in Respect of Climate Change* (n. 1), para. 453.
35 ICJ, *Obligations of States in Respect of Climate Change* (n. 1), para. 455.
36 ICJ, *Whaling in the Antarctic (Australia v. Japan: New Zealand intervening)*, judgment of 31 March 2014, ICJ Rep. 226 (para. 245).
37 ICJ, *Certain Activities Carried Out by Nicaragua in the Border Area (Costa Rica v. Nicaragua)*, Compensation owed by the Republic of Nicaragua to the Republic of Costa Rica, judgment of 2 February 2018, ICJ Rep. 15 (para. 156).

The IACtHR, by contrast, articulated a human rights-centred framework for remedies. Citing Articles 25(1) of the American Convention and XVIII of the American Declaration, the Court asserted that access to reparation is a substantive right that must be guaranteed through domestic judicial and administrative mechanisms.[38] It proposed procedural innovations such as reversing the burden of proof and adopting special evidentiary regimes for structurally disadvantaged groups.

Substantively, the IACtHR laid out a four-part model of reparation: (i) restitution, including ecosystem restoration and mitigation efforts; (ii) rehabilitation, such as medical and psychological care tailored to affected populations; (iii) compensation, adapted to the unique characteristics of climate-related damage; and (iv) guarantees of non-repetition, including institutional reforms, early warning systems, and strengthened environmental governance.[39] It further emphasised that reparation must be grounded in the best available science and respect both the procedural and substantive rights of individuals and communities.[40] The invocation of the doctrine of 'control of conventionality' obliges domestic authorities to implement these standards in good faith.[41]

Together, the ICJ and IACtHR present a two-tiered view of climate reparations. The ICJ establishes the broad legal framework for future climate reparations in cases of violations that may invoke the law of state responsibility, leaving specific details to be settled in future disputes. Complementarily, the IACtHR provides greater clarity on what reparations for climate-related damage could entail, linking them to human rights, equity, and environmental justice. These two levels of reparations address the legal consequences of States' breaches of their obligations vis-à-vis other States or individuals.

38 IACtHR, *Advisory Opinion on Climate Emergency and Human Rights* (n. 1), para. 556.

39 IACtHR, *Advisory Opinion on Climate Emergency and Human Rights* (n. 1), para. 558.

40 IACtHR, *Advisory Opinion on Climate Emergency and Human Rights* (n. 1), para. 559.

41 IACtHR, *Advisory Opinion on Climate Emergency and Human Rights* (n. 1), para. 560.

VI. Concluding Remarks

Despite their structural, historical, geographical, and institutional differences, both Courts affirm the justiciability of climate harm and the applicability of international legal responsibility to climate-related breaches. The ICJ reinforces the doctrinal foundation of climate obligations through the law of state responsibility. The IACtHR, in turn, enhances the accessibility and effectiveness of climate justice through procedural innovations and rights-based reasoning. This means that historical emitters cannot claim that the content of the Paris Agreement, particularly paragraph 51 of the text adopting it,[42] derogates any basis for liability or compensation for loss and damage resulting from climate-related harm.

Together, these approaches create a more holistic legal framework in which human rights, environmental protection, and state responsibility reinforce each other, thereby making the prospect of climate reparations more than a rhetorical aspiration. They offer a roadmap for legal practitioners, scholars, and affected communities seeking to hold States accountable and advance equitable, science-based solutions to the climate crisis. Their convergence on principles such as due diligence, evidentiary flexibility, and differentiated responsibilities paves the way for a more integrated and progressive international legal order responsive to the climate emergency.

Therefore, the ICJ and IACtHR have established the normative and procedural groundwork for a new phase of climate litigation—one that connects formal legal doctrine with transformative hopes for global climate justice. The route toward climate reparations has now, in theory, been made possible, and the otherwise formidable challenges of proving causation and attribution to determine the right remedy should start to fossilise underneath in the strata of attribution science.[43]

---

42 Decision 1/CP.21, *Adoption of the Paris Agreement* (COP-21, 12 December 2015) (UNFCCC), para. 51.

43 For an insightful deployment of geological parlance to understand international law as a discipline in dialectical temporalities, including in stratigraphic moves, see: Moritz Vinken, 'International Law's Fault Lines and Sediments: Geology as Method' (29 May 2025), Max Planck Institute for Comparative Public Law & International Law (MPIL) Research Paper No. 2025–09, available at SSRN: https://papers.ssrn.com/sol3/papers.cfm?abstract_id=5274030.

2. The Proceduralisation of International Environmental Law and its Turn to the Future.

The Advisory Opinion on *Obligations of States in Respect of Climate Change*: Harm Prevention under Customary International Law

Jutta Brunnée[*]

I. Introduction

The International Court of Justice (ICJ) has delivered an Advisory Opinion on *Obligations of States in Respect of Climate Change* that meets the moment.[1] That the members of the Court clearly felt the weight of that moment on their shoulders – with respect to the role of the ICJ in the context of the current pressures on international legality and the existential threat of climate change – is evident from the fact that the Court issued an opinion that is not only robust but also unanimous on all aspects of the opinion's operative part.[2]

The Advisory Opinion covers the wide spectrum of issues raised by the UN General Assembly request of March 2023.[3] While there is much to be said, my focus is on the highly significant pronouncements on States' environmental harm prevention obligation under customary international law. In this short contribution, I highlight some of the most important ways in which the opinion reinforces, clarifies and augments the Court's previous decisions on this pivotal obligation. In so doing, the opinion also speaks to

* Professor of Law & University Professor, Henry N.R. Jackman Faculty of Law, University of Toronto. Member, Institut de Droit International.

1 ICJ, *Obligations of States in Respect of Climate Change*, Advisory Opinion of 23 July 2025.

2 Declaration of Judge Tladi, *Obligations of States in Respect of Climate Change*, Advisory Opinion of 23 July 2025, para. 2.

3 UNGA, *Request for an advisory opinion of the International Court of Justice on the obligations of States in respect of climate change*, Resolution 77/276 (29 March 2023).

debates around the structure and, according to some,[4] 'proceduralization' of international (environmental) law. Far from being a relic of the past, customary international law emerges as a highly relevant, strong normative framework for grappling with global environmental concerns.

II. Five Take-Aways (and One in Five Parts ...)

1. Invoking its 1996 Advisory Opinion on *Nuclear Weapons*,[5] the Court confirms that States' harm prevention obligations under customary law apply to global environmental concerns. The ICJ is explicit that the salient obligations are 'not confined to instances of direct cross-border harm'-[6] Since all of the Court's judgments on the harm prevention rule were rendered in the context of disputes involving transboundary environmental impacts,[7] this is a very welcome statement. The Court had previously confirmed that the harm prevention rule applied to the 'environment of other States or of areas beyond national control'.[8] Its unequivocal affirmation in *Obligations of States in Respect of Climate Change* that the rule also applies to the climate system is all the more significant because several States had argued that it did not apply, given the cumulative and global nature of climate change.[9]

2. The Court notes that the duty to prevent under customary law arises when there is a risk of significant harm to the environment'.[10] This simple, intuitive statement provides a crucial clarification of some of the Court's previous jurisprudence on the harm prevention rule. Its decisions in the

4 See e.g. Martti Koskenniemi, 'The Fate of International Law: Between Technique and Politics' M.L.R. 70 (2007), 1-30; Jan Klabbers, *International Law* (4th edn., Cambridge University Press 2023), 291.

5 ICJ, *Legality of the Threat or Use of Nuclear Weapons*, Advisory Opinion of 8 July 1996, ICJ Rep. 226, para. 29.

6 ICJ, *Obligations of States in Respect of Climate Change* (n. 1), para. 134.

7 ICJ, *The Gabčíkovo-Nagymaros Project (Hungary/ Slovakia)*, Judgment of 25 September 1997), ICJ Rep. 7, para. 53; ICJ, *Pulp Mills on the River Uruguay (Argentina/ Uruguay)*, Judgment of 20 April 2010), ICJ Rep. 14, para. 193; ICJ, *Certain Activities Carried Out by Nicaragua in the Border Area (Costa Rica/ Nicaragua)* and *Construction of a Road in Costa Rica along the San Juan River (Nicaragua/ Costa Rica)*, Judgment of 16 December 2015), para. 104.

8 ICJ, *Legality of Nuclear Weapons* (n. 5); ICJ, *Gabčíkovo-Nagymaros* (n. 7); ICJ, *Pulp Mills* (n 7) [emphasis added].

9 ICJ, *Obligations of States in Respect of Climate Change* (n. 1), paras. 133, 134, 273.

10 ICJ, *Obligations of States in Respect of Climate Change* (n. 1), para. 274.

Pulp Mills case and, in particular, in the *Certain Activities/Construction of a Road* cases, appeared to suggest that the Court considered that a failure to take the requisite prevention measures, notably procedural steps, would not constitute a violation of the rule unless harm had been caused.[11] However, harm *causation* is not in fact an element of the primary rule, which is concerned precisely with harm *prevention*.[12] In *Obligations of States in Respect of Climate Change*, the ICJ could not have been more explicit on this important point, stating that the '[f]ailure of a State to take appropriate action to protect the climate system [...] may constitute and internationally wrongful act',[13] 'whether that act causes harm or not'.[14] Hence, unless the desired remedy is compensation for harm,[15] proof of harm causation is not required when States invoke the responsibility of others for failures to address climate change. So long as it can be established that a State is not taking measures that are commensurate with the risk of climate harm, it may incur legal consequences under the law of State responsibility,[16] including the 'obligations of cessation and non-repetition, which [...] apply irrespective of the existence of harm'.[17]

3. What then is required of States in discharging their harm prevention obligation? As the ICJ previously decided, States must exercise due diligence,[18] the requirements of which in a given situation, according to the ICJ in *Obligations of States in Respect of Climate Change*, 'should be determined objectively'.[19] The ICJ previously held that due diligence 'entails not only the adoption of appropriate rules and measures, but also a certain level of vigilance in their enforcement and the exercise of administrative control applicable to public and private operators'.[20] In *Obligations of States in Respect of Climate Change*, the Court provides a series of important

11 For a discussion see Jutta Brunnée, 'Procedure and Substance in International Environmental Law', in: Hague Academy, *Collected Courses / Recueil des cours*, Vol. 405 (2020) 79, at 141–146.

12 See Brunnée (n. 11), 150–152.

13 ICJ, *Obligations of States in Respect of Climate Change* (n. 1), para. 427.

14 ICJ, *Obligations of States in Respect of Climate Change* (n. 1), para. 433.

15 ICJ, *Obligations of States in Respect of Climate Change* (n. 1), para. 433.

16 See Brunnée (n. 11), 151.

17 ICJ, *Obligations of States in Respect of Climate Change* (n. 1), para. 445.

18 ICJ, *Obligations of States in Respect of Climate Change* (n. 1), para. 135 (citing to ICJ, *Pulp Mills* (n. 7), paras. 101, 197).

19 ICJ, *Obligations of States in Respect of Climate Change* (n. 1), para. 300.

20 ICJ, *Pulp Mills* (n. 7), para. 197. See also ICJ, *Obligations of States in Respect of Climate Change* (n. 1), para. 281 (citing ITLOS, *Request for an Advisory Opinion Submitted*

clarifications regarding the 'elements' that determine the 'conduct required by due diligence'.[21] Here, I highlight only the most significant of these clarifications.

a) Naturally, the 'degree of a given risk of harm is always an important element'.[22] Aligning itself with the conceptualization employed by the International Tribunal on the Law of the Sea (ITLOS) in its 2024 Advisory Opinion on *Climate Change and International Law*, the ICJ finds that '[w]hether an activity constitutes a risk of significant harm' depends upon a combination of 'both the probability or foreseeablility of the occurrence of harm and its severity or magnitude'.[23] Therefore, 'the higher the probability and the seriousness of possible harm, the more demanding the required standard of conduct'.[24]

Indeed, with respect to threats of serious or irreversible harm, the ICJ agrees with ITLOS' conclusion 'that "where there are plausible indications of potential risks", a State "would not meet its obligation of due diligence if it disregarded those risks".'[25] Thus, significantly, the ICJ agrees with ITLOS that 'the "precautionary approach is also an integral part of the general obligation of due diligence" under the duty to prevent significant harm to the environment.'[26]

b) The ICJ also echoes ITLOS' conclusion that the requisite risk can exist in situations involving 'the cumulative effect of different acts undertaken by various States and by private actors subject to their jurisdiction or control'.[27] In short, the fact that risks of harm to the climate system result from

by the Commission of Small Island States on Climate Change and International Law, Advisory Opinion of 21 May 2024, case no. 31., para. 235).

21 ICJ, *Obligations of States in Respect of Climate Change* (n. 1), para. 136.

22 ICJ, *Obligations of States in Respect of Climate Change* (n. 1), para. 275.

23 ICJ, *Obligations of States in Respect of Climate Change* (n. 1), para. 275 (citing to ITLOS, *Request for an Advisory Opinion Submitted by the Commission of Small Island States on Climate Change and International Law* (n. 20), para. 239).

24 ICJ, *Obligations of States in Respect of Climate Change* (n. 1), para. 275.

25 ICJ, *Obligations of States in Respect of Climate Change* (n. 1), para. 295 (citing to ITLOS, *Request for an Advisory Opinion Submitted by the Commission of Small Island States on Climate Change and International Law* (n. 20), para. 131).

26 ICJ, *Obligations of States in Respect of Climate Change* (n. 1), paras. 134, 294 (citing to ITLOS, *Responsibilities and Obligations of States Sponsoring Persons and Entities with Respect to Activities in the Area*, Advisory Opinion of 1 February 2011, case no. 17 , para. 131).

27 ICJ, *Obligations of States in Respect of Climate Change* (n. 1), para. 276 (citing to ITLOS, *Request for an Advisory Opinion Submitted by the Commission of Small Island States on Climate Change and International Law* (n. 20), para. 365).

the multiple States' and private actors' contributions does not relieve individual States from their obligation to take appropriate preventive measures. This conclusion is in line with other judicial decisions to the effect that no State should 'evade its responsibility by pointing to the responsibility of other States' and that 'each State has its own responsibilities within its own territorial jurisdiction in respect of climate change'.[28] Given the growing international and national judicial consensus on this issue, the 'drop in the ocean' argument seems to have [...] run dry.

c) What measures are appropriate to prevent harm is dependent, in particular, upon 'scientific and technological information, as well as relevant rules and international standards', including those adopted under the auspices of the UN climate regime.[29] As is true for the risk to which States' measures must respond, these factors underscore that the standard of conduct can evolve over time, for example in light of 'new scientific or technological knowledge'.[30] The ICJ notes at various points that, given the indisputable scientific evidence of the universal and urgent risks of significant harm to the climate system, 'the standard of due diligence is stringent',[31] requiring 'a heightened degree of vigilance and prevention',[32] that States do their 'utmost',[33] and that they take measures that are 'designed to achieve the deep, rapid, and sustained reductions of GHG emissions that are necessary for the prevention of significant harm to the climate system.'[34]

d) As the Court confirms, 'what is required by due diligence ultimately "calls for an assessment *in concreto*" of what is reasonable under the specific circumstances in which a State finds itself',[35] such that the standard 'will vary depending on each State's respective capabilities'.[36] For the Court, this conclusion follows because the obligation requires a given State to

---

28 ECtHR (Grand Chamber), *KlimaSeniorinnen v. Switzerland,* judgment of 9 April 2024, no 53600/20, paras. 442–443.

29 ICJ, *Obligations of States in Respect of Climate Change* (n. 1), paras. 136, 283–288.

30 ICJ, *Obligations of States in Respect of Climate Change* (n. 1), para. 284.

31 ICJ, *Obligations of States in Respect of Climate Change* (n. 1), paras. 137, 138.

32 ICJ, *Obligations of States in Respect of Climate Change* (n. 1), para. 138.

33 ICJ, *Obligations of States in Respect of Climate Change* (n. 1), para. 246.

34 ICJ, *Obligations of States in Respect of Climate Change* (n. 1), para. 282.

35 ICJ, *Obligations of States in Respect of Climate Change* (n. 1), para. 137 (citing to ICJ, *Application of the Convention on the Prevention and Punishment of the Crime of Genocide (Bosnia and Herzegovina v Serbia and Montenegro),* Judgment on the merits on 26 February 2007, ICJ Rep. 43, para. 430).

36 ICJ, *Obligations of States in Respect of Climate Change* (n. 1), para. 136.

'use all means at its disposal'.[37] I do not have space here to comment on the Court's various observations regarding the principle of common but differentiated responsibilities and respective capabilities. Suffice it to say for present purposes that it considers the principle to be relevant to the 'determination of the applicable standard of due diligence in a particular situation'.[38]

e) Due diligence entails substantive and procedural requirements. Previously, notwithstanding acknowledgement of their 'functional' linkages,[39] the Court appeared to separate these requirements legally speaking, finding a procedural violation while refraining, in the absence of harm causation, from finding a substantive violation.[40] In *Obligations of States in Respect of Climate Change*, the ICJ seems intent on overcoming this much criticized, including by members of the Court,[41] and conceptually unconvincing approach to the relationship between procedure and substance.[42] After all, in the context of the harm prevention rule, procedural elements, such as the obligations to undertake risk or environmental impact assessments, or to notify and consult potentially affected States, are tightly intertwined with the substantive goal of harm prevention, such that the latter could not be achieved without the former. *Obligations of States in Respect of Climate Change* reflects this reality, noting that the 'duty to prevent significant harm to the environment consists of substantive elements [...] and procedural elements, through both of which States fulfill their duty of due diligence'.[43] Accordingly, a State's failure, for example, to assess the risks of harm to the climate system occasioned by activities under its jurisdiction, could amount to a violation of the harm prevention rule. That certainly would be the logical consequence of the Court's observation in *Pulp Mills* that 'due diligence [...] would not be considered to have been exercised if a party

37 ICJ, *Obligations of States in Respect of Climate Change* (n. 1), para. 290 (citing to ICJ, *Pulp Mills* (n. 7), para. 101 and ICJ, *Certain Activities/Construction of a Road* (n. 7), para. 104).
38 ICJ, *Obligations of States in Respect of Climate Change* (n. 1), para. 290.
39 ICJ, *Obligations of States in Respect of Climate Change* (n. 1), para. 289 (citing to ICJ, *Pulp Mills* (n. 7), para. 79).
40 See also *supra* notes 10–17 and accompanying text (discussing the ICJ, *Pulp Mills* (n. 7) and *Certain Activities/Construction of a Road* (n. 7) cases).
41 See e.g. Joint Dissenting Opinion Al-Khasawneh and Simma, *Pulp Mills* (n. 7); and Separate Opinion Donoghue, *Certain Activities/Construction of a Road* (n. 7).
42 For a discussion, see Brunnée (n. 11).
43 ICJ, *Obligations of States in Respect of Climate Change* (n. 1), paras. 289, 136, 295, 299.

[...] did not undertake an environmental impact assessment of the potential effects' of activities that may have a significant adverse impact.[44]

4. In *Obligations of States in Respect of Climate Change* the ICJ confirms that 'States' obligations pertaining to the protection of the climate system and other parts of the environment [...], in particular the obligation to prevent significant transboundary harm under customary international law, are obligations *erga omnes*'.[45] Since 'obligations *erga omnes*, are '[b]y their very nature [...] the concern of all States',[46] it follows that, under the rules on State responsibility, 'climate mitigation obligations [...] may be invoked by any State when such obligations arise under general international law',[47] including a State 'other than an injured State'.[48] This pronouncement marks the first time that the ICJ affirmed the *erga omnes* nature of obligations regarding the prevention of harm to the environment beyond national jurisdiction. Given the Court's reference to '*obligations* pertaining to the protection of the climate system',[49] it stands to reason that all harm prevention obligations are owed *erga omnes*. This would include the procedural requirements detailed by the Court, as well as the all-important obligation to cooperate in good faith,[50] which for reasons of space I cannot discuss here.

5. There is much that could be said about the Court's engagement with States' commitments under the UN Framework Convention on Climate Change (FCCC) and, in particular, the Paris Agreement.[51] For present purposes, the key point is that the ICJ is clear that, contrary to the views expressed by several States, these treaties do not displace States' harm

44 ICJ, *Pulp Mills* (n. 7), para. 204.

45 ICJ, *Obligations of States in Respect of Climate Change* (n. 1), para. 440.

46 ICJ, *Obligations of States in Respect of Climate Change* (n. 1), para. 441 (citing to ICJ, *Barcelona Traction, Light and Power Company, Limited (Belgium v. Spain)*, Judgment of 5 February 1970, ICJ Rep. 3, para. 33).

47 ICJ, *Obligations of States in Respect of Climate Change* (n. 1), para. 442.

48 ICJ, *Obligations of States in Respect of Climate Change* (n. 1), para. 442 (citing to Article 48(1)(b) of the ILC Articles on State Responsibility).

49 ICJ, *Obligations of States in Respect of Climate Change* (n. 1), para. 440 [emphasis added].

50 ICJ, *Obligations of States in Respect of Climate Change* (n. 1), paras. 140–142, 301–302.

51 See e.g. Christina Voigt, 'The ICJ and the UN Climate Regime: Clarifying mitigation obligations under the Paris Agreement', in this volume. But see also the important concerns raised by Daniel Bodansky and Susan Biniaz, 'The ICJ's Advisory Opinion on Climate Change: Does It Throw a Wrench into the Negotiator's Toolbox of Diplomatic Problem-Solving Techniques?', EJIL: Talk!, September 23, 2025.

prevention obligations under customary law.[52] On the contrary – according to the ICJ, the due diligence requirements discussed above inform the interpretation of States' 'obligations of conduct' under the Paris Agreement, including their obligations regarding the mitigation of greenhouse gas emissions.[53]

III. Conclusion

As the ICJ notes in its concluding observations: climate change is 'more than a legal problem'; it is 'an existential problem of planetary proportions that imperils all forms of life and the very health of our planet'.[54] Conscious that international law 'has an important but ultimately limited role' in resolving the climate crisis, the Court expressed the hope that 'its conclusions will allow the law to inform and guide social and political action to address the ongoing climate crisis'.[55] In my assessment, the Court has made a significant contribution to these ends. As I hope to have illustrated, its opinion on *Obligations of States in Respect of Climate Change* reinforces, clarifies and augments its previous decisions on international environmental law's cornerstone obligation. The Court's observations confirm that, in terms of the structure of international law, the harm prevention obligation has emerged as a pivotal part of the international legal regime applicable to the climate crisis. Not only does it provide standards that bind every State, whether party to climate agreements or not, it also provides a robust normative framework. In this framework, the proceduralisation of international environmental law that some observers have detected would seem to be a strength rather than a weakness. Through the harm prevention obligation's due diligence standard, substance and procedure are tightly intertwined to provide adaptable, stringent and remarkably concrete requirements for the conduct of all States in the face of the climate crisis.

---

52 ICJ, *Obligations of States in Respect of Climate Change* (n. 1), paras. 162–171.

53 See ICJ, *Obligations of States in Respect of Climate Change* (n. 1), e.g. paras. 228-229, 241-242, 245- 246, 252, 254.

54 ICJ, *Obligations of States in Respect of Climate Change* (n. 1), para. 456.

55 ICJ, *Obligations of States in Respect of Climate Change* (n. 1), para. 456.

Custom, Entrenchment, Interpretation – How the ICJ's Advisory Opinion on Climate Change Contributes to International Law's Turn Toward the Future

Jochen Rauber[*]

I. Introduction

The vision of international climate change law is as simple as it is unassailable: Keeping the world a liveable place for humans all over the planet. As modest as this vision might sound, it still is a vision, i.e. a substantive conception of what the future should look like. Thus, having to fight climate change is having to shape the future. International rules and conventions tackling the current climate crisis have therefore always been among the most prominent exponents of international law's orientation toward the future. Whereas large parts of classic international law – such as the rules protecting State sovereignty or governing treaty relations – primarily aim to safeguard the conditions necessary for the collective self-regulation of States, international climate change law contains norms designed to substantively shape the world's future state: By calling for mitigation, these norms commit States to upholding the status quo ('*stabilization* of greenhouse gas concentrations in the atmosphere'[1] – emphasis added), as it is considered worth preserving for the future. At the same time, by requiring adaptation, they call for change to make the world more resilient and less vulnerable to the consequences of climate change than it is today (these dimensions might be labelled as 'safeguarding the future' ['Zukunftssicherung'] and 'shaping the future' ['Zukunftssteuerung'] respectively)[2]. In a couple of to some extent inconspicuous ways, the ICJ's advisory opinion on Obligations of States in Respect of Climate Change sharpens the contours of this substantive grasp for the future. In this article, I will focus

* Professor of Public Law, International and European Law, and Legal Philosophy at the University of Hannover.

1 Art. 2 United Nations Framework Convention on Climate Change (UNFCCC), 1771 UNTS 107.

2 Jochen Rauber, 'Zukunftsorientierung und Prozeduralisierung im öffentlichen Recht', AöR 143 (2018), 67–121 (68 et seq.).

on three of them: The customary status of climate change obligations (II), their qualification as obligations *erga omnes* (III) and, most importantly, the Court's finding that intergenerational equity serves as a guiding interpretative principle (IV).

II. Conceptualising the Future Through Custom

It is first and foremost by strengthening States' mitigation obligations that the Advisory Opinion contributes to defining – and in fact expanding[3] – international law's conception of the future. In contrast to what some States claimed during the course of the proceedings,[4] the Court clarified without any further ado that the protection provided by the customary principle of prevention extends to the climate system as well, as it forms 'an integral and vitally important part of the environment'[5]. Considering international law's turn to the future, this is important for two reasons: First, because the substantive vision of the future that customary international law pursues is broadened. It now encompasses an undamaged climate system – or at least one that compared to its current state has not suffered further significant harm. Second, as has already been noted,[6] protecting the climate system under the customary principle of prevention expands the range of duty-bearers under international law's future-oriented obligations. Even States that are not parties to the treaty framework on climate change, namely the UNFCCC, the Kyoto Protocol and the Paris Agreement, are now legally held to contribute to the fight against climate change and, hence, to the realization of international law's idea of what the future should look like.

3 For a similar assessment see: Julian Arato and Justina Uriburu, 'Treaty and Custom in the ICJ's Climate Change Opinion', EJIL:Talk!, 24 July 2025.

4 See inter alia: ICJ, *Obligations of States in Respect of Climate Change*, Written Statement of the United States of America, 22 March 2024, para 4.5 et seqq.; Written Statement of New Zealand, 22 March 2024, para. 96 et seqq.

5 ICJ, *Obligations of States in Respect of Climate Change*, Advisory Opinion of 23 July 2025, para. 273.

6 Maria Antonia Tigre, Maxim Bönnemann and Antoine De Spiegeleir, 'The ICJ's Advisory Opinion on Climate Change: An Introduction', Verfassungsblog, 24 July 2025.

III. Securing the Future by Entrenchment

Quite remarkably, the Court adds that these customary obligations protect a common interest of all States and consequently qualify as obligations *erga omnes*.[7] While the Advisory Opinion elaborates on the effects of this qualification for the question of *ius standi*,[8] it has remained largely unnoticed that it also provides these obligations with a form of legal entrenchment that makes them immune against almost any attempt to evade or disengage from them in the future. As Art. 41 (1) (b) VCLT[9] demonstrates for treaty relations, bilateral modifications or exemptions are no longer an option once every State has a legally protected interest in upholding of the respective obligations.[10] To customary international law this applies as well. Hence, except for the highly unlikely case of a sufficiently universal desuetude with regard to the principle of prevention, there is no way out of the respective climate change obligations. It follows that States' obligations to preserve the climate system and thus to contribute to international law's vision for the future are itself rendered future-proof. The ICJ may not have followed in the footsteps of the Inter-American Court of Human Rights that in its own Advisory Opinion on 'The Climate Emergency and Human Rights' has declared the prohibition of irreversible harm to the environment, including the climate system, part of *jus cogens*.[11] But in terms of temporality, the effects of its finding that the prevention principle contains obligations *erga omnes* are not that different. Neither the obligation nor the vision of the future it purports are going to go away any time soon.

---

7 ICJ, *Obligations of States in Respect of Climate Change* (n. 5), para. 440.

8 ICJ, *Obligations of States in Respect of Climate Change* (n. 5), para. 441 et seqq.; for a deeper analysis of this aspect of the opinion see: Federica Paddeu and Miles Jackson, 'State Responsibility in the ICJ's Advisory Opinion on Climate Change', EJIL: Talk!, 25 July 2025.

9 Vienna Convention on the Law of Treaties of 23 May 1969, 1155 UNTS 331.

10 It is subject to debate, however, whether an agreement that tries to illegally derogate from an *erga omnes* (*partes*) obligation is also invalid or at least inapplicable between the parties of the *inter* se-opt out, see on this discussion Jan B. Mus, 'Conflicts Between Treaties in International Law', NILR 1998, 208–232 (222–227).

11 IACtHR, *Advisory Opinion on Climate Emergency and Human Rights*, 29 May 2025, AO-32/25, para. 291.

IV. Shaping the Future Through Legal Interpretation

This rather firm grip on the future seems to be somewhat at odds with the fact that explicit references to the rights of future generations are – except for the occasional quotes from the General Assembly's request or the preamble of one of the climate change treaties – rather hard to find in the Court's Advisory Opinion. Although the Court directly mentions 'generations unborn' in the context of States' obligations to protect the environment,[12] the Court's silence on the not-yet-living is particularly striking in the human rights context. Taking into account that the most severe consequences of a failure to act now will materialize only after the life-span of current generations has ended and considering that most mitigation efforts will not yield success in the immediate future, the rights to life and a healthy environment would, in my opinion, have suggested a more detailed analysis of those questions. And it does not come as a surprise that the General Assembly had, in its request for the Advisory Opinion, explicitly asked the Court to delineate the obligations that States bear to protect 'present and future generations' and even demanded to outline the consequences of violations of those duties 'with respect to [...] [p]eoples and individuals of the present and future generations'.[13] In one of the many individual declarations appended to the Opinion, Vice-President Sebutinde understandably deplores the reluctance of the Court to deal with this particular aspect of the question put to it.[14] And it is in this regard that the Court could have adopted a more future-oriented stance.

It would not do justice to the Opinion, though, to accuse the Court of outlining States' future-shaping obligations without having due regard to future generations and their (presumed) interests. Instead, in one of the rather jaw-dropping paragraphs of the Opinion, the Court acknowledges intergenerational equity as a principle that – although not establishing self-standing obligations – guides the interpretation of applicable rules.[15] This principle, according to the Court, gives 'expression [to] the idea that present generations are trustees of humanity tasked with preserving dignified living

12 ICJ, *Obligations of States in Respect of Climate Change* (n. 5), para. 155.

13 ICJ, *Obligations of States in Respect of Climate Change*, Request for Advisory Opinion, 12 April 2023.

14 Separate Opinion of Vice-President Sebutinde, *Obligations of States in Respect of Climate Change*, Advisory Opinion of 23 July 2025, para. 7.

15 ICJ, *Obligations of States in Respect of Climate Change* (n. 5), paras. 157, 161.

conditions and transmitting them to future generations'.[16] And it is these 'interests of future generations' that 'need to be taken into account where States contemplate, decide on and implement policies and measures in fulfilment of their obligations under the relevant treaties and customary international law'.[17] With these brief remarks, the Court establishes a previously unarticulated interpretative principle aimed at reinforcing the core imperative of international climate change law: to preserve the world as a liveable place. International law's ambition to shape the future in this particular way is now a legally recognized and mandatory interpretative consideration. And although the Court initially draws on the preamble of the Paris Agreement to back the legal status of intergenerational equity and in its conclusions only refers to the interpretation of the 'most directly relevant legal rules'[18], the interpretative principle it endorses is neither restricted to the former nor to the legal instruments of climate change law in general. Instead, if I read the Opinion correctly, it applies to the entirety of international law – for a simple reason: In the Court's own words, intergenerational equity is nothing but a 'manifestation of equity in the general sense and thus shares its legal significance'[19]. Equity, however, is – as the Court has found before – a 'direct emanation of the idea of justice'[20] and 'a *general* principle directly applicable as law'[21]. Given this general character of the underlying principle of equity, it is difficult to see how the realm that considerations of intergenerational equity apply to could be restricted to the rules and treaties most directly relevant to questions of climate change. When in doubt, any rule of international law has therefore – according to the ICJ's interpretative approach – to be applied in a manner that preserves dignified living conditions for future

16 ICJ, *Obligations of States in Respect of Climate Change* (n. 5), para. 156; for a similar trusteeship-account, see Eyal Benvenisti, 'Sovereigns as Trustees of Humanity: On the Accountability of States to Foreign Stakeholders', AJIL 107 (2013), 295–333 (314–318) who argues for a re-conception of sovereignty as trusteeship for humanity according to which 'national decision makers have an obligation to take into account the interests of others when devising policies (or when reviewing them, in the case of national courts)' (314).

17 ICJ, *Obligations of States in Respect of Climate Change* (n. 5), para. 157.

18 ICJ, *Obligations of States in Respect of Climate Change* (n. 5), para. 161.

19 ICJ, *Obligations of States in Respect of Climate Change* (n. 5), para. 157.

20 ICJ, *Obligations of States in Respect of Climate Change* (n. 5), para. 152; ICJ, *Continental Shelf* (Tunisia v. Libyan Arab Jamahiriya), Judgement of 24 February 1982, ICJ Rep. 18 (para. 71).

21 ICJ, *Obligations of States in Respect of Climate Change* (n. 5), para. 152.

generations. For international law's orientation toward the future this is a new step. Where in classic international law a restrictive interpretation (*in dubio mitius*) would have prevailed in order to keep international law's determinations as minimal as possible, safeguarding States' regulatory freedoms,[22] the Court's interpretative approach potentially strengthens the realization of the modest vision that international climate change law holds for the future. It is somewhat disappointing that in the later passages of the Advisory Opinion the Court does not put its novel approach into practice but largely confines itself to the rather abstract statement of principle that I have just sketched. The Court's finding, for instance, that due diligence requires an environmental impact assessment could have benefitted from drawing on its new interpretative rule: If States are bound to consider the interests of future generations when applying international rules, is the duty to assess how these interests might be affected not an obvious corollary?

V. Conclusion

When it comes to international law's turn toward the future, there is no way around international climate change law. The ICJ's advisory opinion on climate change reinforces this centrality in three key ways: First, by extending the customary principle of prevention to the protection of the climate system, it expands international law's vision of the future to the conservation of the climate; second, by elevating these obligations to the status of *erga omnes*, it safeguards them for the foreseeable future; and third, by declaring intergenerational equity a general principle that guides the interpretation of international legal norms, it obliges States to contribute to international law's vision of the future. So, if the future should fail to be bright, the Court is not to blame.

22 On the discussion whether *in dubio mitius* still is a valid interpretative rule see Luigi Crema 'Disappearance and New Sightings of Restrictive Interpretation(s)', EJIL 21 (2010), 681–700 (686–691).

Timing the Environment in International Law: Reflections on Temporality in the Three Advisory Opinions on Climate Change

David M Scott[*]

I. Introduction

In the closing paragraph of its *Advisory Opinion on the Obligations of States in respect of Climate Change* (one set to be quoted for years to come), the ICJ recalled that 'it has been suggested that these advisory proceedings are unlike any that have previously come before the Court'. While able to answer the legal questions put before it by the General Assembly, the Court acknowledged that climate change represents 'more than a legal problem': it is 'an existential problem of planetary proportions that imperils all forms of life and the very health of our planet', one which '[i]nternational law...has an important but ultimately limited role in resolving'.[1]

I find this hesitancy fascinating. In this paragraph, the ICJ acknowledged a fundamental gap between law and climate justice—a limit to how far law and legal responsibility can ultimately take us in protecting our planet. Yet this paragraph also expresses a feeling I think many of us share. Climate change occurs at such a large, abstract level that it is impossible for us to comprehend its full scale and history. We live in a 'fossil modernity' powered by fuels compacted over millennia in the past, turned into plastics and residues that will remain on the planet for thousands of years after our deaths.[2] How can you begin to conceptualise your personal responsibility for something that monumental, never mind the legal responsibility of states?

In their 2013 book *Hyperobjects: Philosophy and Ecology after the End of the World,* philosopher Timothy Morton designates climate change a titular

---

* British Academy Postdoctoral Fellow, Queen Mary University of London. My thanks to the editors for careful comments on an earlier draft. Any errors remain wholly my own.

1 ICJ, *Obligations of States in respect of Climate Change*, Advisory Opinion of 23 July 2025, para. 456.

2 Andreas Folkers, 'Fossil Modernity: The Materiality of Acceleration, Slow Violence, and Ecological Futures', Time and Society 30 (2021), 223–246.

'hyperobject': something so massively distributed across space and time that it is impossible for us to relate to it fully:

> [O]ne hundred thousand years? It's unimaginably vast. Yet there it is, staring me in the face, as the hyperobject global warming. And I helped cause it. I am directly responsible for beings that far into the future, insofar as two things will be true simultaneously: no one then will meaningfully be related to me; and my smallest action now will affect that time in profound ways.[3]

In this chapter, I want to argue that one of the primary ways in which international law articulates this problem of the 'hyperobject' is through *time*: more specifically, through the creation of temporal boundaries that delimit climate change's start, translating and 'slicing up' the impossibly vast temporality of the climate into the smaller scale of legal responsibility.[4] Following how the ICJ, ITLOS, and Inter-American Court of Human Rights have positioned law and climate change 'in' time, this chapter aims to show not only the different bordering functions of time for each Advisory Opinion, as a kind of jurisdictional scope for international law's grasp on the climate, but also position this as the starting point for a map of something like the climate 'imaginary' of international law—what it is that different legal regimes and courts and tribunals visualise, integrate, and exclude from their minds when they try to think about our changing climate in the terms of the law.

---

3 Timothy Morton, *Hyperobjects: Philosophy and Ecology after the End of the World* (University of Minnesota Press 2013), 60. Note that Morton advocates the use of 'global warming' over 'climate change'—ibid, 7–8: 'Whatever the scientific and social reasons for the predominance of the term *climate change* over *global warming* for naming this particular hyperobject, the effect in social and political discourse is plain enough. There has been a decrease in appropriate levels of concern… *Climate change* as substitute enables cynical reason (both right wing and left) to say that the "climate has always been changing," which to my ears sounds like using "people have always been killing one another" as a fatuous reason not to control the sale of machine guns.' [emphasis original].

4 Thinking here again with Morton (n. 3), 70: 'That's why you can't see global warming… We only see snapshots of what is actually a very complex plot of a super complex set of algorithms executing themselves in a high-dimensional phase space. When the weather falls on your head, you are experiencing a bad photocopy of a piece of that plot. What you once thought was real turns out to be a sensual representation, *a thin slice of an image*, a caricature of a piece of global climate. [Global warming] is a real object, but one that occupies higher dimension than objects to which we are accustomed.' [emphasis added].

II. Establishing the legal time of climate change at the ICJ

At first blush, the ICJ's Advisory Opinion appears to dodge the question of temporality entirely. At paragraph 97, the Court notes that temporality was raised as an issue for both of the questions before it: for question (a), this related to 'crystallization and identification' of relevant obligations to protect the climate system; and for question (b), the need to establish an international obligation 'in force' at the time in which the allegedly wrongful conduct occurred. The Court found that while these temporal questions 'may be particularly relevant for an *in concreto* assessment of the responsibility of States for breaches of obligations pertaining to the protection of the climate system', their specific determination fell outside the scope of the present Advisory Opinion.[5]

Nevertheless, the Court elsewhere provides suggestions as to where it would border the legal start of climate change. In its description of the context of the request for an advisory opinion, the Court begins in December 1968, with General Assembly resolution 2398 (XIII), which the Court identifies as the starting point for the context of the Advisory Opinion before it.[6] From there, the Court then ties awareness of climate change to the reports of the IPCC, created in 1988 to report every five to seven years on the state of knowledge on climate change and recognised by states as 'the best available science on the causes, nature and consequences of climate change'.[7] Considering that this 'best available science' is identified as core to states' obligations of due diligence obligations,[8] the duty to prevent,[9] and risk assessments and environmental impact assessments under the precautionary approach,[10] future litigation on these matters will need to wrestle with how the historical state of knowledge about climate change can be translated into legal obligations at different points in time—that is to say, as an application of the intertemporal doctrine, a point raised in a number of State submissions but unremarked upon by the ICJ.[11]

5 ICJ, *Obligations of States in Respect of Climate Change* (n. 1), para. 97. A similar exclusion is made for attribution and causation at ibid, para. 423.
6 ICJ, *Obligations of States in Respect of Climate Change* (n. 1), para. 51.
7 ICJ, *Obligations of States in Respect of Climate Change* (n. 1), para. 74.
8 ICJ, *Obligations of States in Respect of Climate Change* (n. 1), paras. 137, 254, 258, 284.
9 ICJ, *Obligations of States in Respect of Climate Change* (n. 1), para. 278.
10 ICJ, *Obligations of States in Respect of Climate Change* (n. 1), para. 298.
11 On the use of science here by the ICJ, particularly as relates to the (in part temporally-organised) distinction between 'harmfulness' and 'wrongfulness', see Katalin

While this temporal framing may seem uncontroversial, States had presented divergent views on the matter during written and oral submissions.[12] Large polluters such as the USA,[13] Australia,[14] France,[15] Russia,[16] and the UK[17] had argued for a tighter temporal frame, beginning only in 1992, with the UNFCCC as the *lex specialis* that should govern climate change at the expense of other rules of international law. In contrast, a number of less-developed States, more vulnerable to the immediate impacts of climate change, argued that climate change was 'inseparable from our shared colonial histories' (the Melanesian Spearhead Group),[18] not only in the

Sulyok, 'On the Science-Coloured Glasses of the ICJ: Harmfulness, Wrongfulness, and Climate Accountability', in this volume. For recent productive engagements with intertemporal law, see Steven Wheatley, 'Revisiting the Doctrine of Intertemporal Law', Oxford J. Legal Stud. 41 (2021), 484–509; Rémi Fuhrmann and Melissa Schweizer, 'Ending The Past: International Law, Intertemporality, and Reparations for Past Wrongs', GLJ (2025), 1-21; Sara Wissmann, 'Before *Re*construction: *De*constructing the Prayer of Intertemporality' (forthcoming, on file with author).

12 For more on state submissions before the ICJ, see David M Scott, 'Time and Temporality before the ICJ in the Advisory Opinion on Obligations of States in Respect of Climate Change', EJIL: Talk!, 14 February 2025; David M Scott, 'The Challenge of Time' (18 June 2025). Queen Mary Working Paper No. 452/2025, available at SSRN: https://ssrn.com/abstract=5309578.

13 Submissions of the United States of America, Verbatim record 2024/40, 4 December 2024, describing the UN climate change regime as 'the only international legal régime specifically designed by States to address climate change' (44, para. 21), with '[a]ny other legal obligations relating to climate change mitigation…interpreted consistently with the obligations States have under this treaty régime' (40, para. 7).

14 Submissions of Australia, Verbatim record 2024/36, 2 December 2024, stating that the UN climate treaties are 'the central instruments that provide the framework for international co-operation' (36, para. 5).

15 Submissions of France, Verbatim Record 2024/41, 5 December 2024, noting that awareness of climate change, for the purposes of international law, would begin with the UN General Assembly's resolution on the 'Protection of global climate for present and future generations of mankind' and the 1992 Rio Declaration on Environment and Development (14–15, para. 26).

16 Submissions of Russia, Verbatim record 2024/40, 4 December 2024, stating that 'any legal consequences arising from breaches of "climate obligations" due to harm caused to the climate system can only be invoked from the moment the relevant treaties of the UNFCCC system entered into force for that State' (61, para. 63).

17 Submissions of the United Kingdom, Verbatim Record 2024/48, 10 December 2024, describing the Paris Agreement as 'not only, as a matter of international law, the most relevant applicable international instrument for addressing the challenge, but also, as a matter of fact, the most realistic framework for the concerted action necessary to respond to the crisis' (43–44, para. 13).

18 Submissions of the Melanesian Spearhead Group, Verbatim Record 2024/35, 2 December 2024, 102, para. 7.

'colonialism and racism which largely inform our level of development and vulnerabilities' in the present (the Cook Islands)[19] but also the historical fact that the 'developed' position of industrialised States was 'powered by colonial exploitation' (Timor-Leste) in the first place.[20]

The ICJ tracked a course between these positions. While rejecting the *lex specialis* arguments that would have limited responsibility for climate change to only recent and future acts, the Court also resisted calls to extend climate change back to encompass its roots in colonial exploitation, with its 1968 starting point locating the start of any claim after the process of formal decolonization.[21] In this light, it is also notable that the right to self-determination—featured in many States' submissions—receives only a cursory mention in relation to sea level rise.[22] As such, climate change is rendered by the ICJ as a shared, contemporary responsibility of all States, rather than the outcome of a differentiated and unequal historical process that is already imperilling the presents and near-futures of particular States and peoples—a point forcefully criticised in the Separate Opinions of Judge Sebutinde, Judge Yusuf, and Judge Charlesworth.[23]

---

19 Submissions of the Cook Islands, Verbatim Record 2024/42, 5 December 2024, 11–12, para. 9.

20 Submissions of the Democratic Republic of Timor-Leste, Verbatim Record 2024/51, 12 December 2024, 25, para. 13.

21 ICJ, *Obligations of States in Respect of Climate Change* (n. 1), paras. 162–171.

22 ICJ, *Obligations of States in Respect of Climate Change*(n. 1), para. 357. For substantial discussions of self-determination in oral submissions, see, among others, Submissions of the Melanesian Spearhead Group (n. 18), 103–106, paras. 1–11; Submissions of the Republic of Fiji, Verbatim Record 2024/40, 4 December 2024, 71–72, paras. 18–20; Submissions of the Marshall Islands, Verbatim Record 2024/42, 5 December 2024, 29–30, paras. 6–9; Submissions of Papua New Guinea, Verbatim Record 2024/43, 6 December 2024, 25–26, paras. 10–14; Submissions of Kiribati, Verbatim Record 2024/43, 6 December 2024, 47, paras. 22–25; Submissions of Micronesia, Verbatim Record 2024/45, 9 December 2024, 24–26, paras. 20–27; Submissions of Nauru, Verbatim Record 2024/46, 9 December 2024, 11–13, paras. 13–18; Submissions of Tuvalu, Verbatim Record 2024/51, 12 December 2024, 52–56, paras. 3–21.

23 For example, Separate Opinion of Vice-President Sebutinde, *Obligations of States in respect of Climate Change*, Advisory Opinion of 23 July 2025, para. 5: '[c]limate justice requires, at the very least, a recognition that there is an imbalance between the major polluters (constituting a small number of developed or industrialized countries) and the majority of States (comprising least developed and small island States) whose GHG emissions are negligible'. Separate Opinion of Judge Yusuf, *Obligations of States in respect of Climate Change*, Advisory Opinion of 23 July 2025, para. 20: '[t]he disparities in historical and current contributions of various groups of States to climate change and the distinctions in the responsibilities they bear, over which the Advisory Opinion tries to draw a formalistic veil, is fully recognized and

III. Temporal fragmentation across three tribunals

The work done by the ICJ's temporal boundaries becomes sharper when we compare its Advisory Opinion against those given by ITLOS and the Inter-American Court of Human Rights.

In the ITLOS Advisory Opinion, climate change is understood on a much tighter, narrower scale. At paragraph 47, ITLOS begins its legal history of climate change with UN General Assembly resolution 43/53 of 6 December 1988—passed *after* the drafting of UNCLOS.[24] This creates a different relationship between the law of the sea and climate change. Rather than asking which new obligations must be found to apply to climate change, ITLOS instead asks how climate change can be understood within the existing boundaries of UNCLOS. This means that the Advisory Opinion is not oriented towards preventing the extinction of humanity at large (indeed, the ITLOS Advisory Opinion is almost totally devoid of the existential language that the ICJ uses when describing climate change),[25] and instead asks only how ongoing climate change can be understood and domesticated within the existing parameters law of the sea, with the meaning of the treaty evolving to meet the new challenges presented by climate change.

The Inter-American Court of Human Rights' Advisory Opinion, on the other hand, posed a very different temporality. For the Inter-American Court, we do not simply face an 'urgent' risk from climate change in the future, as the ICJ describes our situation,[26] but are in fact *already living*

well established in contemporary international law relating to the protection of the climate system'. And Separate Opinion of Judge Charlesworth, *Obligations of States in respect of Climate Change*, Advisory Opinion of 23 July 2025, para. 28: emphasising that 'States' obligations to apply the treaty and customary principles of equality and non-discrimination entail that heightened attention must be paid to the situation of climate vulnerable groups'. For discussion, see also Julia Dehm, 'The Evasion of Historical Responsibility?: Colonialism, Temporality and Reparative Justice in the ICJ's Climate Advisory Opinion', Verfassungsblog, 4 September 2025.

24 ITLOS, *Request for an Advisory Opinion submitted by the Commission of Small Island States on Climate Change and International Law*, Advisory Opinion of 21 May 2024, para. 47.

25 The only real recognition of these stakes comes at ITLOS, *Request for an Advisory Opinion submitted by the Commission of Small Island States on Climate Change and International Law* (n. 24), para. 122, where the Tribunal notes that 'climate change is recognized internationally as a common concern of humankind'.

26 ICJ, *Obligations of States in Respect of Climate Change* (n. 1), para. 137.

in a 'climate emergency'.[27] This drawing back leads to two significant differences in the Inter-American Court's treatment of climate change. First, the characterisation of climate change as an already existing harm leads to a much earlier historical starting point: not in the twentieth century legal sources of the OAS, but in *1750*, when human activities first began to influence the global climate.[28] Second, as a consequence, the historical 'complexity' of the climate emergency demands different measures in the present 'to address the *structural* circumstances that led to it', with the Inter-American Court specifically calling for a move towards sustainable development.[29] Rather than casting climate change as a universal, future threat, then, the Inter-American Court looks for structural responses that can undo the past and present harm already occurring.

Does ITLOS's more specific and timebound approach give easier purchase for achievable and measurable action? Is the ICJ simply setting the minimum stage for other courts and tribunals to drive forward real progress? Or is it only the Inter-American Court that properly grasps the significance of our changing climate for the present and the future? Scholars can debate the benefits and drawbacks of each approach.[30] But as legal action on the climate builds on the foundations of these three Advisory Opinions, these temporal differences not only show different ways of thinking about the climate within these regimes, but may also manifest in distinct obligations, with each regime attributing responsibility for historical contributions at different points in time. This has the potential

---

27 Inter-American Court of Human Rights, *Requested by the Republic of Chile and the Republic of Colombia: Climate Emergency and Human Rights*, Advisory Opinion of 29 May 2025, case no. OC-32/25, Chapter V, 16–79.

28 Inter-American Court of Human Rights, *Requested by the Republic of Chile and the Republic of Colombia: Climate Emergency and Human Rights* (n. 27), para. 46.

29 Inter-American Court of Human Rights, *Requested by the Republic of Chile and the Republic of Colombia: Climate Emergency and Human Rights* (n. 27), para. 369 [emphasis added]. See also paras. 204–216.

30 See, among the many blogposts and symposia prompted by the ICJ Advisory Opinion, Mario Prost, 'Disaster Passing as Miracle? A Critical Take on the ICJ's Climate Advisory Opinion', EJIL: Talk!, 14 August 2025; Jorge Alejandro Carrillo Bañuelos and Susan Ann Samuel, 'Judicial Convergence on Climate Change', Verfassungsblog, 16 September 2025; Margaretha Wewerinke-Singh, 'Harmonizing Sources, Hardening Duties', Verfassungsblog, 11 August 2025.

to fragment rather than systemically integrate the law relating to climate change, following the bedrock of these different temporal imaginaries.[31]

IV. International law on a warming planet

So far, I have tried to show an 'internal' view of how climate change is domesticated within the bounds of international law through time—how time can be operationalised to assign or deny particular forms of legal responsibility. But these temporal borderings also have a significant 'external' effect. In giving a definition to 'climate change', they 'synchronise' diverse histories, processes, and future trajectories according to the needs and rationales of *legal* responsibility, in a way that might not do full justice to climate change and its impact on our planet.[32] Grappling with the manifestation of those existential stakes, as expressed through the discipline's sense of time, is thus one clear way to bring into focus what international law's 'important but ultimately limited role in resolving' our climate crisis will be, in contrast to other disciplines and modes of thought.[33]

It is, of course, hard to know what to do when faced with a looming future of extreme climate change. Prior ways of living no longer make sense —established practices need to be adapted or salvaged as sea levels rise. Law, like everything else, is fumbling in the shadow of the hyperobject. As Morton writes:

> [H]yperobjects are impossible to handle just right... [W]e have no time to learn fully about hyperobjects. But we have to handle them anyway.

31 Sarah Thin, 'Playing Fast and Loose with Article 31(3)(c) VCLT: Lessons on Systemic Integration from the ITLOS Climate Change Opinion', NILR 72 (2025), 31–57; Sarah Thin, 'From Paris with Love: The Systemic Integration of Environmental Law in the Interpretation of UN Human Rights Treaties', NQHR 43 (2025), 150–171.

32 On synchronisation, see Helge Jordheim and Espen Ytreberg, 'After Supersynchronisation: How Media Synchronise the Social', Time & Society 30 (2021), 402–422; Scott, 'Time and Temporality before the ICJ' (n. 12). On the difficulties of law as a producer of historical 'truth', see Marko Milanović, 'Establishing the Facts about Mass Atrocities: Accounting for the Failure of the ICTY to Persuade Target Audiences', Geo. J. Int' l L. 47 (2016), 1321–1378; Barrie Sander, *Doing Justice to History: Confronting the Past in International Criminal Courts* (Oxford University Press 2021). On law and its distinct relationship to time, see Reinhart Koselleck, 'History, Law, and Justice' in: Reinhart Koselleck, *Sediments of Time: On Possible Histories* (Stanford University Press 2018), 117–136.

33 ICJ, *Obligations of States in Respect of Climate Change* (n. 1), para. 456.

> This handling causes ripples upon ripples. Entities that are massively distributed in time exert downward causal pressure on shorter-lived entities.[34]

These legal temporalities provide an insight into the ways in which international lawyers make sense of the world in which they work today. Thinking through how the 'causal pressure' of climate change exerts itself on international law brings to the fore how our discipline thinks about itself during environmental collapse: which concepts survive, which change, and which practices are upheld or sanctioned into the future.[35]

34 Morton (n. 3), 67.

35 See also Jochen Rauber, 'Custom, Entrenchment, Interpretation: How the ICJ's Advisory Opinion on Climate Change Contributes to the International Law's Turn toward the Future', in this volume.

The ICJ Advisory Opinion on Climate Change: From Carbon Sovereignty to Trusteeship of the Climate Commons

Jannika Jahn[*], *Nele Suchantke*[**]

I. Introduction

Treated as a corollary of industrial development, the freedom to emit CO_2 and other greenhouse gases within a State's territory has long been regarded as both a prerequisite of economic progress and an expression of sovereignty. The International Court of Justice (ICJ/the Court)'s Advisory Opinion marks a shift, calling on States to protect the climate system, thereby putting their carbon sovereignty under an international-law duty of justification (II.). The Court's interpretation reinforces a public-order conception of international law guided by common interests (III.). The Opinion articulates a vision of sovereignty as trusteeship of the climate commons that emphasises collective environmental responsibility and intergenerational solidarity (IV.). It advances a normative counterpoint to interest-driven, short-term international relations. However, its robustness will yet have to be tested when normative commitments, particularly those of ecological and economic concerns, collide (V.).

II. Prevention and Cooperation: Legal Constraints on Carbon Sovereignty

The ICJ limits States' carbon sovereignty through internal obligations of prevention (1.) and external obligations of cooperation (2.), and characterises the relevant obligations as *erga omnes (partes)*.[1] This places legal constraints on States' exercise of territorial sovereignty when formulating and implementing climate policies and aligns with ITLOS's Climate Change

* Jannika Jahn is a Senior Research Fellow at the Max Planck Institute for Comparative Public Law and International Law.

** Nele Suchantke was a legal intern at the Max Planck Institute for Comparative Public Law and International Law.

1 ICJ, *Obligations of States in Respect of Climate Change*, Advisory Opinion of 23 July 2025, para. 440.

Advisory Opinion which held that the sovereign right in Article 193 UNCLOS 'to exploit their natural resources pursuant to their environmental policies' is subject to the duty to protect and preserve the marine environment.[2]

1. The Duty to Prevent Significant Harm to the Climate System

The Court requires States to employ effective means to advance collective climate-mitigation efforts. It understands the climate system as a global commons,[3] whose safeguarding is a preventive duty incumbent on States. The Court thereby orients the protective purpose of international environmental law toward a common ecological interest. Specific obligations to mitigate CO_2 emissions, and the general duty to prevent significant harm to the environment, arise under the applicable climate treaties and customary international law.[4] The Court narrows the discretion of States under the climate treaty framework, in particular the Paris Agreement,[5] requiring them to justify their conduct against normative standards,[6] particularly the principles of due diligence and common but differentiated responsibilities and respective capabilities (CBDR-RC), in light of national circumstances. Similarly, the customary due diligence duty to prevent significant harm requires effective regulation of public and private conduct,[7] including fossil-fuel production and consumption, licensing and subsidies. The failure to do so may constitute an internationally wrongful act.[8] One might read this

2 ICJ, *Obligations of States in Respect of Climate Change* (n. 1), para. 344, with reference to ITLOS, *Request of the Commission of Small Island States on Climate Change and International Law*, Advisory Opinion of 21 May 2024, paras. 187, 380.

3 ICJ, *Obligations of States in Respect of Climate Change* (n. 1), paras. 308, 440.

4 ICJ, *Obligations of States in Respect of Climate Change* (n. 1), paras. 116 and esp. 230 et seq.; 132 and 272 et seq.; see also Christina Voigt, 'The ICJ and the UN Climate Regime: Clarifying Mitigation Obligations Under the Paris Agreement', in this volume; and Jutta Brunnée, 'The Advisory Opinion on Obligations of States in Respect of Climate Change: Harm Prevention under Customary International Law', in this volume.

5 ICJ, *Obligations of States in Respect of Climate Change* (n. 1), para. 237.

6 Cf. Voigt (note 4).

7 ICJ, *Obligations of States in Respect of Climate Change* (n. 1), para. 282; cf. ICJ, *Pulp Mills on the River Uruguay (Argentina v. Uruguay)*, Judgment, I.C.J. Reports 2010 (I), para. 197; Harro van Asselt, 'The Private Life of the ICJ Advisory Opinion on Climate Change', in this volume.

8 ICJ, *Obligations of States in Respect of Climate Change* (n. 1), para. 427.

as support for an ecologically informed approach to economic governance that prioritizes long-term climate protection over short-term interests.

2. The Duty to Cooperate for the Protection of the Environment

The ICJ further reinforces cooperation as a justiciable duty and situates it within a broader conception of community. Recognising climate change as a 'common concern of humankind', it characterises cooperation as 'a pressing need and a legal obligation'.[9] While the existence, character, and content of a customary obligation to cooperate had previously remained unclear,[10] the Court now confirms such a duty for the protection of the environment.[11] According to the Court, this customary obligation reinforces the Paris Agreement's cooperation duties.[12] Although States retain discretion as to the means of cooperation under treaty and customary law, they must satisfy due-diligence and good-faith standards.[13] In substance, the customary duty to cooperate extends beyond procedural requirements and beyond obligations regarding finance, technology transfer, and capacity-building as set out in the Paris Agreement.[14] It requires that 'States develop, maintain and implement a collective climate policy that is based on an equitable distribution of burdens and in accordance with the principle of common

9 ICJ, *Obligations of States in Respect of Climate Change* (n. 1), para. 308.

10 Cf. Laurence Boisson de Chazournes and Jason Rudall, 'Co-Operation', in: Jorge Viñuales (ed.), *The UN Friendly Relations Declaration at 50: An Assessment of the Fundamental Principles of International Law* (Cambridge University Press 2020), 105 (113); Jutta Brunnée and Ellen Hey, 'Judicial Contributions to the Development of International Environmental Law: Refining the Duty to Cooperate in Environmental Harm Prevention', YIEL, 30 (2019), 45 (46); Rüdiger Wolfrum, 'Entwicklung des Völkerrechts von einem Koordinations- zu einem Kooperationsrecht', in: Peter-Christian Müller-Graf and Herbert Roth (eds.), Recht und Rechtswissenschaft (C.F. Müller 2000), 421 (425–429); see also International Law Commission (ILC), Report of 67th session, 2015, A/CN.4/689, para. 12.

11 ICJ, *Obligations of States in Respect of Climate Change* (n. 1), para. 140, referencing the ITLOS, *Request of the Commission of Small Island States on Climate Change and International Law* (n. 2); cf. Khaled El Mahmoud, 'One Climate, Many Courts: The ICJ Advisory Opinion on Climate Change, Systemic Integration, Cross-Judicial Law-Making and Interjudicialism', in this volume.

12 ICJ, *Obligations of States in Respect of Climate Change* (n. 1), para. 261.

13 ICJ, *Obligations of States in Respect of Climate Change* (n. 1), paras. 262, 306.

14 ICJ, *Obligations of States in Respect of Climate Change* (n. 1), paras. 260 et seq.

but differentiated responsibilities and respective capabilities.'[15] Cooperation emerges as an essential complement to the duty to prevent significant environmental harm, since effective prevention requires coordinated action.[16] This action must be geared to preventing significant climate harm and to fostering solidarity among States.[17] Additionally, the duty to cooperate serves as a legal benchmark for assessing whether further collective action, particularly treaty-based obligations, must be undertaken.[18]

III. Common Interests Guiding Interpretation

The restriction of carbon sovereignty through international legal obligations reflects an interpretive approach that conceives international environmental law as a public order grounded in common interests. The Court distils the content of the common interest from the most pertinent sources of international environmental and human-rights law relevant to the protection of the climate system. It engages in harmonious interpretation, reinforcing and consolidating the common interest within a coherent body of climate obligations through systemic integration: treaty and customary law inform each other[19] and customary rules guide – and may even reinforce – the interpretation of treaty obligations.[20]

With respect to interpreting customary international law, the Court relies not only on bottom-up State consent but proceeds deductively from rules and principles that express a common interest.[21] It extends the duty to prevent significant harm from the transboundary context to the global phenomenon of climate change.[22] Although some States rejected this extension,

15 ICJ, *Obligations of States in Respect of Climate Change* (n. 1), para. 306.

16 ICJ, *Obligations of States in Respect of Climate Change* (n. 1), para. 141, cf. *Pulp Mills* (note 7), para. 77.

17 ICJ, *Obligations of States in Respect of Climate Change* (n. 1), paras. 305–306; 364.

18 ICJ, *Obligations of States in Respect of Climate Change* (n. 1), para. 307.

19 ICJ, *Obligations of States in Respect of Climate Change* (n. 1), paras. 313–314.

20 ICJ, *Obligations of States in Respect of Climate Change* (n. 1), paras. 261, 313.

21 Cf. Stefan Talmon, 'Determining Customary International Law: The ICJ's Methodology between Induction, Deduction and Assertion', EJIL 26 (2015), 417–443; William T. Worster, 'The Application of Logic and Reason in CIL Identification and Interpretation', in: Marina Fortuna et al (eds.), *Customary International Law and Its Interpretation by International Courts: Theories, Methods and Interactions* (Cambridge University Press 2024), 105–129.

22 ICJ, *Obligations of States in Respect of Climate Change* (n. 1), para. 134.

pointing to the diffuse nature of climate change,[23] the Court notes that it has applied this duty to areas beyond national jurisdiction, and thus to global environmental concerns, in earlier pronouncements.[24] It proceeds deductively from a broad prevention principle that protects long-term environmental and not merely present State interests, and by analogy to areas beyond jurisdiction.

Since treaty obligations are interpreted in light of these customary duties, this interpretation results in stricter treaty obligations, as evidenced in the Court's reading of Article 4 (2) and (3) Paris Agreement. The Court treats the clause that successive NDCs 'will' represent a progression prescriptively, explaining that this interpretation is informed by the customary duty to prevent significant environmental harm, which requires States to exercise due diligence, including when setting NDCs.[25] Similarly, the Court adopts a strict reading of 'highest possible ambition'[26] and subjects Parties to stringent due-diligence requirements in implementing domestic mitigation measures.[27]

Furthermore, the Court expressly invokes the common interest in climate protection and the treaty notion of the common concern of humankind to characterise the relevant obligations to protect the climate system as *erga omnes (partes)*.[28] On this basis, any State may invoke responsibility irrespective of injury.[29] This approach differs from earlier reasoning that grounded *erga omnes* status in the universal or quasi-universal character of treaties or in the *jus cogens* nature of the obligations.[30] With this approach, the Court recognizes the broader 'commons' dimension of international environmental law, acknowledging the inherent common interest in protecting shared environmental systems.[31]

---

23 ICJ, *Obligations of States in Respect of Climate Change* (n. 1), para. 133.

24 ICJ, *Obligations of States in Respect of Climate Change* (n. 1), para. 134, citing ICJ, *Legality of the Threat or Use of Nuclear Weapons*, Advisory Opinion, I.C.J. Reports 1996 (I), para. 29.

25 ICJ, *Obligations of States in Respect of Climate Change* (n. 1), paras. 241; see also 133, 139.

26 ICJ, *Obligations of States in Respect of Climate Change* (n. 1), paras. 242 et seq.; 136 et seq.

27 ICJ, *Obligations of States in Respect of Climate Change* (n. 1), para. 254.

28 ICJ, *Obligations of States in Respect of Climate Change* (n. 1), para. 440.

29 ICJ, *Obligations of States in Respect of Climate Change* (n. 1), para. 441.

30 Cf. *Barcelona Traction, Light and Power Company, Limited* (New Application: 1962) (Belgium v. Spain), Second Phase, Judgment, I.C.J. Reports 1970, para. 34.

31 Cf. Brunnée and Hey (n. 10), 52.

IV. Sovereignty as Trusteeship: Responsibility and Solidarity in International Environmental Law

Against this background, the Advisory Opinion forms part of a shift in international environmental law from managing 'neighbourly relations' to pursuing long-term community interests[32] and thus, from a private-law to a public-law paradigm in which state sovereignty is oriented not to individual or aggregate States' interests but to the interest of the international community. Conceptually, the Court transposes the notion that present generations act as trustees of humanity[33] to States, which must give due regard to interests of future generations when exercising sovereign rights affecting the climate system.[34] The trusteeship notion can be regarded as a structural umbrella principle anchored in the common concern concept which the Court invokes alongside intergenerational equity as an interpretative principle to buttress duties of cooperation and prevention.[35] It enshrines the understanding that the atmosphere as a global commons is not owned by anyone and must be preserved for the benefit of present and

32 Cf. Alan Boyle and Catherine Redgwell, 'International Law and the Environment', in: Alan Boyle and Catherine Redgwell (eds.), *Birnie, Boyle, and Redgwell's International Law and the Environment* (4th edn, Oxford University Press, 2021), 1 (40); Rüdiger Wolfrum, 'The International Law of Cooperation', in: Anne Peters (ed.), *Max Planck Encyclopedia of Public International Law* (online edn, Oxford University Press 2010), para. 40.

33 ICJ, *Obligations of States in Respect of Climate Change* (n. 1), para. 156.

34 ICJ, *Obligations of States in Respect of Climate Change* (n. 1), para. 157..

35 Cf. ICJ, *Obligations of States in Respect of Climate Change* (n. 1), paras. 155, 308, 440; Special Rapporteur Murase for the ILC on the 'protection of the atmosphere' called common concern and the obligations of prevention and cooperation the 'trinity for the protection of the atmosphere', Second Report, 2 March 2015, A/CN.4/681, para. 78. For a more elaborate discussion of this interpretation, see the Concluding Chapter by Jannika Jahn, Moritz Vinken and Khaled El Mahmoud, 'The ICJ and the Climate Commons', in this volume, I. 2.

future generations[36] with due diligence and care.[37] The Opinion emphasises collective responsibility, accountability and solidarity, recasting the freedom underpinning sovereignty as contingent on the common goal of climate protection. Accordingly, States must subject their individual interests to the common interest in climate protection by self-limitation, so that all States have equal opportunities in exercising CO_2-related freedoms. Fulfilling this common interest is not only a moral imperative, but also a prerequisite for States' compliance with their human rights obligations[38] and a yardstick for assessing the lawfulness of the exercise of territorial sovereignty in light of States' treaty and customary obligations relating to CO_2 mitigation.

Assuming that emitting CO_2 'appropriates' the atmosphere's absorptive capacity,[39] the conception of sovereignty underpinning the Advisory Opinion aligns with traditions of common-ownership thinking. It moves beyond Grotius's view of the high seas as inexhaustible *res communis* not subject to appropriation (Mare liberum), from which scholarship derived open access and first-come-first-served principles, enabling unrestricted exploitation.[40] Grotius also held that God bestowed the Earth in common and that private

36 For a conceptualisation of ecological trusteeship, see in particular Klaus Bosselmann, *Earth Trusteeship and the Sovereign State* (Routledge 2025); Christina Wood, *Nature's Trust: Environmental Law for a New Ecological Age* (Cambridge University Press 2014); see also Trevor Daya-Winterbottom, Trusteeship for the environment?', in: Harro van Asselt, Seita Vesa and Kaisa Huhta, *Future-Proofing Law in a Time of Environmental Emergency* (Edward Elgar Publishing 2025), 251-272; the concept of ecological trusteeship is closely related to the common law public trust doctrine, see Joseph L. Sax, 'The Public Trust Doctrine in Natural Resource Law: Effective Judicial Intervention', Mich. L. Rev. 68 (1970), 471-566 and must be distinguished from mere stewardship models for environmental goods that do not entail public accountability and were critiqued from a postcolonial perspective, see e.g. Surabhi Ranganathan, 'Global Commons', EJIL 27 (2016), 693–717 (714).

37 See more generally on fiduciary State duties towards humankind, Anne Peters, 'Humanity as the A and Ω of Sovereignty, European Journal of International Law', EJIL 20 (2009), 513–544; see also Evan J. Criddle, Evan, 'Fiduciary Principles in International Law', in Evan J. Criddle, Paul B. Miller, and Robert H. Sitkoff (eds), *The Oxford Handbook of Fiduciary Law* (Oxford University Press 2019); Evan J. Criddle and Evan Fox-Decent, *Fiduciaries of Humanity: How International Law Constitutes Authority* (Oxford University Press 2016).

38 ICJ, *Obligations of States in Respect of Climate Change* (n. 1), paras. 369 et seq.

39 Cf. Darrel Moellendorf, 'Common atmospheric ownership and equal emissions entitlements', in: Denis G. Arnold (ed.), *The Ethics of Global Climate Change* (Cambridge University Press 2011), 104 (106).

40 Nico Schrijver and Vid Prislan, From Mare Liberum to the Global Commons: Building on the Grotian Heritage, Grotiana, 30 (2009), 168 (esp. 180–181).

ownership arose later by convention; access to the original commons had to be preserved in necessity, and harm to commonly used goods avoided.[41] *Vattel* likewise stressed that the Earth was given for human subsistence.[42] The theological idea of divinely granted common ownership has been recast in modern philosophy in terms of human rights: each person holds equal claims to access and use natural resources such as the atmosphere as a CO_2 sink.[43] Building on these ideas, some argue that territorial sovereignty must be complemented by other-regarding duties,[44] or that sovereign rights over territory and resources are legitimate only within a collective, justificatory legal framework that secures equal opportunities to exercise such exclusionary rights.[45] Others transpose Rawls's 'just savings' principle to justify fiduciary duties of States to preserve natural resources for future generations[46] and combine it with common-ownership thinking about the Earth and atmosphere.[47]

It is submitted that, on this common ownership reading, territorial sovereignty should be regarded as implicitly conditioned by the requirements of common use, warranting joint regulation. While the Court does not ground climate-protection duties in extraterritorial human rights law,[48] it develops a legal framework of positive State obligations to prevent harm to the climate commons. Beyond mere remediation, it advances a model of proactive prevention and cooperation attuned to the inter- and intragenerational power asymmetries inherent in territorial rights. By applying CBDR-RC across the relevant obligations, the Opinion treats States not as 'black boxes' but as representatives of populations requiring special protection or bearing particular responsibilities. Accordingly, the Opinion conceives

41 Hugo Grotius, 'II.2 II.1, IV.2 – 4, XI', in: Robert Feenstra and Bernadina Kanter- van Hettinga Tromp (eds.), De iure belli ac pacis 1625 (Scientia Verlag 1993).

42 Emer de Vattel, '§ 81', in: Joseph Chitty (ed.), The Law of Nations or Principles of the Law of Nature Applied to the Conduct and Affairs of Nations and Sovereigns 1758 (Cambridge University Press 2015).

43 Matthias Risse, *On Global Justice* (Princeton University Press 2012).

44 Eyal Benvenisti, 'Sovereigns as Trustees of Humanity: On the Accountability of States to Foreign Stakeholders', AJIL, 107 (2013), 295 (310–311).

45 Cf. Lea Ypi, 'A Permissive Theory of Territorial Rights', Eur. J. Philos. 22 (2012), 288–312, building on Kant.

46 Edith Brown Weiss, 'The Planetary Trust: Conservation and Intergenerational Equity' ELQ, 11 (1984), 495–582.

47 Moellendorf (note 39); Wood, *Nature's Trust* (n. 36).

48 ICJ, *Obligations of States in Respect of Climate Change* (n. 1), para. 402; cf. Helen Keller, 'A Right to a Clean, Healthy and Sustainable Environment: Or Perhaps Not (Yet)?', in this volume.

sovereign territorial rights not as an idealised extension of natural rights of appropriation, but as politically constituted and bound by a duty of justification.

V. From Vision to Practice

The Advisory Opinion advances a normative vision of global community and cooperative pursuit of shared interests despite short-term political or economic incentives. It substantiates this vision with duties of cooperation and prevention that address structural obstacles to effective global climate protection. The duty of prevention requires States to adopt a long-term perspective and regulate emissions by public and private actors.[49] Regulatory measures can remedy market failures, especially where prices fail to internalise the social costs of emissions. Reinforced cooperative obligations may counteract collective-action problems of the climate commons.[50] The recognition of customary obligations prevents States from evading international law obligations on climate protection simply by withdrawing from the Paris Agreement.[51] The risk of legal accountability for non-compliance acts as an incentive to cooperate.

Nevertheless, the legal effectiveness of international environmental law will be tested specifically in its interaction with international economic law.[52] International environmental law's transformative force will depend on the extent to which its objectives and State obligations will be integrated into the legal instruments of global trade, finance and investment, will

49 For the regulation of private actors, see ICJ, *Obligations of States in Respect of Climate Change* (n. 1), paras. 282, 298, 427.

50 See generally, Mancur Olson, *The Logic of Collective Action: Public Goods and the Theory of Groups* (Harvard University Press 1965); in relation to climate change, Daniel C. Esty and Anthony L. Moffa, 'Why Climate Change Collective Action has Failed and What Needs to be Done Within and Without the Trade Regime', Journal of International Economic Law, 15 (2012), 777 (777-781).

51 Cf. also Art. 41(2) Vienna Convention on the Law of Treaties; Jochen Rauber, 'Custom, Entrenchment, Interpretation: How the ICJ's Advisory Opinion on Climate Change Contributes to the International Law's Turn toward the Future', in this volume.

52 Cf. ICJ, *Obligations of States in Respect of Climate Change* (n. 1), para. 173; see also Declaration of Judge Cleveland, para. 21, see also von Jochen von Bernstorff and Ingo Venzke, 'The Struggle Against Fossil Sovereignty: The International Court of Justice in the Climate Crisis', Verfassungsblog, 6 August 2025.

prevail in case of normative conflict, and will materialise in state responsibility. This is where the legal framework will demonstrate if it can act as a catalyst[53] and guide the transformation of the global economy in the interest of a sustainable environment.

53 Cf. Steven Bernstein and Matthew Hoffmann, 'The politics of decarbonization and the catalytic impact of subnational climate experiments', Policy Sciences, 51 (2018), 189–211.

Part II: International Law Beyond the State: A Gradual Softening of the Public/Private Dichotomy

The Private Life of the ICJ Advisory Opinion on Climate Change

Harro van Asselt[*]

I. Introduction

As the various contributions to this volume make abundantly clear, the International Court of Justice's (ICJ) Advisory Opinion on Obligations of States in Respect of Climate Change is a landmark decision in many respects.[1] Yet at first blush it seems rather restrained when it comes to addressing the private sector, particularly coming hot on the heels of the more far-reaching Advisory Opinion by the Inter-American Court of Human Rights (IACtHR).[2]

Keeping in mind that States are the primary addressees of the Advisory Opinion, this contribution discusses what the ICJ said (and what it left out) about the role of the private sector. I suggest that even where the private sector is not addressed directly, the Advisory Opinion still has important implications for business actors.

II. Strengthening Corporate Climate Accountability

As several participants pointed out in the written proceedings, the private sector can be considered responsible for the majority of the world's

* Hatton Professor of Climate Law, Department of Land Economy and Hughes Hall, University of Cambridge, Cambridge, United Kingdom.

1 ICJ, *Obligations of States in Respect of Climate Change*, Advisory Opinion of 23 July 2025.

2 IACtHR, *Climate Emergency and Human Rights*, Advisory Opinion of 29 May 2025, AO-32/25.

greenhouse gas (GHG) emissions.[3] Indeed, the Carbon Majors Database suggests that 180 companies, including private and state-owned fossil fuel companies as well as heavy industrial emitters, are the source of 70 % of global carbon dioxide emissions since the start of the Industrial Revolution.[4]

Corporations can thus be seen as part of the problem, but they are likewise part of the solution. Companies often possess the financial and technological capacity necessary for the impending climate and energy transition. Moreover, many companies have made voluntary commitments to tackle their carbon emissions, with Oxford University's Net Zero Tracker finding that 60 % of the world's largest 1,977 companies (good for 67 % of the world's annual revenue) have set net zero targets.[5]

The integrity of these targets can be questioned, however, with lofty goals often not being accompanied by implementation mechanisms such as credible climate transition plans, annual progress reports, and interim targets.[6] Moreover, some companies and business associations have actively undermined climate action by questioning climate science[7] and/or lobbying against the strengthening of climate policy.[8]

To strengthen corporate climate accountability, States have sought to regulate corporate emissions, including through carbon pricing, setting emissions standards, climate risk disclosure requirements, and mandatory due diligence legislation, such as the European Union's (EU) Corporate Sustainability Due Diligence Directive, which requires covered companies to take due diligence measures to identify, prevent and mitigate environmental harm along their supply chain.[9]

---

3 The Bahamas, 'Written Statement' (22 March 2025), <https://www.icj-cij.org/sites/default/files/case-related/187/187-20240322-wri-04-00-en.pdf>, para. 127; Kenya, 'Written Statement' (22 March 2024), <https://www.icj-cij.org/sites/default/files/case-related/187/187-20240322-wri-33-00-en.pdf>, para. 5.5.

4 InfluenceMap, 'Carbon Majors: 2023 Data Update' (March 2025) <https://carbonmajors.org/briefing/The-Carbon-Majors-Database-2023-Update-31397>.

5 Net Zero Tracker, 'Net Zero Stocktake 2024' (NewClimate Institute, Oxford Net Zero, Energy and Climate Intelligence Unit and Data-Driven EnviroLab 2024) 17.

6 Net Zero Tracker (n. 5) 21.

7 See, e.g., Benjamin Franta, 'Early Oil Industry disinformation on Global Warming', Environ. Polit. 30 (2021), 663; Naomi Oreskes, *Merchants of Doubt* (Bloomsbury 2010).

8 See, e.g., Catherine Rocchi, 'Climate Protagonists? Strategic Misrepresentation and Corporate Resistance to Climate Legislation', Stan. L. Rev. 74 (2022), 1153.

9 Directive (EU) 2024/1760 of 13 June 2024 on Corporate Sustainability Due Diligence and Amending Directive (EU) 2019/1937 and Regulation (EU) 2023/2859 [2024] OJ

In parallel, corporations are increasingly targeted by litigants. By 2024, 230 strategic corporate climate litigation cases had been initiated.[10] In the Netherlands, although the groundbreaking District Court ruling in *Milieudefensie et al. v. Royal Dutch Shell plc* imposing an absolute emission reduction obligation on the company was overturned on appeal, the Court of Appeal still found that companies 'have their own responsibility in achieving the targets of the Paris Agreement'.[11] Companies contributing to climate change have also faced tort law-based challenges in other countries, including in Germany,[12] New Zealand,[13] and the United States.[14] Moreover, myriad climate-washing cases are emerging across the globe.[15]

III. The IACtHR Raises the Bar

While domestic legislators, litigants, and courts have thus sought to strengthen corporate climate accountability, the situation is different at the international level. Notwithstanding the emergence of relevant soft law instruments such as the United Nations (UN) Guiding Principles on Business

---

L2024/1760 (CSDDD). See Andreas Buser, 'Protecting the Climate through EU Supply Chain Legislation? Two Critiques and a Compromise', ELO 3 (2024) 617, (621–622). The Directive initially also included a provision requiring covered companies to adopt and implement climate transition plans (Article 22), but this requirement has been removed as a result of an 'Omnibus' process purportedly aimed at simplifying EU law. See European Commission, 'Prosperity and Competitiveness – Implementation Tracker', <https://commission.europa.eu/priorities-2024-2029/competitiveness/implementation-tracker_en>.

10 Joana Setzer and Catherine Higham, 'Global Trends in Climate Change Litigation: 2024 Snapshot' (Grantham Research Institute on Climate Change and the Environment, London School of Economics and Political Science), 19.

11 *Milieudefensie v. Shell*, 26 May 2021, C/09/571932 / HA ZA 19–379, para. 7.27.

12 OLG Hamm, *Lliuya v. RWE*, 28 May 2025, 5 U 15/17 (Unofficial Translation).

13 *Smith v Fonterra Co-Operative Group Ltd* [2024] NZSC 5.

14 For an overview, see <https://climatecasechart.com/case-category/common-law-claims/>.

15 Juliana Vélez-Echeverri, Catherine Higham and Joana Setzer, 'Climate-washing Litigation: Towards Greater Corporate Accountability?' (Grantham Research Institute on Climate Change and the Environment, London School of Economics and Political Science, 17 April 2024), <https://www.lse.ac.uk/granthaminstitute/news/climate-washing-litigation-towards-greater-corporate-accountability/>.

and Human Rights,[16] and efforts to develop a dedicated treaty on business and human rights,[17] States remain the primary addressees of international law.

Still, only three weeks before the ICJ published its Advisory Opinion, the Inter-American Court raised the bar by spelling out in detail what States must do to regulate companies' activities in combating the climate crisis.[18]

The IACtHR did not shy away from calling out the private sector, finding that it plays an 'essential role'.[19]. Citing the UN working group on business and human rights, the Court found that corporations 'have obligations and responsibilities with respect to climate change, and [their] impacts ... on human rights'.[20]

Moreover, it identified several concrete obligations for States, including: enacting legislation that requires companies to conduct due diligence to identify and address climate-related impacts along the entire value chain (i.e., including through emissions taking place abroad); requiring the disclosure of GHG emissions; and adopting regulations countering greenwashing and undermining corporate lobbying.[21]

The IACtHR also clarified that not all companies are equal, and that 'some of them bear greater responsibility for their impacts on climate change due to the risk created by their activities'.[22] Accordingly, the Court found, States 'must ensure a more demanding supervision and monitoring of [these companies'] activities and, in particular, their compliance with the obligations imposed as a result of those responsibilities', specifically singling out fossil fuel-producing and agro-industrial companies in this regard.[23]

---

16 UN Office of the High Commissioner on Human Rights, 'Guiding Principles on Business and Human Rights: Implementing the United Nations "Protect, Respect and Remedy" Framework' (United Nations 2011).

17 UN Human Rights Council, 'Open-ended Intergovernmental Working Group on Transnational Corporations and Other Business Enterprises with Respect to Human Rights', <https://www.ohchr.org/en/hr-bodies/hrc/wg-trans-corp/igwg-on-tnc>.

18 For an analysis, see Eoin Jackson, 'Advancing Corporate Climate Accountability Post the Inter-American Court Advisory Opinion on Human Rights and the Climate Emergency', EJIL:Talk!, 21 July 2025.

19 IACtHR, *Climate Emergency and Human Rights* (n. 2), para. 345.

20 IACtHR, *Climate Emergency and Human Rights* (n. 2), para. 346.

21 IACtHR, *Climate Emergency and Human Rights* (n. 2), para. 347.

22 IACtHR, *Climate Emergency and Human Rights* (n. 2), para. 350.

23 IACtHR, *Climate Emergency and Human Rights* (n. 2), para. 353.

Lastly, the IACtHR also included observations on the misalignment of investment treaties and climate change. Such treaties can be used by companies to challenge changes in public policies that affect their investments, including for example fossil fuel phase-out policies. The IACtHR finds that 'it is essential to foster a balance that allows States to adopt legitimate regulatory measures to address the climate crisis, without undermining the legal certainty and predictability that international investment agreements seek to provide as essential incentives for foreign direct investment'.[24]

IV. The ICJ Doesn't Follow Suit?

Compared to the Inter-American Court, the ICJ's Advisory Opinion may seem underwhelming. It does not suggest that companies have their own obligations to address climate change (or even acknowledge soft law instruments like the UN Guiding Principles); it does not expound what States' obligations are in any level of detail; it does not touch upon the question of extraterritoriality; and it does not discuss international investment law.[25] Still, it is useful to reiterate what the ICJ *does* say in relation to private actors.

First, the Court finds that the material scope of the questions posed by the UN General Assembly encompasses 'States' obligations concerning all actions or omissions of States, *and of non-State actors within their jurisdiction or effective control*, that result in the climate system and other parts of the environment being adversely affected by anthropogenic GHG emissions'.[26] It thus suggests that the conduct of private actors is relevant to determining the obligations of States as well as the extent to which States have fulfilled those obligations. Moreover, the impacts of those activities are not limited to the impacts on other States, but also on areas beyond national jurisdiction.[27]

---

24 IACtHR, *Climate Emergency and Human Rights* (n. 2), para. 163.

25 With the exception of Declaration by Judge Cleveland, *Obligations of States in Respect of Climate Change*, Advisory Opinion of 23 July 2025, paras. 21–22.

26 ICJ, *Obligations of States in Respect of Climate Change* (n. 1), para. 95 (emphasis added).

27 ICJ, *Obligations of States in Respect of Climate Change* (n. 1), para. 272, with the Court citing ICJ, *Legality of the Threat or Use of Nuclear Weapons*, Advisory Opinion of 8 July 1996, ICJ Rep. 226.

Second, citing last year's Advisory Opinion on climate change by the International Tribunal for the Law of the Sea (ITLOS),[28] the Court posits that Article 4(2) of the Paris Agreement imposes a due diligence obligation 'to take domestic mitigation measures, including in relation to activities carried out by private actors'.[29]

Third, in discussing the contents of the customary due diligence obligation to prevent significant harm, the Court suggests that States ought to adopt 'regulatory mitigation mechanisms that are designed to achieve the deep, rapid, and sustained reductions of GHG emissions that are necessary for the prevention of significant harm to the climate system', and that such 'rules and measures *must regulate the conduct of public and private operators* within the States' jurisdiction or control and be accompanied by effective enforcement and monitoring mechanisms to ensure their implementation'.[30] It hereby echoes its earlier jurisprudence in *Pulp Mills*, in which it found that States' due diligence requires 'a certain level of vigilance in their [appropriate rules and measures] enforcement and the exercise of administrative control applicable to public and private operators, such as the monitoring of activities undertaken by such operators'.[31] In short, States have an obligation to regulate the GHG emissions of private actors, and to ensure those regulations are implemented and enforced.

Fourth, the Court reiterates the importance of regulating private sector activities to safeguard human rights. The Court did not follow the participants, such as Vanuatu,[32] who had referred to a statement by human rights treaty bodies that found that 'States must regulate private actors, including by holding them accountable for harm they generate both domestically and extraterritorially'.[33] The Court nevertheless indicates that States must take the 'necessary measures' to guarantee the effective enjoyment of human rights.[34]

28 ITLOS, *Request for an Advisory Opinion Submitted by the Commission of Small Island States on Climate Change and International Law*, Advisory Opinion of 21 May 2024, case no. 31.
29 ICJ, *Obligations of States in Respect of Climate Change* (n. 1), para. 252.
30 ICJ, *Obligations of States in Respect of Climate Change* (n. 1), para. 282.
31 ICJ, *Pulp Mills on the River Uruguay (Argentina v. Uruguay)*, judgment of 20 April 2010, ICJ Rep. 14, para. 197.
32 Republic of Vanuatu, 'Written Statement' (22 March 2024), para. 254.
33 UN International Human Rights Instruments, 'Statement on human rights and climate change', UN Doc. HRI/2019/1 (14 May 2020), para. 12.
34 ICJ, *Obligations of States in Respect of Climate Change* (n. 1), para. 403.

Last but not least, the Court deals with the role of private actors in the context of establishing state responsibility. Although some participants argued that private conduct generally cannot be attributed to a State, the ICJ makes clear that such attribution is not needed as the relevant conduct for the purposes of state responsibility is a State's failure to regulate private actors. Accordingly, 'a State may be responsible where ... it has failed to exercise due diligence by not taking the necessary regulatory and legislative measures to limit the quantity of emissions caused by private actors under its jurisdiction'.[35] Perhaps surprisingly, given its cross-references to ITLOS jurisprudence throughout the Advisory Opinion, the ICJ does not discuss the possibility raised in the ITLOS *Area* Advisory Opinion that in cases 'where the [private] entity in question is empowered to act as a State organ ... or where its conduct is acknowledged and adopted by a State as its own', it *is* possible to attribute private conduct to a State.[36] Moreover, whereas some participants had argued that the Court should do so,[37] the ICJ does not elaborate on the specific legal consequences of state responsibility in such cases (e.g., guaranteeing non-repetition by requiring the adoption of specific legislation to regulate private GHG emitters).

IV. Reading between the Lines

Although these findings are useful in that they clarify the obligations to regulate corporations under the Paris Agreement, custom, and human rights law, and indicate that breaching such obligations can give rise to state responsibility, the Court, unlike the IACtHR, falls short of spelling out the contents of the obligation to regulate private actors.

Yet it is by reading between the lines that we can see the broader relevance of the Advisory Opinion for business activities. In particular, several findings may more indirectly have major implications for the private sector.

First, the Court's finding that the 1.5°C threshold is the agreed lodestar for climate action[38] will likely have reverberations in the private sector over

35 ICJ, *Obligations of States in Respect of Climate Change* (n. 1), para. 428.

36 ITLOS, Responsibilities and Obligations of States with Respect to Activities in the Area, Advisory Opinion of 1 February 2011, ITLOS Reports 2011, case no. 17, para. 182.

37 Republic of Colombia, 'Written Statement' (22 March 2024), para. 4.10; Republic of Vanuatu, 'Written Comments' (15 August 2024), para. 190.

38 ICJ, *Obligations of States in Respect of Climate Change* (n. 1), para. 224.

time, as private standards and benchmarks tied to the Paris Agreement's 'well below 2°C' goal will become less credible. To be certain, the Court omits crucial details about the specific pathway towards 1.5°C (e.g., with or without overshoot[39]), meaning that it will still not be entirely clear what exactly States (let alone companies) need to align with. Nevertheless, drawing on private standards such as those developed by the Science-Based Targets Initiative,[40] companies – particularly those that want to brandish their climate credentials – are well advised to develop and implement 1.5°C-aligned climate transition plans. Moreover, companies should expect that plaintiffs in strategic corporate climate litigants will draw upon the Advisory Opinion's endorsement of the 1.5°C goal to argue for stronger corporate climate action.

Second, the Court put major fossil fuel-producing and -consuming companies on notice, stating that '[f]ailure of a State to take appropriate action to protect the climate system from GHG emissions – including through fossil fuel production, fossil fuel consumption, the granting of fossil fuel exploration licences or the provision of fossil fuel subsidies – may constitute an internationally wrongful act which is attributable to that State'.[41] Although the addressee here is the State, the wrongful acts listed here mainly benefit private companies (e.g., fossil fuel companies being granted exploration licenses, or receiving tax breaks or other subsidies). Moreover, although the Court discussed the scenario where private conduct is not necessarily attributable to the State, as the aforementioned ITLOS *Area* Advisory Opinion reminds us, in some cases such conduct *is* attributable to the State, notably in the case of state-owned enterprises that are also major GHG emitters.[42]

Third, the Court's findings on environmental impact assessments (EIAs) are clearly relevant to those private activities for which an EIA is required. Specifically, the Court finds that 'possible specific climate-related effects must be assessed ... at the level of proposed individual activities, e.g. for

---

39 On the concept of overshoot, see Uta Kloenne et al., 'Interactive: The Pathways to Meeting the Paris Agreement's 1.5 °C Limit', Carbon Brief, 8 December 2023.

40 Science-Based Targets Initiative, 'SBTi Corporate Net-Zero Standard, Version 1.2' (March 2024).

41 ICJ, *Obligations of States in Respect of Climate Change* (n. 1), para. 427.

42 See Alex Clark and Philippe Benoit, *Greenhouse Gas Emissions from State-Owned Enterprises: A Preliminary Inventory* (Columbia University, Center for Energy Policy 2024).

the purpose of assessing their possible downstream effects'.[43] As Judges Bhandari and Cleveland point out in their joint declaration, this means that EIAs for fossil fuel projects require consideration of the downstream impacts of fossil fuel production (i.e., the combustion of fossil fuels by end users), even if these take place in other jurisdictions.[44] The Judges point to relevant domestic cases, including the 2024 *Finch* ruling by the United Kingdom Supreme Court[45] and a subsequent decision by the Court of the European Free Trade Association.[46] However, the ICJ's Advisory Opinion goes beyond such individual rulings by suggesting that, under customary international law, EIAs for fossil fuel projects also in other jurisdictions should consider end-use emissions. This is likely to pose new hurdles for companies seeking to expand fossil fuel production.

V. Conclusion

Those expecting the Court to set out detailed obligations for States on how to regulate private actors, or suggest that private actors have their own climate obligations, may be disappointed. But such expectations were unrealistic from the start. The Court's pronouncements on States' obligations to regulate private actors and the indication that not meeting those obligations may entail state responsibility are a helpful affirmation of the basic requirements for States vis-à-vis the private sector. Moreover, the Court's findings on the 1.5°C threshold, fossil fuels, and EIAs will likely shape the future of corporate climate accountability.

43 ICJ, *Obligations of States in Respect of Climate Change* (n. 1), para. 298.

44 Declaration by Judges Bhandari and Cleveland, *Obligations of States in Respect of Climate Change*, Advisory Opinion of 23 July 2025, paras. 11–17.

45 *R (on the application of Finch on behalf of the Weald Action Group) v. Surrey County Council and Others* [2024] UKSC 20.

46 EFTA Court, *Norwegian State v. Greenpeace Nordic, Nature and Youth Norway*, judgment of 21 May 2025, E-18–24.

Both a 'Global' and an 'International' Court of Justice*

*Lillian Robb*** *and Vishal Prasad****

I. Introduction

The ICJ is a State-centric body – it handles disputes between States, and only representatives of States have an audience with the Court. However, the proceedings of the ICJ in the Obligations of States in respect of Climate Change Advisory Opinion ('Climate AO')[1] have exhibited elements symptomatic of an international legal system operating beyond a purely State-centric paradigm.

In their editorial to this book, Khaled El Mahmoud, Jannika Jahn, and Moritz Vinken introduce structural and systemic transformations of the international legal order, of which the ICJ Advisory Opinion is both a reflection and a catalyst. Their list describes an emerging international legal architecture that is integrative, rooted in multilateral cooperation, ecologically orientated, and reaching increasingly into the domestic sphere through a gradual piercing of the sovereign veil. This contribution argues that a further structural transformation regards the recognition, influence, and interrelationship of the different subjects of international law, indicative of a legal order in which the classical legal categories are questioned, challenged, and potentially reshaped.

While the authority of this Advisory Opinion ('AO') derives from its status as an opinion of the ICJ, and its associated State-centric mandate, there are also elements of significance that lie behind it and play out in the spaces surrounding its institutional consideration. They reveal an international legal order in a phase of broadening and opening to a diversity of actors

---

* Disclaimer: this piece is part of an ongoing monograph project involving a variety of methods, including two-way research, ethnography, and interviews. While that work is forthcoming, and explains those methods in full, some insights presented here draw on the larger work and its methodology

** PhD Candidate in International Law at the Graduate Institute of International and Development Studies in Geneva.

*** Director of the Pacific Islands Students Fighting Climate Change.

1 ICJ, *Obligations of States in respect of Climate Change*, Advisory Opinion of 23 July 2025.

and influences beyond the State. The associated shifts in influence and legitimacy of a diversity of actors are evidenced in and around the Climate AO through interrelated procedural and substantive symptoms of a broader questioning. Viewing this AO through too narrow an analytic frame runs the risk that significant elements (such as the 'archive of narrative microhistories' discussed by Rashmi Dharia in this book) become lost within the classical narratives of international law, and these 'subject' related structural transformations become overlooked as falling outside of the State-focused frame of consideration.

II. The Stage and the Actors

The four types of actors at the forefront of this piece are: the State, as the traditionally considered base unit or subject of the international legal system, including recently decolonised States whose membership of the 'international community of States' is more recent; civil society, a catch-all term that can include a wide range of actors, including individuals, networks, and organisations and which refers broadly to those actors operating 'below the level of the State';[2] the individual, whose accommodation in international law has been the subject of recent legal scholarship;[3] and Indigenous peoples, whose status in international law has been progressively recognised, including through international agreements of 1989[4] and 2007,[5] and whose status continues to be developed and clarified.

While the interrelationship and status of these actors as 'subjects' of the international legal order is in constant flux, the ICJ is an organ in which the primacy of the State is concretely embedded. This embedding is both procedural and substantive, and exists in both its contentious and advisory jurisdictions. The jurisdiction of the Court is activated through State request: either by States directly in the case of its contentious jurisdiction, or indirectly in the case of its advisory jurisdiction. The advisory jurisdiction is activated at the request of UN Organs or specialised agencies, whose

2 Peter Stoett and Pamela Teitelbaum, 'The Hague Appeal for Peace Conference: Reflections on "Civil Society" and NGOs', International Journal 55 (1999), 35-44.
3 See, for example, Tom Sparks and Anne Peters (eds), *The Individual in International Law: History and Theory* (Oxford University Press 2024).
4 ILO, Indigenous and Tribal Peoples Convention, 27 June 1989 (No. 169).
5 UN General Assembly, United Nations Declaration on the Rights of Indigenous Peoples: resolution / adopted by the General Assembly, A/RES/61/295, 2 October 2007.

authority derives from State consent (most often the UN General Assembly which as requested which has requested 18 AOs[6]).

The Climate AO falls within the advisory jurisdiction of the Court and results from a request[7] originating in the UN General Assembly, which was adopted by a consensus[8] of the member States. Behind that request lies an extensive campaign carried out by, among others, the Pacific Islands Students Fighting Climate Change,[9] a civil society organisation representing Pacific Youth who have worked alongside a coalition[10] of civil society actors (see the contribution of Lovleen Bhullar to this book). That campaign has also significantly shaped oral and written statements, as well as the atmosphere surrounding the Climate AO. This contribution places focus on that 'behind the scenes' activity.

III. Symptoms of Wider Structural Transformations

1. Procedural: Emphasis on Testimonies

Civil society holds significant, and potentially increasing, influence in the international legal order. The symptoms of this can be seen procedurally in relation to the Climate AO. Civil society was influential in: the commencement of the proceedings, including by campaigning among member States of the UN General Assembly; the drafting of written pleadings; the preparation of oral arguments; and presenting during Oral proceedings as invited by State delegations.[11] The presence and influence of civil society is, in itself, symptomatic of an open and porous international legal order, but the contributions of these actors, and the matters which they emphasised,

6 ICJ, Organs and Agencies Authorized to Request Advisory Opinions, available at: <https://icj-cij.org/organs-agencies-authorized>, accessed 6 August 2025.

7 Request for Advisory Opinion Transmitted to the Court pursuant to General Assembly resolution 77/276 of 29 March 2023, *Obligations of States in Respect of Climate Change*, Advisory Opinion of 23 July 2025.

8 UNGA, Official Records, 64th plenary meeting Wednesday, 29 March 2023, 10 a.m. New York, UN. Doc. A/77/PV.64.

9 Pacific Island Students Fighting Climate Change, 'Seeking an Advisory Opinion from the ICJ', available at: <https://www.pisfcc.org>, accessed 6 August 2025.

10 Pacific Islands Students Fighting Climate Change, 'Alliance for a Climate Justice Advisory Opinion: Seeking an Advisory Opinion from the ICJ', available at: <https://www.pisfcc.org>, accessed 6 August 2025.

11 Information based on interviews conducted by the first author, and personal experience of the second.

are further symptomatic of, and significant contributions to, the structural shifting and questioning around 'subjecthood'.

The Alliance for a Climate Justice Advisory Opinion,[12] a civil society coalition, placed significant emphasis on individual and community voices from the grassroots, including those of Indigenous peoples. In some cases, they did so internally to the proceeding with the objective of encouraging States to include witness testimony in their submissions,[13] which they hoped[14] would be influential even if not cited directly (such as the Book of Exhibits[15] contained in the written submissions of Vanuatu discussed by Rashmi Dharia in this book, or the Witness Statements[16] provided in the written statements of the Melanesian Spearhead Group).

In addition, the 'People's Petition'[17] was created – a 102-page document containing testimonies from affected communities couched in a legal analysis, and presented during oral proceedings in an effort to ensure that individuals impacted at the grassroots were represented, and that legal concepts were considered with that reality in mind. This document, as a civil society submission, faced challenges regarding its weight and the procedure for its submission, as do all NGO or Civil Society submissions and reports before the ICJ,[18] which, consistently with other UN organs, are increasingly common in ICJ proceedings. Thus, while not traditional 'subjects' with a right to audience before the Court, the testimony of individuals and communities, together with civil society, were significant features which permeated an otherwise State-centric process.

---

12 Pacific Islands Students Fighting Climate Change (n. 10).

13 Isabella Kaminski, 'The "one Shot" Campaign to Get a Strong Legal Statement on Climate Change', The Wave, 6 September 2023.

14 Isabella Kaminski, 'How Youth Activists Are Mobilising Ahead of a Landmark Climate Hearing', The Wave, 29 November 2024.

15 Written Submissions of the Republic of Vanuatu, '*Book of Exhibits*;', *Obligations of States in Respect of Climate Change*, Advisory Opinion of 23 July 2025, submitted by Republic of Vanuatu 21 March 2024.

16 Written Statement of the Melanesian Spearhead Group, Index of Exhibits 22 March 2024, *Obligations of States in Respect of Climate Change*, Advisory Opinion of 23 July 2025.

17 The People's Petition: A Collective Climate Justice Call for the ICJ, available at: <https://static1.squarespace.com/static/6090cc1eec59dc2ed057b027/t/67907a7d4135cf7a4c1fb2a7/1737521808020/People%27s%2BPetition.pdf>, accessed 6 August 2025.

18 Anna Riddell and Brendan Plant, *Evidence Before the International Court of Justice* (British Institute of International and Comparative Law 2009), 247–250, 366–368.

2. Interlinked Procedural and Substantive: A Global Audience

The effort to hear from individuals and communities extended beyond the courtroom, also finding expression in forums addressing a global audience. The size of that audience, and efforts to address it directly, indicate that these proceedings are viewed as more than a purely interstate concern by civil society and the global public alike.

While decisions of the ICJ have always been of concern to States, they have not always been of such significant public concern or the subject of such public attention. Outside of the courtroom, the global public was addressed through many mechanisms, among them the 'Witness Stand for Climate Justice',[19] which aimed[20] to ensure that human experiences were centred and those on the frontline were platformed. This involved a library of testimonies on climate impact, which could be accessed physically in the Hague through touch screens as well as online. A People's Assembly[21] was held, in which witnesses presented testimony publicly. Vishal Prasad explained that one objective of the Pacific Islands Students Fighting Climate Change campaign was a 'visionary' one in which the global nature of the case would be reflected in the accessibility of the process by addressing not only the judges but also ordinary people. The hearings were also accompanied by a significant presence outside the Peace Palace, and the progress of the proceedings was reported on multiple platforms.

Juliette McIntyre discusses, in relation to the recent Provisional Measures Hearings concerning Gaza,[22] how the Court in those hearings, as perhaps in all hearings, engaged in a performance by which the courtroom becomes a theatre of justice both for the Court and for the general public, who mobilised to observe those proceedings to a new extent.[23] That novel level of mobilisation was seen, if not expanded on, in the Climate hearings. The level of public attention placed on the Court's recent cases could arise from

19 Witness Stand, 'The Witness Stand for Climate Justice', available at: <https://witnessstand.live/>, accessed 6 August 2025.

20 Kaminski (n. 13).

21 Just Peace, 'The People's Assembly: Setting the Stage for Climate Justice', available at_ <https://www.justpeacethehague.org/en/event/the-people-s-assembly-setting-the-stage-for-climate-justice>, accessed 6 August 2025.

22 ICJ, *Application of the Convention on the Prevention and Punishment of the Crime of Genocide in the Gaza Strip* (South Africa v. Israel), merits, Oral Proceedings.

23 Juliette McIntyre, 'Telling Stories at the International Court of Justice: The Provisional Measures Hearings in South Africa v. Israel', Völkerrechtsblog, 16 January 2024.

many factors, surely in part because the ICJ is considering the type of issues of general concern to the international public. The question considered in the Climate AO, which is one whose drafting was significantly influenced by civil society involvement, touches on all layers of the international community (non-exclusively: individuals, civil society, communities, peoples, and States). The text of the question itself asked the Court to consider not only the obligations of States with respect to harm caused to other States,[24] but also with respect to the harm caused to individuals and peoples.[25] But there seems to be something more: Is it because of the ease of engaging with these proceedings in the internet era? Is it because the 'international community' has shifted somehow into a global community in which individuals, communities, and civil society feel a part and experience a concern for? Or is it simply because the international legal order has now developed to such an extent that, together with the thinning of the sovereign veil, it now addresses topics of wide public concern far beyond States.

3. Substantive: Mixed Legal Vocabularies

A substantive consequence of the inclusion of individual voice and narrative in State submissions is the introduction of mixed legal vocabularies. In the Climate AO mixed legal vocabularies were represented, for example, on the futurity of international law and the concept of intergenerational equity.

As a procedural matter, the Court does not often hear testimonies, though States can include them in their oral submissions.[26] In the Chagos AO[27] the Court heard from Madame Elyse, a 65 year old Chagossian woman who spoke of the colonial history of the Chagos in a moment that has been called 'ground breaking' for its inclusion of the voice of the community in an interstate proceeding, and an example of the hearing of Indigenous testimony at the ICJ which introduced mixed legal vocabularies

24 Request for Advisory Opinion Transmitted to the Court pursuant to General Assembly resolution 77/276 (n. 7).
25 Separate Opinion of Vice-President Sebutinde, *Obligations of States in Respect of Climate Change*, Advisory Opinion of 23 July 2025.
26 Riddell and Plant (n. 18) 309–311.
27 ICJ, *Legal Consequences of the Separation of the Chagos Archipelago from Mauritius in 1965*, Advisory Opinion of 25 February 2019, ICJ Rep. 95.

to the consideration of self-determination.[28] In the Climate AO, mixed legal vocabularies are presented by Cynthia Houniuhi, President and founding member of the Pacific Islands Students Fighting Climate Change, who presented on behalf of the Republic of Vanuatu and the Melanesian Spearhead Group.[29] She referenced testimony of another witness before the ICJ, Lijon Eknilang from the Marshall Islands, who spoke on the impact of nuclear weapons on her family and community[30] (providing the kind of narrated *in concreto* assessments discussed by Rashmi Dharia in this book). In her own statement, Cynthia Houniuhi presented the legal principle of intergenerational equity in the context of, and as an expression of, the duty to protect the environment for future generations as it exists in her culture, thus presenting a vocabulary through which to understand the legal concept under consideration. That vocabulary is also reflected in the submission of Vishal Prasad in his rebuttal of the idea that future generations are 'abstract' and his reference to international justice, and the role of the Court, as one of 'wayfinding', a practice connecting past and future – those who came before with those who will follow.[31] Both of these submissions present a vocabularies through which to grapple with the futurity of international law (potentially contributing to the Courts 'substantive grasp' of the future through the finding of intergenerational equity as an interpretative principle discussed by Jochen Rauber in this book).

Mixed legal vocabularies also found expression through representatives of States (rather than as attached to State written submissions). While this is a legally important distinction in the context of a State-centric Court, it is perhaps an artificial distinction in a case in which State delegations and witnesses often spoke from comparable positions regarding their experience of climate impacts. In their role supporting especially the delegations of Pacific and Small Island Developing States that had not pre-

---

28 Shreya Shankar, 'The Chagos Islands Case: The Vocabularies of Self-Determination', Leiden Law Blog, 17 November 2022.

29 Verbatim Record of the Public Sitting held on Monday 2 December 2024, at 10 a.m. at the Peace Palace, President Salam presiding, UN Doc. CR 2024/35, 115–117, *Obligations of States in Respect of Climate Change*, Advisory Opinion of 23 July 2025.

30 Verbatim Record of the Public Sitting held on Tuesday 14 November 1995, at 10:35 a.m., at the Peace Palace, President Bedjaoui presiding, UN Doc. CR 95/32, 24–28, *Legality of the Use by a State of Nuclear Weapons in Armed Conflict*, Advisory Opinion of 8 July 1996.

31 Verbatim Record of the Public Sitting held on Friday 13 December 2024, at 10 a.m. at the Peace Palace, President Salam presiding, UN Doc. CR 2024/53, 34, *Obligations of States in Respect of Climate Change*, Advisory Opinion of 23 July 2025.

viously presented before the ICJ, civil society actors encouraged mixed legal vocabularies, including Indigenous legal vocabularies. They did so, *inter alia*, by: encouraging representation by citizens, rather than hiring external representation by professional lawyers as is the norm in ICJ proceedings; and by embracing the culture and traditions of those States, including presenting legal principles and arguments in 'a Pacific way' and in Pacific languages. Indeed, these oral hearings were the first in which Global North States' submissions were outnumbered by those of the Global South, and saw the highest number of Indigenous people presenting before the ICJ in comparison to any previous hearing.

IV. The Opinion

While it's impossible to know how much civil society influenced the Court, or how any of these ideas permeated the thinking of the bench, the AO delivered by the Court on 23rd July 2025 aligns in many ways with the campaign conducted by civil society, indicating that these actors and their ideas and goals likely permeated this process in at least some aspects. The AO places great emphasis on human rights obligations (see the discussion of Helen Keller in this book), including the quite remarkable finding that the right to a clean, healthy, and sustainable environment is a 'precondition' to, and inherent in, the enjoyment of other human rights.[32] This strong human rights stance is aligned with the focus of the coalition of civil society actors operating around the Climate AO, who encouraged an approach that recognised the very real impact on individuals. The separate opinion of Judge Charlesworth even cites directly to witness testimony in considering the legal, and particularly human rights, questions posed.[33]

While text of the AO did not reference directly the mixed legal vocabularies used in relation to, for example, the concept of intergenerational equity, it did make references that relate to the different understandings of this concept as expressed by the parties[34] and emphasised its importance,[35] including by acknowledging that the human rights of future generations

32 ICJ, *Obligations of States in Respect of Climate Change* (n. 1), para. 393.

33 Separate Opinion of Judge Charlesworth, , *Obligations of States in Respect of Climate Change*, Advisory Opinion of 23 July 2025, paras. 17–22.

34 ICJ, *Obligations of States in Respect of Climate Change* (n. 1), para. 155.

35 ICJ, *Obligations of States in Respect of Climate Change* (n. 1), paras. 157, 273.

are dependent on environmental preservation.[36] It also made a very significant finding on the recognition of intergenerational equity as a form of equity[37] (and as an interpretative principle, see the contribution of Jochen Rauber in this book). These concrete findings on the concept of future generations are consistent with the emphasis encouraged by the coalition of civil society. Perhaps inspired by the Oral presentations, several judges even used sayings or mixed vocabularies in their separate opinions, including in the separate opinions of Judge Bhandari[38] referring to Bhūmi Devi, Vice-President Sebutinde with the 'wise African saying' '[w]e do not inherit the Earth from our ancestors; we borrow it from our children'[39], and Judge Tladi with the Cree proverb '[o]nly when the last tree has been cut, only when the last river has been poisoned, only when the last fish has been caught, only then we will realize, that money cannot be eaten'.[40]

On the question of the subjectivities 'peoples and individuals of the present and future generations', the separate opinion of Vice-President Sebutinde[41] criticises this element of the Court's decision as 'not going far enough'.[42] She argues that the Court conflated the issue of the legal obligations owed to peoples and individuals, as categories of subject beyond the State[43] which include both those currently living and those yet to be born,[44] with the question of '*locus standii*', being their ability to bring a claim as against a State. By doing so, she argues that the AO falls short of addressing the questions posed regarding the obligations owed to non-state categories,[45] and argues that the Court should have gone further in addressing the status and interrelationship of subjects beyond the State in international law.

---

36 ICJ, *Obligations of States in Respect of Climate Change* (n. 1), paras. 373, 377.

37 ICJ, *Obligations of States in Respect of Climate Change* (n. 1), para. 157. Including as an interpretative principle, see Jochen Rauber, 'Custom, Entrenchment, Interpretation – How the ICJ's Advisory Opinion on Climate Change contributes to international law's turn toward the future', in this volume.

38 Separate Opinion of Judge Bhandari, *Obligations of States in Respect of Climate Change*, Advisory Opinion of 23 July 2025, para. 10.

39 Separate Opinion of Vice-President Sebutinde (n. 25), para. 7.

40 Declaration of Judge Tladi, *Obligations of States in Respect of Climate Change*, Advisory Opinion of 23 July 2025, fn. 34.

41 Separate Opinion of Vice-President Sebutinde (n. 25).

42 Separate Opinion of Vice-President Sebutinde (n. 25).

43 Separate Opinion of Vice-President Sebutinde (n. 25), para. 4.

44 Separate Opinion of Vice-President Sebutinde (n. 25), para. 7.

45 Separate Opinion of Vice-President Sebutinde (n. 25), paras. 3–7.

V. Conclusion

This piece argues that the Climate AO and its proceedings, both inside and outside the Courtroom, illustrate an international legal order that is permeated by, and receptive to, actors and influences beyond the State. While it is too early to judge the extent or outcome of a 'structural transformation' regarding the recognition, influence and interrelationship of 'subjects' of international law beyond the State, symptoms of a current questioning of these classical legal categories and associated State-centrism, and signs of potential resulting transformations, are seen. These symptoms are visible throughout the Climate AO, especially in: the overall influence of civil society in all stages of the proceeding, and potential penetration of civil society ideas into the opinion of the Court; the focus on the voices of individuals and communities in written and oral submissions; the focus on diverse legal vocabularies, including Indigenous legal vocabularies, in written and oral submissions; the addressing of questions of broad public concern beyond the State; the formulation of a question that explicitly asks the Court to consider subjects beyond the State; the criticism in the separate opinion of Vice-President Sebutinde that the Court did not go far enough in addressing questions around subjects beyond the State; and the interest in this proceeding expressed by a global community of non-state subjects, who became a global audience addressed during it.

'Vanishing Yams'

A Food Microhistory in the *Climate Change* Advisory Opinion

Rashmi Dharia[*]

इतिहास देते साक्षी वारली कधी भी भुकेनं मेला नाही
'History is witness; the Warli has never died of hunger'
Swadeshi ft. Prakash Bhoir, 'The Warli Revolt'[1]

I. Introduction

The nature of a 'landmark' decision is that it creates a narrative 'before' and 'after'. This is as true for the Climate Change Advisory Opinion as for any of the ICJ's previous 'historic' rulings. Indeed, in its concluding remarks, the Court acknowledges the unprecedented nature of these advisory proceedings. However, it hastens to outline the limited role international law plays in resolving this 'existential problem of planetary proportions.'[2]. The reader is encouraged to be circumspect about the role of the Court; she is reminded that a quest for a 'lasting and satisfactory solution' to this 'daunting, self-inflicted' problem needs the 'contribution of all fields of human knowledge' along with 'human will and wisdom.'[3]

This Opinion is an event that makes the quest for climate justice more hopeful, more ambitious[4]- and all the more challenging. This is particularly the case for small island developing States, who did much of the heavy

* PhD candidate at Sciences Po Law School and Junior Lecturer at the American University in Paris.

1 Available at: https://www.youtube.com/watch?v=sYADNgIkelY (translation from Marathi to English is my own).

2 ICJ, *Obligations of States in Respect of Climate Change*, Advisory Opinion of 23 July 2025, para. 456.

3 ICJ, *Obligations of States in Respect of Climate Change* (n. 2), para. 456.

4 Sera Sefeti, '"We were heard": the Pacific students who took their climate fight to the ICJ – and won', The Guardian, 25 July 2025, avalable at https://www.theguardian.com/world/2025/jul/25/pacific-students-who-won-climate-case-icj-international-court-of-justice-hague.

lifting[5] in the advocacy efforts leading up to the proceedings and who remain the most vulnerable to the ravages of climate change. But there is one monumental contribution on their part that may be overlooked: an archive of narrated microhistories[6] in the corpus of the ICJ.

II. Small Island States and Personal Narratives in the ICJ

Narration is central to legal discourse.[7] The law recognises and puts limits on its own narrativity by imposing rules about the kind of narration permitted in the courtroom – what can be said, and by whom. For example, international human rights law and international criminal law explicitly recognise the individual as a subject under their frameworks,[8] making the first-person voice and the recounting of personal histories legally significant narrative techniques. However, the ICJ has been limited in this regard by its jurisdictional mandate[9] and retains the largest share of 'main character energy' for States.

5 Bernadette Carreon, 'Vanuatu to seek international court opinion on climate change rights', The Guardian, 26 September 2023, available at: https://www.theguardian.com/world/2021/sep/26/vanuatu-to-seek-international-court-opinion-on-climate-change-rights.

6 Isabella Kaminski, '"A human face on an abstract problem": ICJ forced to listen to climate victims', The Guardian, 11 December 2024, available at: https://www.theguardian.com/law/2024/dec/11/international-court-of-justice-icj-forced-to-listen-to-climate-victims.

7 See for example Peter Brooks, 'The Law as Narrative and Rhetoric', in: Peter Brooks and Paul Gewirtz (eds), *Law's Stories: Narrative and Rhetoric in the Law* (Yale University Press 1996), 14–22; See also Robert Cover, 'Nomos and Narrative', Harv. L. Rev. 97 (1983), 4–68; Ian Ward, *Law and Literature: Possibilities and Perspectives* (Cambridge University Press 1995). For more contemporary work, see for example Andrew Benjamin Bricker, 'Is Narrative Essential to the Law? Precedent, Case Law and Judicial Emplotment', LAW CULT HUMANIT (2016), 1–19; Jerome Bruner, 'Narrative and Law: How They Need Each Other', in: Brian Schiff, A. Elizabeth McKim and Sylvie Patron (eds), *Life and Narrative: The Risks and Responsibilities of Storying Experience* (Oxford University Press 2017), 3–10.

8 Convention for the Protection of Human Rights and Fundamental Freedoms (European Convention on Human Rights, ECHR) of 4 November 1950, 213 UNTS 221, Arts 34–35; American Convention on Human Rights (ACHR) of 22 November 1969, 1144 UNTS 123, Art 3. Rome Statute of the International Criminal Court (Rome Statute) of 17 July 1998, 2187 UNTS 90, preamble and Art 25.

9 Article 34 ICJ-Statute. See also Court's characterisation of itself in ICJ, *Obligations of States in Respect of Climate Change* (n. 2), para. 456.

It is remarkable, therefore, that small island States have long been pioneers in using singular personal narratives before the ICJ[10]. Notably, in the *Nuclear Weapons* Advisory Opinion (hereafter *Nuclear Weapons),*[11] Marshall Islander Lijong Eknilang participated in the oral proceedings, recounting the horrific effects of the Castle Bravo nuclear tests on the Rongelap Atoll.[12] She recalled that it was the first time the islanders had seen snow- a sense of wonder quickly effaced, as they realised the 'snow' was radioactive fallout. She recounted how arrowroot and makmok (tapioca) plants had stopped bearing fruit, and how those that grew caused blisters in mouths and on lips: *'our staple foods had never made us ill before.'*[13] She described how Marshallese women *'suffer silently and differently'*: frequent miscarriages, and the births of what she called 'monster babies,' buried in secrecy and shame.

Eknilang stated that her purpose before the Court was to prove that these effects were not abstract predictions, but the concrete everyday lives of Marshall Islanders[14]. Her statement finds no mention in the main text of *Nuclear Weapons*, even as the Court recognises that 'the environment is not an abstraction.'[15] Her story remains lodged in the *Nuclear Weapons* archive, a small yet indelible fragment in the collective cultural memory of international law.

In the *Legal Consequences of the Separation of the Chagos Archipelago from Mauritius in 1965* (hereafter *Chagos*),[16] Liseby Elyse recounted before the Court her exile from the island. She described how the islanders, having always had access to fresh food, were plunged into a state of hunger and precarity after they were summarily ordered to leave. *'Afterwards, the ships which used to bring food stopped coming. We had nothing to eat. No*

10 See Lilian Robb and Vishal Prasad, 'Both a 'Global' and an 'International' Court of Justice', in this volume.

11 ICJ, *Legality of the Threat or Use of Nuclear Weapons*, Advisory Opinion of 8 July 1996, ICJ Rep. 226, para. 29.

12 Statement by Lijong Eknilang, *Nuclear Weapons* (n. 11) Verbatim Record CR 95/34, 19 October 1995, 45–46.

13 Statement by Lijong Eknilang (n. 12).

14 Statement by Lijong Eknilang (n. 12).

15 ICJ, *Nuclear Weapons* (n. 11), para. 29.

16 ICJ, *Legal Consequences of the Separation of the Chagos Archipelago from Mauritius in 1965*. Advisory Opinion of 25 February 2019, ICJ Rep., 95.

medicine. Nothing at all.'[17] In the written submissions of Mauritius, she stated that for approximately six months, they had no rice, flour, oil, or milk.[18] On the ship they were made to board to leave the island, they '*were like animals and slaves. People were dying of sadness on that ship.*'[19] She was pregnant at the time; her child was born after her exile, and only lived a few days.[20]

Philippe Sands, counsel for Mauritius, clarifies that the words of Madame Elyse were not offered as testimonial evidence, but 'simply as a member of the delegation of Mauritius.'[21] This is an interesting, and deliberate, distinction to make. The Mauritian delegation included her statement despite knowing that it did not carry much weight before the Court from the formal point of view. In doing so, they transformed what could not count as evidence into something arguably more powerful: a symbolic act of presence within the Court's record. Although the Court summarised the history of the displacement of the Chagossian people in Part III of the Opinion, the personal narratives presented before it did not form part of this historicisation. Like Eknilang's statement in *Nuclear Weapons*, Elyse's personal story becomes a fragment that lodges itself into the Court's State-centric grammar.

Small island States have used such fragments adeptly before the ICJ to give concrete, affective dimensions to international law's legal categories. Their contributions in the *Climate Change* Advisory Opinion, including the personal narratives of marginalised communities,[22] enrich this epistemic vein even as they (still) do not form part of the Court's formal reasoning.[23] Placed alongside the personal narratives in previous advisory opinions, the submissions of small island States in *Climate Change* form part of the

17 ICJ, *Legal Consequences of the Separation of the Chagos Archipelago from Mauritius in* 1965 (n. 16), Oral Proceedings, Verbatim Record CR 2018/20, 3 September 2018, 74–75.

18 Written Comments of the Republic of Mauritius, *Legal Consequences of the Separation of the Chagos Archipelago from Mauritius in* 1965 (n. 16), para 4.114 (this paragraph also contains personal narratives by four other Chagossians who were all present in the Peace Palace for the oral proceedings).

19 ICJ, *Legal Consequences of the Separation of the Chagos Archipelago from Mauritius in* 1965 (n. 16), Oral Proceedings, Verbatim Record CR 2018/20, 3 September 2018, 74–75.

20 Oral Proceedings, *Chagos* (n. 19).

21 Oral Proceedings, *Chagos* (n. 19), 72.

22 Isabella Kaminski (n. 6).

23 Separate Opinion of Judge Charlesworth, *Obligations of States in Respect of Climate Change*, Advisory Opinion of 23 July 2025, paras. 13–29 for an exception.

emerging archive of microhistories at the ICJ. Each offers a glimpse of lived experience- radioactive fallout, exile, miscarriages, the loss of staple food- and each in turn is woven into the Opinions' corpus without forming explicit part of its reasoning.

In this chapter, I foreground one such narrative, a 'microhistory' in Vanuatu's extraordinary 736-page *Book of Exhibits*, which is absent from the main Advisory Opinion yet has the narrative tools to fill its gaps and throw its limits into relief: the vanishing yam.[24] The vanishing yam of Yakel, stands in continuity with earlier voices, part of a longer story of how small island States have used personal narrative to make the Court's archive speak beyond its main Opinion.

III. The Microhistory of the Vanishing Yam

Microhistory, as a historical method, examines the everyday lives of previously overlooked subjects to gain insight into larger-scale global events and processes.[25] It analyses 'primary documents'- letters, personal accounts etc. – and maps them onto larger structures of history to capture what they might miss, and to add marginalised voices to the 'grand narrative.'

Nothing demonstrates this as clearly as the motif of the vanishing yam in Yakel Village, Tanna, Vanuatu (Exhibits F-N in Vanuatu's *Book of Exhibits*).[26] This set of documents narrates the history of how the yam vanished in Yakel through nine personal testimonies. Read together, they give us the rich and complex story of how the loss of the yam struck an unimaginable blow to their everyday lives.[27]

Through these testimonies, we find out that Yakel is a Kastom village. It lives by the old ways. The yam, or *Neok*, is integral to Kastom ceremonies and occupies a special place in the political, socio-economic, and cultural

24 Written Submissions of the Republic of Vanuatu, '*Book of Exhibits*,' Exhibits F–N (*Book of Exhibits*), *Obligations of States in Respect of Climate Change*, Advisory Opinion of 23 July 2025, submitted by Republic of Vanuatu 21 March 2024.

25 Carlo Ginzburg, 'Microhistory: Two or Three Things That I Know about It', Crit. Inq. 20 (1993), 10–35, 12.

26 *Book of Exhibits* (n. 24).

27 In this section, I attempt to follow closely the phrasing and cadence of the testimonies contained in Vanuatu's *Book of Exhibits*. The descriptive sentences are drawn from the testimonies themselves, and should therefore be read as paraphrases or condensations thereof. They are not ethnographic interpretations. I have indicated the exact exhibits as often as possible.

life of this community. It is the subject of origin stories, cautionary tales, and myths in a way that is entangled with agricultural practices, food habits, social norms, and economic structures.

We also learn that *Kalbapeng*, a God from the mountains, made the yam. We are told the story of the Yam Spirit and the Taro Spirit, of how the Yam came to be king of crops in Tanna because He stayed, while His wife Taro and the other crops went to the Americas. We learn that Wildcane is the Chief of the Yam because the two plants always go together. Mangau Iokai is *Tupunis* of the yam in Yakel and has an ancestral spiritual connection to it that allows him to oversee the yam crop.[28] The yam is the primary offering in many Kastom ceremonies, which are inconceivable without it.

However, the testimonies agree that four years ago, *the yam vanished altogether.* After the cyclones (Pam, Kevin, Judy, La Nina, Harold, Lola), the erratic unseasonal rain made the yam crop shrink and die, along with wildcane and banana. Incidentally, Iokai has not tasted a banana since 2023. His connection to the Yam Spirit has been severed, leaving him heartbroken. Nine women in a collective statement[29] narrate how the food shortage and dangerous weather have disrupted social and familial harmony. *The yam has vanished entirely,* they repeat. They can no longer access yam for the ceremonies; this feels wrong, shameful, in ways they cannot explain.

The reefs are dead too, and so are the fish.[30] Yam can no longer be traded for fish with the coastal villages- alternative financial arrangements must be made.[31] The knowledge of the yam can no longer be passed on to the next generation. It will exist only in the past (Exhibit K).[32]

The microhistory of the yam in Yakel village is absent from the main Advisory Opinion. It might be more relevant before a human rights tribunal or a relevant treaty body, like the Court has implied.[33] However, it has a strategic role in this case that goes beyond being formally 'useful' information. It is a narrative singularity that can fill gaps in the law and demonstrate its epistemic limits.

---

28 *Book of Exhibits* (n. 24) Exhibit H.
29 *Book of Exhibits*, (n. 24) Exhibit I and Exhibit P.
30 *Book of Exhibits* (n. 24) Exhibit G.
31 *Book of Exhibits* (n. 24) Exhibits G and H.
32 *Book of Exhibits* (n. 24) Exhibit K.
33 ICJ, *Obligations of States in Respect of Climate Change* (n. 2), para. 111.

IV. On the Deferred In Concreto *Assessment*

The narrative boundaries of Advisory Opinions are drawn by the Court's reading of the questions posed to it. While clarifying the scope of question (b), the Court has drawn such a boundary (Paras 101–111).[34] It does not speculate on questions of responsibility that, in its view, require an *in concreto* assessment.[35] The motif of the '*in concreto* assessment' comes up in the following observations of the Court:

(i) That international responsibility of a State/group of States requires an *in concreto* assessment, and that the Court is only called upon to establish in general the applicable legal framework of state responsibility[36]
(ii) That 'specially affected' or 'vulnerable' States are entitled to the same remedies as other injured States. Whether there are any specific legal consequences to any particular injured State would be a question for an *in concreto* assessment.[37]
(iii) That causal links between wrongful acts and omissions of a State and the damage arising from climate change, though tenuous, are not impossible to draw, but must be established through an *in concreto* assessment.[38]
(iv) That the forms of reparation may be difficult to determine in a climate change context and must be assessed on a case-by-case basis[39], but that once the general conditions of state responsibility, including

34 ICJ, *Obligations of States in Respect of Climate Change* (n. 2), paras. 101–111. Question (b) is as follows: 'What are the legal consequences under these obligations for States where they, by their acts and omissions, have caused significant harm to the climate system and other parts of the environment, with respect to: (i) States, including, in particular, small island developing States, which due to their geographical circumstances and level of development, are injured or specially affected by or are particularly vulnerable to the adverse effects of climate change? (ii) Peoples and individuals of the present and future generations affected by the adverse effects of climate change?'.

35 See Juan Auz, 'The Legal Consequences of Climate Harm: Complementarity Between the Advisory Opinions of the International Court of Justice and the Inter-American Court of Human Rights', in this volume.

36 ICJ, *Obligations of States in Respect of Climate Change* (n. 2), paras. 106, 423.

37 ICJ, *Obligations of States in Respect of Climate Change* (n. 2), para. 107.

38 ICJ, *Obligations of States in Respect of Climate Change* (n. 2), para. 438.

39 ICJ, *Obligations of States in Respect of Climate Change* (n. 2), paras. 449–454.

> a direct and certain causal nexus, are established, the injured State is entitled to 'full reparation.'[40]

Judge Nolte observes that the Court has 'not elaborated much' on the limits of climate change-related claims, leaving the deliberation of these limits to *in concreto* assessments. He cautions that this might lead to 'false expectations.'[41] The irony that the *in concreto* assessments take place in the abstract future is not lost on anyone. However, the vanishing yam enables us to map this abstract-future '*in concreto* assessment' onto the past and present landscape of Yakel village. The ravages of the cyclones, the disappearance of the yam, and the resulting hunger and heartbreak of the inhabitants of Yakel are as '*in concreto*' as it gets.

As such, the vanishing yam becomes a metonym for everything that the Court has deferred for '*in concreto*' assessments. It foreshadows the problems of 'concrete' assessments of state responsibility and reparations. Reading this microhistory makes us do the complex temporal-imaginative work of drawing the causal nexus between the worsening cyclones in Vanuatu, the disappearance of the yam, the resulting damage to the State of Vanuatu, and state responsibility.

IV. Vanishing Yams and the Tenuous (But Possible) Causal Nexus

The 'tenuous, but not impossible'[42] causal nexus is particularly interesting when read alongside the vanishing yam testimonies. State responsibility seems to hinge on the drawing of the causal nexus – an event[43] of injury, and the attribution of this injury to a breach of international obligations by a particular State or States. The narrativity[44] of state responsibility thus emerges from this causal nexus; this nexus is the *plot* that configures the

40 ICJ, *Obligations of States in Respect of Climate Change* (n. 2), Operative Clause 4 (c).

41 Declaration of Judge Nolte, *Obligations of States in Respect of Climate Change*, Advisory Opinion of 23 July 2025, para. 14.

42 ICJ, *Obligations of States in Respect of Climate Change* (n. 2) para. 438.

43 See Fleur Johns, Richard Joyce, and Sundhya Pahuja (eds), *Events: The Force of International Law* (Routledge, 2011) 1–3. Particularly evocative is their statement '... [i]nternational lawyers listen, above all, for the screech accompanying an event, when that hum seems to recede and reparation of one kind or another is urged...of the episodic, international law makes an everyday.'

44 For a deeper reading of narrativity, see generally Hayden White, 'The Value of Narrativity in the Representation of Reality', Crit. Inq. 7 (1980), 5–27.

events into an intelligible and meaningful whole. Paul Ricœurhas argued that it is emplotment that mediates between chronological sequences to form a coherent story in which the past, present, and future are held in relation.[45] Rooted in this causal nexus, therefore, is the notion of time.

The vanishing yam of Yakel offers us readings of time that push the boundaries of the 'causal nexus' beyond chronological cause and effect. It becomes a window to let these readings of time refigure the interpretive tools of climate change discourse, perhaps making it possible to adapt them to the diffuse temporality of climate change. In the following section, I reflect on how the vanishing yam as part of the textual corpus of the Opinion enriches the temporal imagination of the reader.

1. Reading Time in the Causal Nexus: The Precautionary Principle and Intergenerational Equity

Judge Charlesworth in her Separate Opinion suggests that the Court could have offered more guidelines on the dynamic between the obligation of prevention and the precautionary principle in the context of climate change. In doing so, she reads these concepts not only as legal doctrines but also as temporalities. She observes that prevention speaks to 'risk' while precaution speaks to 'uncertainty',[46] and that these two are in a temporal continuum with each other: 'it is possible for a certain conduct to be initially governed by the precautionary principle, and subsequently, as greater scientific certainty is gathered in connection with the conduct in question, for the obligation of prevention to apply.'[47] Although the Court acknowledges the precautionary principle as an important 'guiding principle for the interpretation and application of most directly relevant rules,'[48] it does not dwell on this continuum. Its statement that 'States should...not refrain from or delay taking actions of prevention in the face of scientific uncertainty' hints at the link but leaves it underdeveloped.

---

45 PaulRicœur, 'Narrative Time', *Crit. Inq.* 7 (1980), 169–190, 171. See also Hayden White (n. 44).

46 Separate Opinion of Judge Charlesworth, *Obligations of States in Respect of Climate Change*, Advisory Opinion of 23 July 2025, para. 4.

47 Separate Opinion of Judge Charlesworth (n. 46), para. 6. While doing so, she cites International Law Association, Resolution 2/2014, 'Declaration of legal principles relating to climate change', Article 7B. 3 which also sets out this continuum between precaution and prevention.

48 ICJ, *Obligations of States in Respect of Climate Change* (n. 2), para. 161.

Judge Charlesworth's opinion presses further. She stresses that although the high level of scientific certainty and consensus on scientific facts about climate change gestures towards the heightened scope of the obligation of prevention, the precautionary principle retains an underexplored but distinct scope of obligations. In her view, the Court ought to have offered some guidelines as to applying the precautionary principle in cases of scientific *uncertainty* in the context of climate change. Her suggestion is to look to ITLOS, which has drawn more directly on the precautionary principle to flesh out States' obligations to conduct environmental impact assessments as part of the general obligation of due diligence.[49]

Judge Charlesworth's framing of prevention and precaution as temporal postures (*initial* precaution as interpretive principle, *subsequent* prevention as obligation), juxtaposed with the vanishing yam, allows us to read time differently into the Advisory Opinion. The testimonies of the inhabitants of Yakel[50] fold together and open multiple readings of time. First, we read mythic time- the stories of Kalbapeng, of the Wildcane, and of the Yam Spirit and the Taro Spirit belong to a 'sacred' time that is made cyclically present through their community rituals.[51] Mythic time does not move forward; it is grounded in the present by returning, through periodic rituals, to the register of a timeless primordial beginning. Secondly, we read historical time- more familiar to us as international lawyers.[52] The cyclones with the oddly banal names (Pam, Kevin, Judy, Lola) that destroyed the yam harvests are 'events' arranged in a chronology of cause and effect. This

49 Separate Opinion of Judge Charlesworth (n. 46), para. 7, citing ITLOS, *Request for Advisory Opinion submitted by the Commission of Small Island States on Climate Change and International Law*, Advisory Opinion of 21 May 2024, case no. 31, paras. 353, 361.

50 See *Book of Exhibits* (n. 24) Exhibits F-N.

51 Mircea Eliade has called this *illud tempus* ('that time'), in which primordial events are re-enacted in ritual. He contrasts linear time (*profane* time) with cyclical time (*sacred* time) and argues that 'sacred time' is indefinitely recoverable and repeatable. It is an 'eternal mythical present that is periodically reintegrated by means of rites.' Mircea Eliade, *The Sacred and the Profane: The Nature of Religion*, trans. Willard R. Trask (Harcourt, Brace & World 1959), esp. 'Profane Duration and Sacred Time', 68–79.

52 See for example Thomas Kleinlein and Jean d'Aspremont, 'The Turn to Historiography in International Law: Limitations and New Horizons', J. History Int' l L. 27 (2025), 7-35. See also Anne Orford, *International Law and the Politics of History* (Cambridge University Press, 2021). For work specific to climate change, see for example Eliana Cusato, Progress and Linear Time: How to Rethink International Law to Account for Ecologically Precarious Presents?, Völkerrechtsblog, 19 September 2023.

is the time of the causal nexus, where the loss of the yam can be linked to climate change in the grammar of state responsibility. Thirdly, there is proleptic time, a 'flash forward' foreshadowing.[53] The knowledge of the yam will no longer be passed to future generations. There is a collective shame that ceremonies will never be the same. There is grief that children will never taste the yam of the past. This is the collective anticipation of loss, a future grief folded into the present.

PaulRicœur's account of narrative time clarifies what the vanishing yam adds to the precautionary principle that the Court in the main Opinion cannot. ForRicœur, time becomes human time only when it is narrated. The *plot* of a narrative gathers episodic succession into a configuration that holds past, present, and future in tension.[54] To explain briefly, narrative time always moves across three interwoven registers- repetition (the retrieval of foundational or mythic beginnings), extension (the historical chain of datable events), and anticipation (the sense of narrative closure that draws the story forward).[55] These are not distinct kinds of time but entangled layers of temporal experience in a narrative. Seen through this lens, the vanishing yam is not merely a chronicle of loss lodged into the margins of *Climate Change* Advisory Opinion dossier, but a *narrative configuration* in which mythic repetition, historical extension, and proleptic anticipation coexist. The inhabitants of Yakel narrate a story that synthesises the temporal modes that the Court's mandate cannot accommodate.

At the center ofRicœur's framework lies the idea of care.[56] He argues that to exist in time is to *care*, to act within a web of inheritances and possibilities that bind us to what has been and what may come.[57] Care here does not mean sentiment or benevolence, but involvement. It is the unity of remembering, acting, and anticipating that makes time meaningful. Narrative gives this care a discernible form. It gathers what is remembered, done, and hoped for into a structure that can be inhabited. In the personal narratives that form the microhistory of the vanishing yam, the people of Yakel live this temporality of care through cultivation and ritual; their land and soil itself become a medium of remembrance and foresight.

53 Ricœur(n. 45), 182.
54 Ricœur (n. 45), 171.
55 Ricœur (n. 45), 182.
56 Ricœur (n. 45), 171.
57 Ricœur (n. 45), 171.

The precautionary principle is a notion broadly conceived. As a general 'interpretive principle' of applicable rules on climate change, it can be read more generously than the 'obligation' of prevention but does not have the latter's teeth. As part of the 'general obligation of due diligence,'[58] it remains shaped by impact assessments and scientific projections of risk. However, the precautionary principle as a *temporal gesture* (as noted by Judge Charlesworth) is greatly enriched by multiple understandings of time when read with the vanishing yam. The narrative of the vanishing yam allows precaution to be emplotted as *care*- a temporality of attention, tending, and preservation rather than risk assessment and calculation.

This can also be read into the Court's engagement with intergenerational equity. The Advisory Opinion also treats intergenerational equity as an interpretive principle- a 'manifestation of equity in the general sense' to be read alongside sustainable development and precaution in giving effect to States' climate obligations.[59] The word 'intergenerational' indicates a role in the emplotment of climate change narratives; as a temporal gesture, it converges the past, present, and future into a coherent narrative as theorised byRicœur. The Court does not read much into the principle of intergenerational equity,[60] perhaps because of its State-centric mandate. The vanishing yam offers that missing embodiment. In its emplotment of mythic, historical, and proleptic time, the yam performs the very work that intergenerational equity names but cannot perform in this Opinion. It gives the principle a narrativity rooted in lived experience. In this sense, the vanishing yam transforms intergenerational equity from an interpretive principle into a lived practice of temporal care, an enactment of continuity that international law recognises but cannot itself perform.

InRicœur's terms, the vanishing yam performs the configuration that the Advisory Opinion cannot. It allows us to read both precaution and intergenerational equity as interpretive principles with a rich, multi-layered *temporal imagination*, one that keeps the future and the past co-present. These principles, as narrated through the vanishing yams of Yakel, are not only about *acting under uncertainty* but about *inhabiting uncertainty*

58 ITLOS, *Request for Advisory Opinion submitted by the Commission of Small Island States on Climate Change and International Law* (n. 49), paras. 353 and 361.

59 ICJ, *Obligations of States in Respect of Climate Change* (n. 2), para. 146.

60 This contrasts with the Inter-American Court of Human Rights. IACtHR, *Advisory Opinion on Climate Emergency and Human Rights*, 29 May 2025, AO-32/25. See Ignacio Vásquez Torreblanca, 'Not Only Humans, Not Only the Present – The Leap Toward Intergenerational Justice', Opinio Juris, 2 October 2025.

as a form of care. It discloses that the task international law attributes to the precautionary principle, acting before full knowledge, is already being actively sought through the simple presence of the vanishing yam in the Court's corpus. The story of the Yam Spirit is already a cautionary tale in Vanuatu's folklore.[61] When annexed in the Advisory Opinion, the vanishing yam becomes another kind of spirit, the trace of a *precautionary* tale. It signals to international legal discourse that there are temporalities beyond its grammar, and that these other temporalities may already embody the ethical stance that law seeks but cannot yet perform.

It must be noted here that I do not critique the linear temporality of international law's progress narratives in this piece; a significant body of scholarship already makes this argument convincingly.[62] My attempt is to highlight, rather, how reading the vanishing yam into the Opinion can contribute to refiguring this linearity; it does not yield to a tidy chronology, but presents a palimpsest of mythic, historical, and proleptic time. It also demonstrates the entanglement of time with *space* by showing that a people's lived experience of time is inseparable from their connection with land and biodiversity,[63]

61 *Book of Exhibits* (n. 24) Exhibits F–N (for personal testimonies from Yakel on yam cosmology and ceremonies). See also the explanatory note by the authors where they mention the cautionary tale.

62 See for example Jean d'Aspremont, 'Critical Histories of International Law and the Repression of Disciplinary Imagination', Lond. Rev. Int. Law 7 (2019), 89–115; Eliana Cusato, 'Against temporal abstractions: the battle for colonial and climate reparations in international law,' Int. J.L.C. (2025), 281–299; Damien Cueni and Matthieu Queloz, 'Theorising the Normative Significance of Critical Histories for International Law,' J. History Int' l L. 24 (2022), 561–587; Valentina Vadi, 'International Law and its Histories: Methodological Risks and Opportunities,' Harv. Int'l. L.J. 58 (2017), 311–353. For time and decoloniality, see Katharina Hunfeld, 'The Coloniality of Time in the Global Justice Debate: Decentering Western Linear Temporality', Globalizations 19 (2022), 1–18; For general critique on the progress narrative and international law as a history of events, see Thomas Skouteris, *The Notion of Progress in International Law Discourse* (TMC Asser Press 2010), and Nathaniel Berman, *Passion and Ambivalence: Colonialism, Nationalism and International Law* (Martinus Nijhoff Publishers 2011).

63 On the entanglement of nature, time, and ontology, see Anne Salmond, 'Ontological pluralism and the politics of nature, Cult. Anthropol. 29 (2014), 623–637.

2. Reading Time in the Causal Nexus: Reparations

Precaution and intergenerational equity, read through the vanishing yams, name an ethic of continuity and anticipation in reading the Advisory Opinion. Reparations, the last element in the 'causal nexus' of the deferred *in concreto* assessment, names international law's demand for narrative closure. The braiding of temporalities in the story of the vanished yams now meets the hard edge of doctrine – operative clause 4(c) and its promise of 'full reparations' to future injured States. What happens when a harm emplotted as cumulative and diffuse is asked to settle into the grammar of attribution and remedy? Put differently, what becomes of the reparations regime when the 'event' of harm is not a single moment in the past?[64] The narrative of *care* presses on the juridical register of *repair*. Can a reparations framework built for discrete injury receive a loss that arrives as attrition, recurrence, and proleptic grief?

The Opinion affirms that an injured State is entitled to 'full reparation' once the general conditions of responsibility are met (attribution and the breach of an international obligation) and is quick to specify that 'specially affected' or 'vulnerable' States are subject to the same remedies as 'other injured States'. The general conditions of responsibility include a 'direct and certain causal nexus' between the injury and an internationally wrongful act attributed to a particular State or group of States. It states that this nexus, though 'tenuous,' is not impossible to draw scientifically in the context of climate change.[65] It even goes so far as to concede that the forms of reparation are hard to imagine in climate-related cases but insists that they are not excluded altogether. Reparations, along with state responsibility, are to be decided case-by-case through future *in concreto* assessments.

In the Court's narrative, this seems to make sense. There cannot be reparations without a specific injury to curate them for. The reparations regime in operative clause 4 (c) returns us to the juridical demand for narrative closure; it is telling that the Court brings it up at the very end of the Advisory Opinion. Reparations are the law's narrative devices for ending a particular story of state responsibility. They presume an identifiable event, a coherent linear plot, and finally a restoration of equilibrium (in narrative terms, even if this may not always translate into material

64 Eliana Cusato engages with these questions in detail. My analysis on reparations attempts to add a narratological element to her prolific work on climate change and time. See Cusato (n. 52), and Cusato (n. 62).

65 ICJ, *Obligations of States in Respect of Climate Change* (n. 2), para. 438.

reality). By deferring the matter of reparations to case-by-case assessments in the future, the Court both insists on reparation as narrative closure and distances itself from this closure in the present Opinion. It gestures towards an achievable, if challenging, closure and in the same breath defers this closure to a future case; it cannot be *this* Opinion that provides it. Once again, it limits itself both in terms of its mandate in advisory opinions, and its reading of the questions posed to it.

There is a significant amount of scholarship on intangible harm and reparations in scholarship on cultural heritage and international law; it is not my attempt here to draw from or add to this exceptional and convincing vein of work.[66] My reflection here is based on how reparations are emplotted in a narrative of state responsibility, and whether this emplotment works for climate harm. There are two narrative dimensions to be considered here. The first is that of the 'event' and its attribution,[67] and the second is that of the tension between reparations as closure and the diffuse and continuing temporality of climate harm.

Attribution requires, at the very least, an event that can be traced to a certain State or States. But what, here, is the 'event'? In the testimonies from Yakel, the vanishing yam is not a single moment of rupture but an accumulation of storms (the recurring motifs of Pam, Judy, Kevin, Harold, Lola) that destroyed crops and coral reefs in an erratic and lateral timeline. The vanishing yam resists being emplotted as an 'event' leading to a seamless attribution of responsibility to specific States. It becomes, once again, a metonym for the diffuse, cumulative, and fragmented time-space of climate harm.

This difficulty of speculating and adjudicating around an 'event' in the abstract recalls *Nuclear Weapons*. There, too, the Court was asked to imagine state responsibility for a catastrophe that had not yet occurred,[68] and stopped itself from doing so even as it left a window open for an absurd situation in which the legitimacy of 'self-defence if the very survival of a

66 See for example Ana Filipa Vrdoljak, *International Law, Museums and the Return of Cultural Objects* (Cambridge University Press 2006); Francesco Lenzerini, 'Intangible Cultural Heritage: The Living Culture of Peoples', EJIL 22 (2011), 101–120; Philippe Sands and Ashrutha Rai, 'After the Dust Settles: Transitional Justice and Identity in the Aftermath of Cultural Destruction', in: James Cuno and Thomas G. Weiss (eds), *Cultural Heritage and Mass Atrocities* (Getty Publications 2022), 357–372.

67 Johns, Joyce, and Pahuja (n. 43).

68 Derrida calls this a 'non-event'. See Jacques Derrida, 'No Apocalypse, Not Now (Full Speed Ahead, Seven Missiles, Seven Missives)' Diacritics 14 (1984) 2, 20–31.

State is at stake' would be confirmed in a concrete judicial assessment in a future ridden with the fallout of a nuclear war.[69] Yet, though *Nuclear Weapons* already demonstrates this absurdity, there is an important distinction to be made here with the present Opinion that complicates the matter further: attributability. The wrongfulness of a future nuclear war in terms of survival-based self-defence was still eminently attributable in a future contentious case, hence subject to closure in the grammar of reparations. Although *Climate Change* also envisages future 'events' that would eventually be subject to *in concreto* assessments, the event of climate harm is everywhere and nowhere at once. It is an event without eventfulness. The vanishing yam does not vanish in a single blast followed by radioactive fallout, but in the attritional churn of seasons, erratic rainfall, and violent cyclones.[70] It resists the attributional closure that the Court's reparations framework presupposes.

This resistance disrupts the framing of the 'injured State' that the Opinion links to the reparations regime. The classic model of reparation assumes an injured State and an injuring State, a subject and an object, with the harm between them bridged by causal nexus. The vanishing yam testimony does not fit this template. For example, the nine women who mourn the absence of yam in ceremonies are not 'victims' in the sense that the reparations regime (as expressed in the Opinion) can articulate.[71] The harm they suffer is not episodic or quantifiable; it is not reducible to calories lost or income foregone. It is an affective rupture of ritual, a severing of ancestral bonds, a shame they 'cannot explain.' In the story of the vanishing yam, it is hard to code the narrative symmetry between act and consequence.

In this context, the vanishing yam marks a tension between international law and the lived experience of climate harm. The Court's schema of restitution, compensation, and satisfaction depends on a story with identifiable actors, a definable act, and a reparable end. The vanishing yam refuses this closure. Restitution is impossible; no cyclone can be undone, no crop restored. Compensation collapses into absurdity; the notion that any currency could measure the broken tie between Mangau Iokai and the Yam Spirit is a little baffling to wrap one's head around.[72] This also has a

69 ICJ, *Nuclear Weapons* (n. 11), para. 105 (1) (E).

70 See generally Rob Nixon, *Slow Violence and the Environmentalism of the Poor* (Harvard University Press, 2011) on the attritional lethality of environmental crises.

71 *Book of Exhibits* (n. 24), Exhibit I.

72 *Book of Exhibits* (n. 24), Exhibit H.

cynical air reminiscent of compensation's colonial logic, the belief that all loss can be rendered legible through the currencies of the 'most responsible States'.[73] An attempt to 'price' loss like this reinscribes the same extractive logic that made the loss possible in the first place. Satisfaction, extended to encompass symbolic or moral repair, might be even more absurd and cynical. A memorial or apology cannot return yam to the everyday life of Yakel.

The reparations regime falls flat in the face of the complex, multi-layered personal narratives brought forth by Vanuatu's *Book of Exhibits*. The yam thus becomes a narrative marker of something that cannot be repaired. Its very presence in the archive is a reminder that some harms remain beyond the reparations framework, not only because they are 'unreal' or 'intangible' but because they do not conform to the narrative grammar of causality and closure that the reparations regime requires. The Court's deferral to future *in concreto* assessments is less a promise than an acknowledgement that it has reached the edge of what it can say.

In this sense, the yam does double work. It exposes the structural limits of the reparations regime by unraveling its reliance on discrete events, causal certainty, and an injured-injuring framing. It also functions as a counter-narrative, one that insists on the presence of irreparable harm in the corpus of international law. The vanishing yam does not allow for closure through reparation. It lodges instead as a wound, reminding the reader that some stories cannot have closure, and that deferral to an *in concreto* assessment may be the Court's only way of naming this impossibility.

VI. The Epistemic Limits of the ICJ

In our reading of the *Climate Change* Advisory Opinion, the yam disappears twice. One is a narrated disappearance by the inhabitants of Yakel; we read of it in Vanuatu's *Book of Exhibits*. The second is a disappearance

73 See Anthony Anghie, *Imperialism, Sovereignty and the Making of International Law* (Cambridge University Press, 2004) on the colonial genealogy of valuation in international legal thought. See also Sundhya Pahuja, *Decolonising International Law: Development, Economic Growth and the Politics of Universality* (Cambridge University Press, 2011), arguing that the logic of compensation reiterates the developmentalist premise that all value can be rendered economic. On the moral economy of reparations and its limits, see Vasuki Nesiah, 'Reparations, Redemption and the Moral Economy of Law' (2006) 22 Constellations 10.

in the reading experience of the 'main text' of the Advisory Opinion; we read its absence into the Court's formal reasoning. The Court in its advisory function cannot speculate.[74] The presence of the yam in the *Climate Change* archive, however, gives the *reader* tools to speculate. This Opinion carries history and futurity,[75] both of which involve narration and speculation. The vanished yam becomes a narrative point of departure into the past and the future; it collapses the Court's deferral to the future to a *present* reckoning based on an *in concreto* past. It enables Vanuatu to demonstrate that its past is already the future that the Opinion is attempting to improve.

The vanishing yam, therefore, fills the gap left by the narrative limits of the Advisory Opinion by giving us a microscopic window into what an '*in concreto* assessment' might look like for the people of Yakel, Vanuatu. It even goes beyond this; it puts the Opinion in conversation with the broader context of our present. If the yam has a microhistory, so do the olive tree,[76] the sorghum,[77] the tuna.[78] The reader is pushed to consider other contexts of hunger (and starvation) in international law.

Nonetheless, some might ask why we bother with personal narratives before the ICJ when they are superfluous to the Court's formal reasoning. After all, the Court did not *need* the microhistory of the yam to come to its conclusions. Of course, we are bound to lose something when we translate particular stories into the totalising language of international law. This may not be a bad thing in itself; totalising language is sometimes necessary to maintain the law's legitimacy and norm-making capacity.

The vanishing yam becomes, in the language of international law, something else. It is either subsumed into the register of rights or ignored altogether in the face of the State as protagonist. But having it *in* the corpus of the Court plays an important function: it is proof of this epistemic

74 ICJ, *Nuclear Weapons* (n. 11), para. 15.

75 Eliana Cusato, 'Progress and Linear Time: International Environmental Law and the Uneven Distribution of Futurity' HJIL 84 (2024) 865-893.

76 Ruwaida Amer, 'The olive tree, symbol of Palestine and mute victim of Israel's war on Gaza', Aljazeera 22 January 2024, available at: https://www.aljazeera.com/features/2024/1/22/the-olive-tree-symbol-of-palestine-and-mute-victim-of-israels-war-on-gaza.

77 'Staple grains vanish in Sudan's besieged El Fasher, prices soar' Sudan Tribune, 30 July 2025, available at https://sudantribune.com/article/303407.

78 Benjamin Long, 'Climate change threat to 'tuna dependent' Pacific Islands economies', University of Wollongong Australia Media Centre30 July 2021, available at: https://www.uow.edu.au/media/2021/climate-change-threat-to-tuna-dependent-pacific-islands-economies.php.

translation, the erasure that results from it, and of the gaps that it leaves and fills. Its function is to make the gap, the lacuna, a *part* of the historical account instead of setting it *outside* the account.[79]

It is not so important, therefore, for the ICJ to *use* microhistories like the vanished yam in its legal reasoning, the way it has used science[80] or economics. It is crucial, however, for them to be present in the Court's corpus anyway: to signal the places where international law cannot go, and to build narrative bridges for these places to exist in the cultural memory of the discipline nonetheless. Their absent-present nature makes the narrative limitations of international law clear for the reader to encounter. Even if incommensurable with modernist framings of law, their presence de-necessitates a totalising 'theory of everything' in which only one truth or reality is possible.[81]

VII. Concluding remarks

This chapter has traced how the microhistory of the vanishing yam from Vanuatu's *Book of Exhibits* unsettles the ICJ's narration of its own limits. By reading the vanishing yam as a narrative device within the Court's corpus, I have shown how small island States use personal testimony before the Court in a way that expands the epistemic and temporal horizons of international law. Juxtaposed with motifs of precaution, intergenerational equity, and reparation, the vanishing yam reveals the limits of the Court's emplotment of state responsibility, exposing both its proclivity for erasure and the (not so secret) fragility of its storyworld.

International courts and tribunals are obliged to curate their narration to be in line with their mandates, and to abide by the unspoken rules of the interpretive community to stay within the 'grand narratives' of progress, State-centrism, etc. Indeed, the Court's repeated invocation of its own limits is very much part of international law's 'grand narratives.'[82] My attempt

79 Ginzburg (n. 25), 28.

80 See Katalin Sulyok, 'On the science-coloured glasses of the ICJ: harmfulness, wrongfulness, and climate accountability', in this volume.

81 See generally Anne Salmond, *Tears of Rangi: Experiments Across Worlds* (Auckland University Press, 2017).

82 I note here that although the constraints on the Court (limited jurisdiction, State-centrism etc.) are often invoked as if they were objective constraints on judicial narration, this chapter posits that they too are narrative constructs. The language

here is not to reiterate the now-familiar postmodern skepticism towards these narratives; their historical and ongoing misuse by powerful actors is hardly new information. This is perhaps why the Court concludes the Opinion by cautioning us that international law can only do so much, and that climate change can only be combatted through collaboration.[83]

The *Book of Exhibits* of the Republic of Vanuatu subverts our expectations of what such collaborations might look like. In foregrounding the '*Book of Exhibits*' as part of law's archive, we not only encounter the limits of legal narration but also its latent possibilities. Having less utility for the ICJ in normative terms, the *Book* poses less risk of being distorted by those in power for their benefit. At the same time, it pushes the epistemic and narrative boundaries of international law, and enables the reader to imagine forms of care, continuity, and accountability that the Court itself cannot yet name. It is this unique paradox that makes the vanishing yam a quiet motif of resistance in the archive of the Climate Change Advisory Opinion.

---

of jurisdictional restraints, cautious readings of questions posed, and strict interpretations of the advisory function are not neutral descriptions, but narrative moves that bolster the Court's self-characterisation as a prudent, State-centered institution. The invocation of mandates and jurisdiction is not based on an unyielding external normative framework but is itself an act of emplotment that shapes the story of the Court's authority.

83 ICJ, *Obligations of States in Respect of Climate Change* (n. 2), para. 456.

Part III:
The Integration of Science into Law

On the Science-Coloured Glasses of the ICJ: Harmfulness, Wrongfulness, and Climate Accountability

*Katalin Sulyok**

I. Introduction

In its July 2025 Advisory Opinion on Climate Change,[1] the International Court of Justice (ICJ) gave a thoroughly science-based reading of State obligations with respect to climate change. This, in and of itself, is not very surprising considering the standard practice of domestic and human rights courts to cite scientific findings in climate change. Indeed, references to the findings of the International Panel on Climate Change (IPCC) appears to be an essential ingredient in climate litigation judgments.[2] The Advisory Opinion, nevertheless, stands out, first, as compared to the ICJ's own previous environmental case-law, and second, for the way in which the Court interpreted the scope of state obligations with respect to the climate crisis, and how it paved the way towards establishing state responsibility for climate harm with climate science evidence.

The Advisory Opinion sends a strong message that scientific evidence is no longer a nuisance that should be avoided by the reasoning of the ICJ as much as possible,[3] or an extra-legal knowledge that is irrelevant

---

* Associate Professor in International Law and Sustainability at Durham University.

1 ICJ, *Obligations of States in respect of Climate Change*, Advisory Opinion of 23 July 2025.

2 Cf. for instance Dutch Supreme Court, *Urgenda Foundation* v. *The State of the Netherlands*, 20 December 2019, no.19/00135; The Hague District Court, *Vereniging Milieudefensie v. Royal Dutch Shell Plc*, judgment of 26 May 2021, C/09/571932 / HA ZA 19–379, para. 2.3.5.; German Constitutional Court, *Neubauer et al. v. Germany*, decision of 24 March 2021, 1 BvR 2656/18; ECtHR (Grand Chamber), *Verein KlimaSeniorinnen Schweiz and Others v Switzerland*,. judgment of 9 April 2024, No. 53600/20.

3 See *Pulp Mills on the River Uruguay (Argentina v. Uruguay)*, Judgment of 20 April 2010, para. 167.

for deciding the legal controversy. Long gone the days when members of the bench argued that adjudging science-heavy legal questions (in the material case, whether Japan's whaling program can be deemed scientific in nature) is 'more suited to scientists rather than lawyers'.[4] Nor did the Court deem sufficient to make only symbolic gestures towards scientific authority. Instead, it engaged with climate science meaningfully, assigning a central role to scientific knowledge in how the Court defined the content of state obligations.

The Court spared no efforts in weaving together legal and scientific knowledge in translating the 'more than legal problem'[5] of climate change to the language of international obligations and state responsibility. This short contribution will comment on how the Court was balancing factual and legal aspects in operationalizing the duty to prevent harm to the climate system and will discuss the ways in which climate science informs the content of legal concepts, with a special focus on how scientific evidence now may pave the way to a new legal paradigm of climate accountability.

II. Science as the Backbone of State Obligations with Respect to Climate Change

References to climate science run through the Opinion as a consistent thread. With the 76 appearances of the term 'science' or 'scientific' across the 133 pages, the Opinion reads like the Court is using climate science knowledge as the main compass for navigating the uncharted waters of state responsibility for climate harm.

This was made possible likely due to a pre-hearing meeting the Court held with scientists of the IPCC. The goal of the day-long exchange was 'to enhance the Court's understanding of the key scientific findings'[6] which the IPCC has delivered through its periodic assessment reports. Even though the exact questions and answers were not revealed to the public, it seems quite likely that but for this substantive engagement with leading scientists, climate science could hardly fly so high in Court. After all, the scientific fact-finding powers used by a judicial body fundamentally

4 Separate Opinion of Judge Sebutinde, *Whaling in the Antarctic (Australia v. Japan: New Zealand intervening)*, judgment of 31 March 2014, para. 9.

5 ICJ, *Obligations of States in respect of Climate Change* (n. 1), para. 456.

6 See the IPCC anouncement: https://www.ipcc.ch/2024/11/25/ipcc-icj/.

shape the extent to which the judgment will rely on scientific knowledge meaningfully.[7]

Having declared that IPCC reports 'constitute the best available science on the causes, nature and consequences of climate change'[8], the Court went on reiterating the main findings of these reports,[9] which is a standard practice of domestic courts in climate cases. What is perhaps more surprising is that the ICJ also used IPCC science as the starting point for basic legal definitions, such as 'the climate system' or 'mitigation', even though these very terms are also defined in climate treaties.[10]

The science-coloured glasses of the ICJ also enabled giving a holistic solution to the problem before it. Given the scientific fact that the climate crisis is inextricably linked to other human-enhanced planetary challenges, such as the ecological crisis or desertification, the Court included the Convention on Biological Diversity and the Convention to Combat Desertification among 'the most directly relevant applicable laws', and it did so again on the basis of primarily scientific justifications.[11]

Furthermore, just like climate science, which is not confined to inquires studying the impacts of rising emissions only, but also includes research into the various other anthropogenic drivers behind the climate crisis (e.g. land use change, ozone destruction, pollution, etc.), the ICJ also defined the 'material scope of its inquiry' very broadly, encompassing 'the full range of human activities that contribute to climate change as a result of emissions of GHGs, including both consumption and production'.[12] This science-based narrative paints a very broad picture of the various human (and state) conduct, which is now placed within the scope of international law obligations.

Moreover, climate science evidence served as the main epistemic justification for reaching almost every novel conclusion as to the content of legal obligations. More specifically, climate science laid the foundations for several key legal findings, including:

7 Katalin Sulyok, 'Science, Epistemology and Legitimacy in Environmental Disputes - The Epistemically Legitimate Judicial Argumentative Space', LJIL 37 (2024), 139 (163).

8 ICJ, *Obligations of States in respect of Climate Change* (n. 1), para. 74.

9 ICJ, *Obligations of States in respect of Climate Change* (n. 1), paras. 72-87.

10 But the respective legal definitions come only second in the Opinion after the scientific definitions, see ICJ, *Obligations of States in respect of Climate Change* (n. 1), paras. 75, 85.

11 ICJ, *Obligations of States in respect of Climate Change* (n. 1), paras. 325, 331.

12 ICJ, *Obligations of States in respect of Climate Change* (n. 1), para. 94.

- that the harm prevention principle is applicable in the context of climate change and poses corresponding obligations for all States,[13]
- that the standard of due diligence must be stringent, as every fraction of the degree matters, and 'may also become more demanding in the light of new scientific or technological knowledge',[14]
- that the determination of 'significant harm to the climate system and other parts of the environment' must take into account the IPCC reports, which identify 'harms associated with climate change as including sea level rise, extreme weather events and severe consequences for ecosystems and biodiversity',[15]
- that risks caused by GHG emissions should be assessed as part of States' EIA obligations, including 'their possible downstream effects',[16]
- that the 'primary' temperature goal of the Paris Agreement is 1.5°C, and notes that this interpretation is the one that is consistent with best available science,[17]
- that State efforts to 'enhancing adaptive capacity, strengthening resilience and reducing vulnerability to climate change' must also conform to best available science,[18]
- that scientific evidence informs what measures are deemed necessary within the meaning of Article 194 (1),[19] and
- that sea-level rise is 'not without consequences for' the right to self-determination.[20]

Additionally, the Court also showed how scientific data will inform the legal analysis around causal questions in the context of state responsibility. This merits further discussion given the complexity of the issue, to which I will return later in Section IV.

Finally, despite unanimous acceptance of climate science at large, judges of the Court had slightly different takes on climate science evidence, as transpires from several individual opinions. The main point of contention among members of the bench lies in whether the Court went *far enough*

13 ICJ, *Obligations of States in respect of Climate Change* (n. 1), para. 137.
14 ICJ, *Obligations of States in respect of Climate Change* (n. 1), paras. 245, 284.
15 ICJ, *Obligations of States in respect of Climate Change* (n. 1), para. 278.
16 ICJ, *Obligations of States in respect of Climate Change* (n. 1), para. 298.
17 ICJ, *Obligations of States in respect of Climate Change* (n. 1), para. 224.
18 ICJ, *Obligations of States in respect of Climate Change* (n. 1), para. 258.
19 ICJ, *Obligations of States in respect of Climate Change* (n. 1), para. 334.
20 ICJ, *Obligations of States in respect of Climate Change* (n. 1), para. 357.

in relying on climate science. Judge Yusuf deemed the Court's reasoning as 'scientifically ill-grounded'[21] for stopping short of legally recognizing what scientific evidence, in his view, suggested for States' responsibility for climate harm. Judge Nolte defended the Opinion's approach to conceptualizing wrongful acts,[22] whereas Judge Xue would have preferred more extensive reliance on per capita emission data provided by the IPCC.[23]

III. Harmfulness vs Wrongfulness of Emissions

A particularly consequential finding of the Advisory Opinion pertains to operationalizing the duty of prevention in the climate context. In this respect I will focus only on the Court's firm distinction between *harmful* emissions (in the ordinary, and scientific, sense) and *wrongful* emissions (in the legal sense). This element in the reasoning reveals how the 'scientific' and 'legal' narrative on climate change may conflict with each other, even though they relate to the same element of the factual reality, namely, the effects of anthropogenic emissions.

Scientifically speaking, every tonne of GHG emissions contributes to global emissions, which mix up in the atmosphere, and collectively, cause harmful climate impacts well beyond the territory of the State of origin. However, the Court points out that 'the internationally wrongful act in question is not the emission of GHGs per se'[24] only those that contravene international law obligations. As a result, with the words of Judge Nolte, 'only a limited amount of all anthropogenic GHG emissions since industrialization has been caused by *wrongful* acts.'[25]

This conceptualization of the unlawful State conduct is in line with the approach that the European Court of Human Rights took towards assessing climate obligations in the *Verein KlimaSeniorinnen Schweiz and Others v Switzerland* case, which also assessed domestic climate policies, and resulting GHG emissions, as part of States' positive obligations under

---

21 Separate Opinion of Judge Yusuf, *Obligations of States in respect of Climate Change*, Advisory Opinion of of 23 July 2025, para. 16.

22 Declaration of Judge Nolte, *Obligations of States in respect of Climate Change*, Advisory Opinion of of 23 July 2025, paras. 24–27.

23 Separate Opinion of Judge Xue, *Obligations of States in respect of Climate Change*, Advisory Opinion of 23 July 2025, paras. 9–10.

24 ICJ, *Obligations of States in respect of Climate Change* (n. 1), para. 427.

25 Declaration of Judge Nolte (n. 22), para. 27.

human rights law.[26] The alternative view would have appraised domestic climate laws, and the resulting emissions, as part of the negative obligations of States, under which States have an obligation to refrain from infringing on the protected sphere of private and family life. Under this approach, greenhouse gas emissions *per se* would have been deemed unlawful, for being the cause of the human rights violation. Notably, the European Court of Human Rights instead found that it was the lack of 'effective protection by the State authorities from serious adverse effects of climate change on' the individuals' life and wellbeing that constituted the breach of positive obligations under the right to private life,[27] and not the emissions themselves, which were coming mainly from corporate sources.

Nevertheless, the view taken by the ICJ on the breach of international obligations is not fully backed by all members of the bench despite the Opinion being adopted unanimously. Judge Yusuf finds this reconstruction of the relevant processes problematic, calling it 'completely detached from empirical realities and the scientific findings relating to the causes and consequences of climate change'.[28] He concludes that the Opinion's finding that 'climate change is inherently a consequence of activities ... *of all States* (emphasis added) is scientifically ill-grounded'.[29]

It is argued here, however, that rejecting the harmfulness of the emissions of all States disregards the scientific fact that every tonne of emissions (regardless of its source) has equal warming potential (and hence, *harmful* in the scientific sense). This is not to say, of course, that all States' emissions are equally *blameful* or *wrongful,* in a moral and legal sense. Only, that the difference between the different portions of emissions lies in the normative part of the wrongfulness calculus and not in the scientific dimension of harmfulness.

Moreover, Judge Yusuf focuses his legal inquiry on IPCC data confirming a disparately bigger portion of emissions of the Global North compared to developing States as far as historical emissions are concerned.[30] In his reading, these data would justify a system of State responsibility for climate harm that is proportionate to the respective State's cumulative emissions,

26 ECtHR (Grand Chamber), *Verein KlimaSeniorinnen Schweiz and Others v Switzerland* (n. 2), para. 292.
27 ECtHR (Grand Chamber), *Verein KlimaSeniorinnen* (n. 26), para. 519.
28 Separate Opinion of Judge Yusuf (n. 21), paras. 8.
29 Separate Opinion of Judge Yusuf (n. 21), para. 16.
30 Separate Opinion of Judge Yusuf (n. 21), para. 15.

including historical emissions dating back to 1850. In contrast, Judge Nolte invokes IPCC data showing a growing share of emissions post 1990 in all anthropogenic emissions, which by now has reached the same order of magnitude than emissions prior 1990 (42 %-58 %, respectively).[31] This is possible given that *current* levels of emissions are dominated by emerging economies, and not by historically high emitting States from the Global North.

These competing judicial narratives building on different sets of equally robust scientific data highlights the importance of the broader question of the appropriate role of scientific knowledge in adjudication. As I argued elsewhere, even though scientific evidence is crucially relevant and can (and should) *inform* the judicial decision on legal responsibility for climate harm, climate science alone cannot answer the legal question directly, nor such answer is *dictated* by climate science.[32] Evidence needs to be legally contextualized and interpreted for purposes of answering the legal question put before a court. The hard limit, in this respect, lies in that the judicial narrative on factual processes should not contradict robust climate science knowledge. Doing so would undermine the epistemic legitimacy of the reasoning.[33] Nevertheless, the presence of scientific evidence cannot exempt judges from their task of undertaking normative considerations in deciding (science-heavy) legal dilemmas. The climate crisis throws into the limelight the inevitable role and importance of making (scientifically informed) value judgments. These new legal standards can be best spelt out in legislation, or in the persistent lack thereof, in judicial decisions.

After all, the Court seems to strike a careful balance between scientific and normative components in reconstructing the legally relevant process leading from anthropogenic GHG emissions to harmful climate impacts. The Opinion remains within the bounds of epistemically legitimate reasoning when distinguishes the harmfulness of emissions from their wrongfulness. It is argued here that equating the two would have 'scientized' the issue of state responsibility to an excessive extent by eliminating the normative aspects of the (essentially legal) calculus, which would have undermined the epistemic legitimacy of the reasoning.

31 Declaration of Judge Nolte (n. 22), para. 25.
32 Katalin Sulyok, 'Speaking in the Language of Law or Science? Epistemic Hard Cases and Reasoning Dilemmas for Courts in Adjudicating Climate Change', NZJEL 28 (2024) 21–27.
33 Katalin Sulyok (n. 7), 163.

Nevertheless, the Advisory Opinion did avoid answering the hard question of which portions of emissions (i.e. whose emissions?) are *harmful.* This is primarily a normative assessment, which will have to be done in future cases, should those reach the Court. Any such assessment will revolve around the application of the various standards[34] that the Court specified under the obligation of due diligence.

IV. Attribution, Causation: Climate Science in Establishing the International Responsibility of Individual States

The Court, as shown above, preserves room for normative appraisals in the assessment of the wrongfulness of emissions. The Opinion, in fact, swings the door wide open to finding the responsibility of individual States (or group of States) established for climate harm in future contentious proceedings, and, importantly for present purposes, the chances of success of any such claims will, for a large part, hinge on climate science. Relevant scientific questions include causal determinations and assessing whether the respective State took measures that are reasonable, appropriate and necessary to prevent harm to the climate system.

The Court finds that 'the rules on State responsibility admit the possibility of determining the responsibility of States in the climate change context',[35] and the extent of liability must be established 'in concreto',[36] that is, in individual contentious proceedings.

The success of climate damage claims hinges on whether the respective court is willing to accept climate attribution science, a field of climate research that studies whether individual climate impacts, such as extreme weather impacts, can be attributed to anthropogenic climate change (impact attribution), or even further back to individual emitters, based on their share from the global emissions (source attribution).[37] The Advisory Opinion openly welcomes the insights deriving from attribution science. It finds, first, that source attribution studies can have bearing on a state

34 ICJ, *Obligations of States in respect of Climate Change* (n. 1), paras. 280–300.

35 ICJ, *Obligations of States in respect of Climate Change* (n. 1), para. 431.

36 ICJ, *Obligations of States in respect of Climate Change* (n. 1), para. 437.

37 Carly A. Phillips, Delta Merner and Friederike Otto, 'Attribution Science', in: Margaretha Wewerinke-Singh and Sarah Mead (eds), *The Cambridge Handbook on Climate Litigation* (Cambridge University Press 2025), 79–102.

responsibility, by emphasizing that 'it is scientifically possible to determine each State's total contribution to global emissions, taking into account both historical and current emissions'.[38] Moreover, it also acknowledges impact attribution findings by citing IPCC data 'clearly linking the human contribution to climate change to observed increases in heatwaves, flooding and drought'.[39]

While attribution science causally links a portion of emissions to certain harmful impacts and the sources of emissions, respectively, legal causation must still be established separately in the context of state responsibility. This requires the demonstration of a causal link between a wrongful act and a specific climate harm. This is sometimes called as attribution in the climate law sense, which is used for purposes of assigning a given climate impact to a certain emitter.[40] Importantly, this type of attribution must be distinguished from the notion of attribution used in the law of state responsibility,[41] used most notably under the Articles on Responsibility of States for Internationally Wrongful Acts,[42] and equally also from the scientific notion of attribution as used by scientists in climate attribution studies.[43]

Importantly, the Court stresses that finding a causal nexus 'is not impossible' and will have to be done in each case 'through an *in concreto* assessment'.[44] The difficulties presented by scientific uncertainty burdening causal evidence 'must be addressed as and when they arise in light of ... the evidence presented to the Court'.[45] This wording of the Court suggests that the certain factual scenarios may be sufficient for the Court to find causali-

38 ICJ, *Obligations of States in respect of Climate Change* (n. 1), para. 429.

39 ICJ, *Obligations of States in respect of Climate Change* (n. 1), para. 437.

40 For a more detailed discussion, see Petra Minnerop, 'Climate Causality – From Causation to Attribution', in: Margaretha Wewerinke-Singh and Sarah Mead (eds), *The Cambridge Handbook on Climate Litigation* (Cambridge University Press 2025), 421–427.

41 Gábor Kajtar, 'The fragmentation of attribution in international law', in: Gábor Kajtár, Basak Çaliand Marko Milanovic (eds), *Secondary Rules of Primary Importance in International Law – Attribution, Causality, Evidence, and Standards of Review in the Practice of International Courts and Tribunals* (Oxford University Press 2022).

42 ILC, Articles on Responsibility of States for Internationally Wrongful Acts, 2001, General Assembly Resolution 56/83 of 12 December 2001, and corrected by document. A/56/49(Vol. I)/Corr.4.

43 Sulyok (n. 32).

44 ICJ, *Obligations of States in respect of Climate Change* (n. 1), para. 438.

45 ICJ, *Obligations of States in respect of Climate Change* (n. 1), para. 437.

ty established despite the Court's insistence on its causal standard requiring 'a sufficiently direct and certain causal nexus between the wrongful act... and the injury suffered'.[46]

The ICJ's findings on the possibility of establishing (individual) state responsibility for (individual) climate harm may seem progressive, surprising or even radical to some. Yet, there exists robust scientific evidence that is capable of establishing causality, not only in the scientific sense, but also in legally appreciable terms. Any friction is, therefore, not between the logic of (climate) science and the logic of (international) law, but rather between two legal worldviews: the old paradigm of climate impunity and the new paradigm of climate accountability.

46 ICJ, *Obligations of States in respect of Climate Change* (n. 1), para. 436.

Part IV:
Re-negotiation of the Postcolonial International Legal Order

The Advisory Opinion on Climate Justice and the 'Global North-South Divide'

Lovleen Bhullar[*]

I. Introduction

The International Court of Justice (ICJ or Court)'s Advisory Opinion on the *Obligations of States in respect of Climate Change*[1] has the potential to contribute to the future of international law and climate governance and the pursuit of climate justice in different ways.[2] This contribution focuses on the challenges and limitations of international law and the ICJ in addressing the historical and current power asymmetries underlying the so-called 'Global North–South Divide' to achieve climate justice. For this purpose, it starts by explaining two key terms – 'Global South' and 'climate justice' – while acknowledging that the former is not uncontested and the latter may have multiple meanings. This is followed by an examination of the Court's engagement with climate justice and a related concept 'equity' whose temporal and spatial dimensions are captured in the principles of inter-generational and intragenerational equity or justice. Then it considers how the Court engages with the distinction between developed and developing countries and the request for determination of specific legal

* Assistant Professor in Environmental Law at at the Department of Land Economy, University of Cambridge.

1 ICJ, *Obligations of States in Respect of Climate Change*, Advisory Opinion of 23 July 2025.

2 See Martina Igini, '"Landmark Moment for Climate Justice": Reactions Pour in After ICJ Delivers Historic Opinion on States' Climate Change Obligations', Earth.Org 24 July 2025, https://earth.org/landmark-moment-for-climate-justice-reactions-pour-in-after-icj-delivers-historic-opinion-on-states-climate-change-obligations/. See the contributions to this volume as well as Maria Antonia Tigre, Maxim Bönnemann & Antoine De Spiegeleir (eds.), *The ICJ's Advisory Opinion on Climate Change* (Verfassungsbooks, 2025)..

consequences of obligations of States. The penultimate section revisits some cautionary notes about the potential influence of the Advisory Opinion on the future of climate litigation.

II. Two Key Terms: 'Climate Justice' for the 'Global South'

The Global South refers to the world's developing economies and least developed countries[3] that account for 80 percent of the total population. More fundamentally, this term 'references an entire history of colonialism, neo-imperialism, and differential economic and social change through which large inequalities in living standard, living expectancy, and access to resources are maintained'.[4] These factors have contributed to or exacerbated the vulnerability of these countries to the adverse impacts of climate change, and therefore influenced their demands for climate justice.[5] Climate justice, according to Sultana, 'fundamentally is about paying attention to how climate change impacts people differently, unevenly, and disproportionately, as well as redressing the resultant injustices in fair and equitable ways.'[6]

III. Climate Justice and Equity

Climate justice for the Global South is at the heart of the request for the Advisory Opinion from the ICJ. The very idea of seeking this Advisory Opinion is traceable to an extracurricular task of promoting climate justice given to a group of law students at the University of the South Pacific in Fiji.[7] In addition, achieving climate justice was an important objective of the core group of States' initiative to seek an Advisory Opinion.[8] The

---

3 See UNCTAD, *Country classification*, 20 March 2025, <https://unctadstat.unctad.org/EN/Classifications/ClassificationsNewsletter_March2025_US_EN.pdf>.

4 Nour Dados and Raewyn Connell, 'The Global South', Contexts 11(1) (2012), 12-13.

5 Gurminder K Bhambra and Peter Newell, 'More than a metaphor: "climate colonialism" in perspective', GSCJ 2(2) (2023), 179-187, (183).

6 Farhana Sultana, 'Critical climate justice', The Geographical Journal 188(1) (2022), 118-124, (118).

7 Aditi Shetye and Manon Rouby, 'Climate Justice: Advisory Opinion of the International Court of Justice and the Impact of Youth Advocacy', CLJP – JDCP 27 (2022) 79-94, (81–83).

8 UN General Assembly resolution A/RES/77/276 (4 April 2023).

Court received submissions from several countries as well as organizations in the Global South. However, neither the Court nor any of the country submissions use the term Global South. Further, the Court 'ignores or circumvents' the climate justice focus of the request for an Advisory Opinion.[9] However, Judge Xue deals with climate justice in her Separate Opinion. She emphasizes the historical roots of the climate change issue,[10] and the need to consider the transfer of GHG emissions, for example, due to the relocation of carbon-intensive production, from developed to developing countries in conformity with the principle of equity[11].

The Court does recognize the principle of equity and its relationship with justice generally.[12] It further identifies the principles of common but differentiated responsibilities and respective capabilities (CBDR-RC) and intergenerational equity as manifestations of equity.[13] In fact, the 'legal questions' in respect of which the Advisory Opinion was requested concerned the obligations of States under international law to ensure protection for, and legal consequences of acts or omissions that have caused significant harm with respect to, present and future generations.[14] Further, according to the Court, the principle of CBDR-RC reflects the need for equitable distribution of the burdens of obligations in respect of climate change.[15]

Another aspect of equity is the principle of intragenerational justice among members of a generation.[16] The principle of CBDR-RC and the equitable distribution of the burdens of obligations in respect of climate change can capture some elements of this principle but the latter is broader. It also seeks to address disparities between states, for instance, through financial and technical support.[17] Judge Xue explicitly mentions 'intragen-

9 Separate Opinion of Vice President Sebutinde, *Obligations of States in Respect of Climate Change*, Advisory Opinion of 23 July 2025, paras. 5, 9.

10 Separate Opinion of Judge Xue, *Obligations of States in Respect of Climate Change*, Advisory Opinion of 23 July 2025, para. 72.

11 Separate Opinion of Judge Xue (n. 10), para. 74.

12 ICJ, *Obligations of States in Respect of Climate Change* (n. 1), para. 152.

13 ICJ, *Obligations of States in Respect of Climate Change* (n. 1), paras. 151 and 157. For a critique of this framing, see Rebecca Breukers 'Equity in the International Court of Justice's Climate Change Advisory Opinion' CILJ Blog, 24 September 2025.

14 ICJ, *Obligations of States in Respect of Climate Change* (n. 1), paras. 1, 40.

15 ICJ, *Obligations of States in Respect of Climate Change* (n. 1), para. 148.

16 See Oscar Schachter, *Sharing the World's Resources* (Columbia University Press 1977), 16.

17 Catherine Redgwell, 'Principles and Emerging Norms in International Law: Intra- and Inter-generational Equity', in: Kevin R Gray, Richard Tarasofsky, Cinnamon P.

erational equity' and identifies the underlying issue of the persistent gap between developed and developing countries as the reason why developed countries are asked to take the lead in combating climate change and its adverse effects.[18] Notably, the Court does refer to the obligations, in the Paris Agreement, for developed States to provide support to developing States with respect to their mitigation and adaptation responsibilities as forming part of the duty of cooperation.[19] Developed States are to implement these obligations 'at a level that allows for the achievement of the objectives listed in Article 2', and the evaluating factors include 'the capacity of developed States and the needs of developing States'.[20] The inclusion of the capacity of developed States may increase their level of support to developing States. Conversely, the former's capacity may be considered before the latter's needs. In fact, the Court notes: 'The duty of cooperation is founded on the recognition of the interdependence of States, requiring more than the transfer of finance or technology, in particular efforts by States to continuously develop, maintain and implement a collective climate policy[...]'.[21] This should not lead to an inequitable distribution of the burdens of obligations between developed and developing countries or de-emphasise the importance of transfer of technology or finance from the former to the latter for mitigation as well as adaptation measures.

IV. Obligations of States: Developed and Developing Countries

Following the text of the United Nations Framework Convention on Climate Change (UNFCCC), the Kyoto Protocol and the Paris Agreement, the Court refers to 'developed countries' and 'developing countries'. This distinction is based on the level of development of countries, as defined by the United Nations.[22] Judge Xue, in her Separate Opinion, notes in the context of the international climate regime that this distinction is 'not just about a criterion but a crucial factor for States to participate in a meaning-

Carlarne (eds), *The Oxford Handbook of International Climate Change Law* (Oxford University Press 2016), 185-201.

18 Separate Opinion of Judge Xue (n. 10), para. 28.

19 ICJ, *Obligations of States in Respect of Climate Change* (n. 1), para. 227.

20 ICJ, *Obligations of States in Respect of Climate Change* (n. 1), para. 265.

21 ICJ, *Obligations of States in Respect of Climate Change* (n. 1), para. 306.

22 UN, *Country classification* (2014), <www.un.org/en/development/desa/policy/wesp/wesp_current/2014wesp_country_classification.pdf>.

ful way in the global response to climate change'.[23] However, the Court attempts to redefine this distinction by placing the most developed States, States that have undergone considerable development since the UNFCCC, and the least developed States on a spectrum.[24] According to the criteria of the International Monetary Fund and the World Bank, this spectrum corresponds to 40 most developed States, 110 developing States in the middle and 44 least developed States.[25] In this regard, Judge Xue notes: 'Without any specific and credible criteria, this new division of the developing countries has no legal basis in the treaties, which may be perceived as a deviation from the current burden sharing of obligations between developed and developing countries under the UNFCCC, the Kyoto Protocol and the Paris Agreement'.[26]

The Court further notes that the insertion of the phrase 'in the light of the different national circumstances' in the Paris Agreement to the principle of common but differentiated responsibilities as set out in the UNFCCC recognises that 'the status of a State as developed or developing is not static. It depends on an assessment of the current circumstances of the State concerned'.[27] According to Judge Xue, this interpretation is likely to further weaken the principle's role in the international climate change regime.[28] This is because the distinction 'underlies the legal structure of the climate change treaty regime'.[29] Further, this interpretation fails to acknowledge the role of historical events in shaping the differences in current circumstances in developed and developing countries, which do not make it from the negotiations to the text.

There is a significant difference in the Court's level of engagement with the contribution of the Global South to historical and present GHG emissions. In respect of historical emissions, the Court rightly recognises the significant contribution of the most developed States 'to the overall amount of GHG emissions since the Industrial Revolution' and the minimal contri-

23 Separate Opinion of Judge Xue (n. 10), para. 3.
24 ICJ, *Obligations of States in Respect of Climate Change* (n. 1), para. 150.
25 Separate Opinion of Judge Xue (n. 10), para. 64.
26 Separate Opinion of Judge Xue (n. 10), para. 64.
27 ICJ, *Obligations of States in Respect of Climate Change* (n. 1), para. 226. See also Ielyzaveta Badanova, 'Dynamic Differentiation and Common But Differentiated Responsibilities Under the Paris Agreement: Some Clarification But Not Yet Clarity', CILJ Blog, 30 August 2025.
28 Separate Opinion of Judge Xue (n. 10), para. 65.
29 Separate Opinion of Judge Xue (n. 10), para. 67.

bution of the least developed States.[30] However, it does not refer to the minimal contribution to historical emissions of the States in the middle,[31] which include 110 developing countries in the Global South. In contrast, in respect of present emissions, the Court notes that the least developed States 'have only a limited capacity to transform their economies' while the States in the middle 'have progressed considerably in their development since the conclusion of the UNFCCC[...], and some of which now contribute significantly to global GHG emissions'.[32] It is true that some developing States in the middle are now among the major CO2 emitters, and their total emissions are approaching those of the most developed States.[33] However, the per capita GHG emissions of most of the developing States in the middle 'remain relatively low'.[34]

V. Determination of specific legal consequences

The Advisory Opinion was requested in respect of the legal consequences of obligations for States where they, by their acts or omissions, have caused significant harm to the climate system and other parts of the environment, with respect to (a) States, including, in particular, small island developing States, which due to their geographical circumstances and level of development, are injured or specially affected by or are particularly vulnerable to the adverse effects of climate change; and (b) peoples and individuals of the present and future generations affected by the adverse effects of climate change.[35] As mentioned above, the Global South is home to a majority of these States as well as peoples and individuals.

In response to (a), the Court recognises that certain States have faced and are likely to face greater levels of climate change-related harm owing to their geographical circumstances and level of development.[36] It acknowledges some of the nine categories of developing countries with specific needs and concerns 'arising from the adverse effects of climate change

30 ICJ, *Obligations of States in Respect of Climate Change* (n. 1), para. 150.
31 See Separate Opinion of Judge Yusuf, *Obligations of States in Respect of Climate Change*, Advisory Opinion of 23 July 2025, paras. 12-19.
32 ICJ, *Obligations of States in Respect of Climate Change* (n. 1), para. 150.
33 See International Energy Agency, *Global Energy Review* (2025).
34 Separate Opinion of Judge Xue (n. 10), para. 15 (referring to the IPCC reports).
35 ICJ, *Obligations of States in Respect of Climate Change* (n. 1), para. 1.
36 ICJ, *Obligations of States in Respect of Climate Change* (n. 1), para. 110.

and/or the impact of the implementation of response measures', as identified in Article 4, paragraph 8 of the UNFCCC,[37] by referring to the IPCC's report that highlights the high risk of harms associated with climate change in Arctic ecosystems and dryland regions, small island developing States (SIDS) and least developed countries, and to the written submissions from low-lying coastal States and SIDS.[38] However, it reframes the first part of the question from where States 'have' caused to 'may have' caused,[39] and decides not to determine any specific legal consequences[40].

The Court's response to (b) focuses almost exclusively on the entitlement of 'individuals' to bring claims against States.[41] It does not engage with 'peoples' reflecting the general reluctance in international law to engage with peoples' rights outside specific treaty contexts. However, Vice-President Sebutinde, in her Separate Opinion, goes beyond the Court to offer a definition of 'peoples' that attempts to engage with State responsibility. She notes:

> '[t]he phrase "peoples" refers to distinct ethnic groups, nations or communities whose habitat and way of life is adversely affected by the effects of climate change. These include, for example, the indigenous peoples of many small island States whose very existence and way of life is threatened by rising sea levels and disappearing territory'.[42]

At the same time, the Court recognises that individuals and peoples are right-holders under international human rights law.[43] It mentions specific right-holder groups included in the preamble of the Paris Agreement: indigenous peoples, local communities, migrants, children, persons with disabilities and people in vulnerable situations, women and intergenerational

37 These nine categories are small island countries, countries with low-lying coastal areas, arid and semi-arid areas, forested areas and areas liable to forest decay, areas prone to natural disasters, areas liable to drought and desertification, areas of high urban atmospheric pollution and areas with fragile ecosystems, including mountainous ecosystems, countries whose economies are highly dependent on income generated from the production, processing and export, and/or on consumption of fossil fuels and associated energy-intensive products, and land-locked and transit countries.

38 ICJ, *Obligations of States in Respect of Climate Change* (n. 1), para. 212.

39 ICJ, *Obligations of States in Respect of Climate Change* (n. 1), para. 108. See also Separate Opinion of Judge Yusuf (n. 31), para. 4.

40 ICJ, *Obligations of States in Respect of Climate Change* (n. 1), para. 109.

41 ICJ, *Obligations of States in Respect of Climate Change* (n. 1), para. 111.

42 Separate Opinion of Vice President Sebutinde (n. 9), para. 6.

43 ICJ, *Obligations of States in Respect of Climate Change* (n. 1), para. 371.

equity.[44] The Court further considers that climate change may impair the enjoyment of human rights of groups such as women, children and indigenous peoples drawing on the work of UN bodies and the IPCC.[45] This is not a giant leap but it represents a promising tentative step for international law.

VI. Future of Climate Litigation

The Advisory Opinion is not legally binding but it has 'the potential to open a new front in climate litigation'.[46] The Declaration of Judge Nolte provides several cautionary notes about the Advisory Opinion's influence on the behaviour of countries.

1. The 'general manner' in which the Court responds to the questions concerning the law of State responsibility and its application may encourage States 'to pursue litigation which, if successful at all, may entail only symbolic legal consequences'.[47]
2. The Advisory Opinion may raise 'false hopes that climate litigation can supplement the mechanisms of financial transfers and the remedies for loss and damage contained in the climate change treaties'[48].
3. Litigation may lead to 'counterproductive effect on the political processes within the framework of the Paris Agreement and beyond'.[49] 'States may in the future shy away from accepting new treaty obligations or maintaining procedures that could subject them to unpredictable legal consequences'.[50]
4. States may challenge 'the distributive implications of court decisions which, in their view, unjustifiably isolate parts of the problem from the whole' and 'the very legitimacy of courts, particularly international

44 ICJ, *Obligations of States in Respect of Climate Change* (n. 1), paras. 374, 382.
45 ICJ, *Obligations of States in Respect of Climate Change* (n. 1), paras. 382–84.
46 Jorge Viñuales, 'The 'world court' and climate change', University of Cambridge Stories, 24 July 2025.
47 Declaration of Judge Nolte, *Obligations of States in Respect of Climate Change*, Advisory Opinion of 23 July 2025, para. 31.
48 Declaration of Judge Nolte (n. 47), para. 31.
49 Declaration of Judge Nolte (n. 47), para. 31.
50 Declaration of Judge Nolte (n. 47), para. 32.

courts, when these appear to unduly limit the exercise of States' political and administrative discretion'.[51]

The impact of the Advisory Opinion also needs to be considered in light of the growing complexity of domestic and regional climate litigation, which may be used to challenge climate injustice or to deny climate justice. Scholars have highlighted the different understandings of climate litigation in the Global South including the strategic decision not to use climate change language, mitigation, adaptation or loss and damage focus, vulnerabilities of specific individuals, groups and peoples, and use of rights-based approaches etc.[52] The general understanding of the Advisory Opinion will further influence the nature and scope of future climate litigation and its contribution to achieving climate justice in and for the Global South.

VII. Conclusion

The Global South origin of the Advisory Opinion highlights the uneven nature and scale of the vulnerability of countries to the adverse effects of climate change. The Global North-South Divide frames the obligations of developed countries in respect of historical GHG emissions and support for adaptation measures in the Global South as well as a context-driven understanding of the mitigation and adaptation obligations of all countries. The equitable distribution of the burden of these obligations is key to climate justice and the future of peoples and our planet. For this reason, while we must pursue the opportunities offered by the Court, we must also continue to challenge the limits of international law and seek solutions to this planetary crisis beyond international law.

51 Declaration of Judge Nolte (n. 47), para. 32.

52 Melanie Jean Murcott and Maria Antonia Tigre, 'Developments, Opportunities, and Complexities in Global South Climate Litigation: Introduction to the Special Collection', J. Hum. Rights Pract. 16(1) (2024), 1-24.

The ICJ's Historic Nod to Self-Determination and Climate Change Impacts

*Dave-Inder Comar**

I. Introduction

This chapter analyses the July 2025 Advisory Opinion from the International Court of Justice (ICJ), *Obligations of States in Respect of Climate Change* (Advisory Opinion),[1] with respect to the principle and right of self-determination. While the ICJ did not explicitly rely on the principle and right of self-determination in its core discussion of 'the most directly relevant applicable law,'[2] the ICJ did not completely ignore it. In discussing the specific impacts of sea-level rise, the Court observed the possibility of 'adverse consequences' on vulnerable States, including forced displacement and impacts on territorial integrity and permanent sovereignty over natural resources. '[S]ince these principles are closely connected with the right to self-determination, sea level rise is not without consequences for the exercise of this right.'[3]

While the Court's discussion in paragraph 357 is brief, it is also remarkable. The Court's conclusion that certain climate change impacts, particularly sea-level rise, will have consequences on the self-determination of affected States represents a novel application of the right to self-determination by the Court beyond its prior treatment in the context of decolonisation (e.g., *Western Sahara* (1975),[4] *Chagos Archipelago* (2019)[5]) or occupation (*Legal Consequences arising from the Policies and Practices of Israel in the Occupied Palestinian Territory, including East Jerusalem*

---

* PhD candidate at The Grotius Centre for International Legal Studies at Leiden University.

1 ICJ, *Obligations of States in respect of Climate Change*, Advisory Opinion of 23 July 2025.

2 ICJ, *Obligations of States in respect of Climate Change* (n. 1), para. 114.

3 ICJ, *Obligations of States in respect of Climate Change* (n. 1), para. 357.

4 ICJ, *Western Sahara*, Advisory Opinion of 16 October 1975, ICJ Rep., 12.

5 ICJ, *Legal Consequences of the Separation of the Chagos Archipelago from Mauritius in 1965*, Advisory Opinion of 25 February 2019, ICJ Rep., 95.

(2024)[6]). The Court further appears to be aligning its own jurisprudence with the conclusions of the International Law Commission (ILC) and related recommendations from the International Law Association (ILA) concerning the relevance of self-determination in protecting the existence and survival of peoples from climate impacts. In that sense, paragraph 357 represents the Court's opening statement of a potentially much larger doctrinal exploration of climate change and self-determination in the years ahead.

II. Self-Determination in Relation to Existential Climate Impacts

The relevance of self-determination in relation to climate change impacts, particularly for vulnerable States, has been identified by the ILA and the ILC as part of their overlapping but separate assessments on sea-level rise. In a 2024 report focused on statehood and sea-level rise,[7] the ILA specifically identified self-determination as an 'important element' in shaping decisions related to the preservation of statehood and the protection of rights of the population, concluding that the right of self-determination 'becomes particularly significant for peoples affected by sea level rise when most or all of the territory of low-lying SIDS becomes uninhabitable or submerged.'[8] Separately, the ILC released its final conclusions on sea-level rise and international law in 2025, capping a six-year review conducted by an open-ended Study Group. In their final consolidated report, the Co-Chairs of the Study Group articulated that the right to self-determination was 'a fundamental principle' to be taken into account under all three subtopics reviewed by the Study Group: the law of the sea, statehood, and the protection of persons.[9] The final report of the Study Group itself concluded that the right to self-determination supports the continuity of statehood in the context of climate change-related sea-level rise and that peoples cannot be

6 ICJ, *Legal Consequences arising from the Policies and Practices of Israel in the Occupied Palestinian Territory, including East Jerusalem*, Advisory Opinion of 19 July 2024.

7 International Law Association, 'Athens Conference (2024): International Law and Sea Level Rise', (2024), 49.

8 International Law Association (n. 7), 23.

9 ILC, 'Sea-level rise in relation to international law: Final consolidated report of the Co-Chairs of the Study Group on sea-level rise in relation to international law, Patrícia Galvão Teles, Nilüfer Oral and Juan José Ruda Santolaria', (2025) A/CN.4/783, para. 409.

deprived of the continuity of statehood without their consent.[10] Respect for self-determination also requires good faith consultation as to alternative solutions that can preserve the identities of peoples and their international legal personality.[11] Fundamental principles of international law, including that of self-determination, 'should not be undermined by climate change-related sea-level rise.'[12]

The ICJ acknowledged the work of the ILC in the Advisory Opinion[13] and affirmed certain aspects of its conclusions, for example, that UNCLOS does not require States parties 'to update their charts or lists of geographical co-ordinates that show the baselines and outer limit lines of their maritime zones once they have been duly established' in the context of climate-change related sea-level rise.[14] The separate opinions and declarations appended to the Advisory Opinion suggest a level of disagreement regarding the proper analysis of self-determination, statehood, and sea-level rise, with some expressing a degree of dissatisfaction on the lack of engagement on the topic. Vice President Sebutinde, noting that the issue of self-determination had been raised by many States (including small island States) in the context of sea-level rise and statehood, advocated for a more thorough discussion of self-determination and climate change impacts including 'confirming in the operative paragraph 457 the obligation incumbent upon all States to take all necessary measures to protect the right of the most vulnerable States to self-determination.'[15] Judge Aurescu urged more analysis related to UNCLOS and the law of the sea, including with respect to the ICJ's conclusion that there is no obligation under UNCLOS to update charts or lists of geographical co-ordinates that show the baselines and outer limit lines of their maritime zones once they have been duly established.[16] Judge Aurescu suggested that this conclusion could be derived, among other things, 'from the obligation to respect the right

---

10 ILC, 'Final report of the Study Group on sea-level rise in relation to international law', (2025) ILCYB, Vol. II, Part Two, paras. 38, 39.

11 ILC, Final report on sea-level rise (n. 10), para. 39.

12 ILC, Final report on sea-level rise (n. 10), para. 53.

13 ICJ, *Obligations of States in respect of Climate Change* (n. 1), para. 361.

14 ICJ, *Obligations of States in respect of Climate Change* (n. 1), para. 362.

15 Separate Opinion of Vice-President Sebutinde, *Obligations of States in Respect of Climate Change*, Advisory Opinion of 23 July 2025, para. 8.

16 Separate Opinion of Judge Aurescu, *Obligations of States in Respect of Climate Change*, Advisory Opinion of 23 July 2025, para. 2.

to self-determination (closely connected, inter alia, with territorial integrity and permanent sovereignty over natural resources)'.[17]

In contrast, Judge Tomka wrote in his declaration that he would have preferred a 'more prudent approach' on the question of statehood and self-determination.[18] In his view, self-determination and statehood were 'heavily tied to territory'; therefore, the inexistence of land from climate change impacts 'would tend to result in the demise of that [impacted] State as a subject of international law.'[19] Judge Tomka conceded that 'a growing number of States' had expressed to the ILC the view that 'statehood may survive even in the case of the total disappearance of territory.'[20] However, the discussions before the ILC were not sufficient in Judge Tomka's view to indicate 'a collective *opinio juris* reflecting a new rule of custom' that was 'judicially cognizable'. For jurists and scholars holding the same views as Judge Tomka, more will be needed from States, including 'a firm and public position on this issue' before it can be said that 'a customary rule has crystallized around this point.'[21]

III. Doctrinal Implications Moving Forward

Despite the brevity of the Advisory Opinion's reference to self-determination, paragraph 357 nevertheless contains significant doctrinal implications concerning self-determination and climate change, particularly in relation to 'forced displacement of populations' from sea-level rise and impacts on the principles of 'the territorial integrity of States and their permanent sovereignty over their natural resources.' First, the Court's conclusion that 'sea level rise is not without consequences for the exercise of [the right to self-determination],' while cursory, represents a historic expansion of its jurisprudence related to self-determination and confirmation of its applicability outside the contexts of decolonisation and occupation (which the Co-Chairs of the ILC Study Group also affirmed in their final consolidated report).[22] While some scholarship has argued that self-determination's role

17 Separate Opinion of Judge Aurescu (n. 16), para. 3.
18 Declaration of Judge Tomka, *Obligations of States in Respect of Climate Change*, Advisory Opinion of 23 July 2025, para. 10.
19 Declaration of Judge Tomka (n. 18), para. 8.
20 Declaration of Judge Tomka (n. 18), para. 6.
21 Declaration of Judge Tomka (n. 18), para. 6.
22 ILC, Final consolidated report of the Co-Chairs (n. 9), para 295.

is narrow or even irrelevant in addressing climate change impacts (for example, Stoutenburg's conclusion in 2015 that the right was inapplicable on the issue of territorial loss and statehood in the context of sea-level rise),[23] the ILC, ILA, and now the ICJ have expressly shifted the doctrine towards application of the right to self-determination in the face of climate impacts. And even while the ICJ did not explicitly mention self-determination in its review of applicable legal obligations,[24] self-determination is necessarily implicated through the ICJ's references to the Charter of the United Nations (UN Charter),[25] the International Covenant on Civil and Political Rights (ICCPR),[26] and the International Covenant on Economic, Social and Cultural Rights (ICESCR),[27] which each demand the dual protection and promotion of self-determination as a fundamental element of the international legal order (for example, in Articles 1(2) and 55 of the UN Charter, and common Article 1of the ICCPR and ICESCR).

Second, the Court's conclusion that climate change impacts and sea-level rise will have consequences for self-determination serves to further develop the substantive law of self-determination. The ICJ recently summarised the law of self-determination in *Legal Consequences arising from the Policies and Practices of Israel in the Occupied Palestinian Territory, including East Jerusalem* (2024) in a manner that could be directly relevant to issues of sea-level rise and climate impacts more generally. In that Advisory Opinion, the ICJ concluded that territorial integrity and permanent sovereignty over natural resources were fundamentally interwoven with self-determination,[28] and that self-determination further protects a people 'against acts aimed at dispersing the population and undermining its integrity as a people.'[29] The ICJ further held that self-determination 'is the right of a people freely to determine its political status and to pursue its economic, social and

---

23 Cait Storr, 'Islands and the South: Framing the Relationship between International Law and Environmental Crisis', EJIL 27 (2016), 519–540 (525–526).

24 See, e.g., ICJ, *Obligations of States in respect of Climate Change* (n. 1), paras. 172, 457.

25 Charter of the United Nations (signed 26 June 1945, entered into force 24 October 1945), 1 UNTS XVI.

26 International Covenant on Civil and Political Rights (adopted 16 December 1966, entered into force 23 March 1976) 999 UNTS 171.

27 International Covenant on Economic, Social and Cultural Rights (adopted 16 December 1966, entered into force 3 January 1976) 993 UNTS 3.

28 ICJ, *Legal Consequences arising from the Policies and Practices of Israel in the Occupied Palestinian Territory, including East Jerusalem* (n. 6), paras. 237, 240.

29 ICJ, *Legal Consequences arising from the Policies and Practices of Israel in the Occupied Palestinian Territory, including East Jerusalem* (n. 6), para. 239.

cultural development,'[30] in turn connected to international legal concepts enshrined in UNGA Resolution 1514(XV) (1960),[31] the 1970 Friendly Relations Declaration,[32] and the ICCPR and ICESCR. Similarly, in the climate Advisory Opinion, paragraph 357 explicitly references territorial integrity and permanent sovereignty over natural resources, and its mention of forced displacement can be directly connected to protecting the 'integrity' of a people. The Court's current jurisprudence on self-determination can be clearly and logically extended to address the adverse or existential impacts of climate change on vulnerable peoples and States.

Third, the activation of self-determination in relation to climate change impacts may, as a practical matter, help promote the existence and survival of vulnerable peoples and States in a rapidly changing climate system, including Indigenous Peoples. While the Advisory Opinion referenced Indigenous Peoples as a vulnerable group,[33] it stopped short of any discussion of specific doctrinal protections that may apply to Indigenous Peoples under international law, including Indigenous existence and survival and related principles of self-determination as recognised, inter alia, by Articles 3 and 4 of the United Nations Declaration on the Rights of Indigenous Peoples.[34] For many Indigenous Peoples, climate change represents an immediate existential threat wrought by emitter States, threatening their self-determination and cultural integrity.

Fourth, comments from States submitted to the ILC on the issue of continuity of statehood (collected in paras 148–299 of the final consolidated report of the Co-Chairs of the ILC Study Group), as well as the discussion contained in the separate opinions and declarations of the ICJ Advisory Opinion itself, all point towards a larger reexamination of the law of self-determination in the context of adverse climate change impacts. If self-determination is necessarily implicated by issues of displacement and loss of territory and resources from climate change, then the door is seemingly now open for claims of breach of self-determination from injured peoples and States. Such claims may be cognisable not just by small island and low-lying States impacted by sea-level rise; a State rendered permanently

30 ICJ, *Legal Consequences arising from the Policies and Practices of Israel in the Occupied Palestinian Territory, including East Jerusalem* (n. 6), paras. 233, 241.
31 UNGA Res 1514 (XV) of 14 December 1960, A/RES/1514(XV).
32 UNGA Res 2625 (XXV) of 24 October 1970, A/RES/2625(XXV).
33 ICJ, *Obligations of States in respect of Climate Change* (n. 1), para. 382.
34 UNGA Res 61/295 of 13 September 2007, A/RES/61/295 (annex) ('United Nations Declaration on the Rights of Indigenous Peoples').

uninhabitable by extreme heat[35] would also face similar issues of displacement and loss of resources (including subsistence resources protected by common Article 1, section 2 of the ICCPR and ICESCR) underscored by the ICJ in paragraph 357. Arctic Indigenous Peoples, now experiencing significant environmental degradation of cold Arctic conditions, are arguably being 'displaced' from such cold conditions through irrevocable loss of cultural life, even if physical displacement does not take place.[36] The positive obligation to promote self-determination contained, *inter alia*, in common Article 1, section 3 of the ICCPR and ICESCR may further impose an affirmative obligation on States to promote the desired will of impacted peoples and States with respect to their international legal personality and ongoing existence and survival. Ultimately, such solutions will only work to the extent that States are willing to cooperate to effectuate them, which includes the critical task of actually stopping the emissions-generating conduct that is now producing such existential risks.

35 Daniel J. Vecellio, Qinqin Kong, W. Larry Kenney, and Matthew Huber, 'Greatly enhanced risk to humans as a consequence of empirically determined lower moist heat stress tolerance', PNAS 120 (2023), 1–9.

36 Dave-Inder Comar, 'Displaced from the cold: Threats to the self-determination, including the cultural self-determination, of Sámi Indigenous Peoples in the Nordic region from climate change impacts', in: Miriam Cullen and Matthew Scott (eds), *Nordic Approaches to Climate-Related Human Mobility* (Routledge 2024), 101–116.

Conclusion

The ICJ and the Climate Commons:

Cautious Transformations in the Structural Architecture of International Law

Jannika Jahn, Moritz Vinken**, Khaled El Mahmoud****

I. Introduction

The climate change advisory proceedings before the International Court of Justice (ICJ or the Court) indicate that international *law* and the Court itself have become a central site of contestation over the legal governance of the climate system. Prior to the Advisory Opinion, it was debated whether and to what extent international law limits State discretion in the field of climate protection.

While the Paris Agreement was widely regarded as an innovative legal framework fostering experimentalist and polycentric forms of governance,[1] it was generally understood to establish procedural, rather than substantive legal obligations, geared towards aspirational targets.[2]

---

* Senior Research Fellow at the Max Planck Institute for Comparative Public Law and International Law.

** Research Fellow at the Max Planck Institute for Comparative Public Law and International Law.

*** Law Clerk at the Higher Regional Court of Berlin.

1 Veerle Heyvaert, *Transnational Environmental Regulation and Governance* (Cambridge University Press, 2019); Andrew Jordan, Dave Huitema, Harro van Asselt, Johanna Forster (eds), *Governing Climate Change: Polycentricity in Action?* (Cambridge University Press, 2018); Elinor Ostrom, 'Polycentric systems for coping with collective action and global environmental change.' GEC 20(4) (2010), 550–557; Gráinne De Búrca, Robert Keohane, Charles Sabel, Global Experimentalist Governance, BJPolS 44(3) (2014), 477–486.

2 See e.g. Dan Bodansky, The Paris Climate Change Agreement: A New Hope?, AJIL 110(2) (2016), 288-319 (289); Laurence Boisson de Chazournes, Editorial on Paris Agreement, EJIL 27(2) (2016), 253-265 (254); Meinhard Doelle, The Paris Agreement: Historic Breakthrough or High Stakes Experiment?, CLLA 6(1–2) (2016), 1-20 (20); for a criticism of the qualification of the Paris Agreement as bottom-up,

Against this background, the advisory proceedings raised the question of whether international law provides a meaningful framework for guiding State conduct towards the long-term common interests of the international community, or indeed of humankind, rather than the short-term preferences of individual States. Beneath this inquiry lay a more fundamental issue: whether the core branches of international law are capable of accommodating the imperatives of intergenerational solidarity and collective responsibility that have become particularly salient in the context of climate protection.

The Court was called upon to respond to these questions at a moment in which international law had moved beyond mere coexistence towards cooperation and global governance.[3] At the same time, however, international law's authority is increasingly contested, placing renewed pressure on its capacity to provide normative orientation, command compliance and structure collective action. The challenge confronting the Court, therefore, was not only whether international law's structural development could be advanced and further articulated in response to the demands of climate protection, but also whether this could be achieved in a manner capable of reinforcing its legitimacy and authority.

We suggest that the climate change Advisory Opinion has advanced international law's turn towards fiduciary governance as an expression of intergenerational solidarity grounded in preventive self-limitation and mandatory cooperation. Our analysis builds on the contributions to this volume that have examined the content, methodology, and unresolved tensions of the Opinion along four central fault lines[4]: the sovereignty/community interest divide, the public/private divide, the science/politics divide and the North/South divide. Our conclusion is divided into three parts that make observations on the refinement, consolidation, and reinforcement of the role of international law in the governance of the global commons.

First, the Court advances international law towards a more principled and conceptually coherent framework for addressing the collective chal-

see Christina Voigt, 'The ICJ and the UN Climate Regime: Clarifying mitigation obligations under the Paris Agreement', in this volume.

3 Seminally, Wolfgang G. Friedmann, *The Changing Structure of International Law* (Columbia University Press, 1964), 60 et seq.

4 See introduction at p. 10; Moritz Vinken, 'International Law's Fault Lines and Sediments: Geology as Method', *Max Planck Institute for Comparative Public Law & International Law (MPIL) Research Paper Series*, No. 2025–09, available at https://papers.ssrn.com/sol3/papers.cfm?abstract_id=5274030.

lenge of climate protection. It reorients the purpose of protection away from present State interests towards common interests of present and future generations, conceptualising States as trustees of these shared interests (II.). As such, States are required to prevent significant harm to the climate system and to cooperate in avoiding such harms.

Second, the Court consolidates international law around the obligations flowing from these concepts and principles in a coherent manner (III.). It thereby cautiously reads international law as a comprehensive public legal order.[5]

Third, while reinforcing international law's capacity not only to govern climate change but also to contribute to a more just distribution of responsibility,particularly by equipping civil society and States with legal tools to enforce State obligations, the Court leaves open the future role of climate litigation for climate governance (IV.). More fundamentally, the ICJ bench appears deeply divided on whether the Court should, in future, engage

5 International law has arguably progressively developed characteristics of a public legal order. This has led to a range of public law approaches to international law. Global Constitutionalism, for instance, has focused on identifying and theorising the core constitutional principles of the international legal order – democracy, rule of law and human rights, seminal, Jan Klabbers, Anne Peters, Geir Ulfstein, *The Constitutionalization of International Law* (expanded ed., Oxford University Press, 2011); Anne Peters, 'Global Constitutionalism' in: Michael T. Gibbons (ed), *The Encyclopedia of Political Thought* (John Wiley & Sons, 2015). Other approaches have focussed on the emergence of complex administrative structures and the growing range of instruments of international institutions that are capable of determining or conditioning the behaviour of States and other actors, including individuals. Among those is the Global Administrative Law (GAL) approach, see Benedict Kingsbury, Nico Krisch and Richard B. Stewart, 'The Emergence of Global Administrative Law' L&CP 68 (2005), 15–62; Benedict Kingsbury, 'Global Environmental Governance as Administration: Implications for International Law' in Daniel Bodansky, Jutta Brunnée and Ellen Hey (eds), *The Oxford Handbook of International Environmental Law* (1 edn, Oxford University Press, 2008). Similar but distinct to the GAL approach, is the International Public Authority approach, that aims to reconstruct public law frameworks for those instruments of international institutions that constitute exercises of international public authority, see Armin von Bogdandy, Matthias Goldmann and Ingo Venzke, 'From Public International to International Public Law: Translating World Public Opinion into International Public Authority' EJIL 28 (2017), 115–145.
For an assessment of the ICJ's Advisory Opinion from the perspective of international administrative law, see Caroline E. Foster, Bella Belcher, 'International Law's Administrative Law Turn and the Paris Agreement' in: Maria Antonia Tigre, Maxim Bönnemann & Antoine De Spiegeleir (eds.), *The ICJ's Advisory Opinion on Climate Change* (Verfassungsbooks, 2025), 109-122; also on Verfassungsblog 11.9.2025.

more deeply with demands of intragenerational justice including those of distributive justice.

II. Normative and Structural Refinement of International Law: Fiduciary Governance of Climate Commons[6]

The Advisory Opinion contributes to a turn of international law towards fiduciary governance, reflecting an emerging conception of intergenerational solidarity grounded in self-restraint and mandatory cooperation.[7] 'From Carbon Sovereignty to Trusteeship'[8] analyses this development as a conceptual turn: States do not merely cooperate as neighbours but act as fiduciaries of a shared atmospheric resource, answerable both to the international community and to future generations. This shift carries significant implications for international law's understanding of State sovereignty, its purposes, and the international legal obligations constraining State discretion. The Court refines the customary duties to prevent and to cooperate by extending the underlying purpose of international law to the collective management of the global commons. In doing so, it limits State discretion in a qualitatively new manner (1.). We suggest that these normative refinements signal the emergence of a structural principle of trusteeship, which operationalises the intertemporal dimension of solidarity in international law (2.).

---

6 Cf. Eyal Benvenisti, 'Sovereigns as Trustees of Humanity: On the Accountability of States to Foreign Stakeholders', AJIL 107 (2013), 295–333. See also Jannika Jahn and Nele Suchantke, 'The ICJ Advisory Opinion on Climate Change: From Carbon Sovereignty to Trusteeship of the Climate Commons', in this volume.

7 On the idea of fiduciary duties of States in international law, cf. Anne Peters, 'Humanity as the A and Ω of Sovereignty', EJIL 20(3) (2009), 513–544; Criddle, Evan J., 'Fiduciary Principles in International Law', in: Evan J. Criddle, Paul B. Miller, and Robert H. Sitkoff (eds), *The Oxford Handbook of Fiduciary Law* (Oxford University Press, 2019); Criddle, Evan J., and Evan Fox-Decent, *Fiduciaries of Humanity: How International Law Constitutes Authority* (Oxford University Press, 2016); in the context of international environmental law, see Klaus Bosselmann, *Earth Trusteeship and the Sovereign State Transforming International Environmental Law* (Wiley, 2025).

8 See Jahn and Suchantke (n. 6) in this volume.

1. Normative Refinement

The customary prevention rule and that of cooperation form the epicentre of the wider normative framework applicable to climate change. Their interpretation reveals the shifting purpose of international law in this regard: from the individual State interest not to be harmed, to the aggregate State interests of preserving and sharing the benefits of a natural resource beyond national jurisdiction, to the long-term interests of present and future generations to protect the life-sustaining stability of the climate system.[9] It is through the refinement of their scope, their procedural and substantive dimensions, as well as their implications for the broader body of international law applicable to climate protection that these rules render international environmental law capable of informing and guiding the societal transformation required to meet the challenges of anthropogenic climate change.

The Advisory Opinion expands the scope and positive dimension of the prevention rule and reinforces the duty of cooperation for the protection of the environment. As Brunnée astutely observes in her contribution, the prospectively oriented harm prevention rule has its origins in its retrospective complement: the no harm rule. It was firmly rooted in the coexistential international law of neighbourly relations, entailing negative duties to abstain from neighbourly nuisances.[10] From the 1972 Stockholm Declaration (Principle 21) and the 1992 Rio Declaration (Principle 2) onwards, the no harm rule was tilted towards the prevention of harm and extended to areas beyond national jurisdiction. During this reorientation, the rule transcended its coexistential focus and acquired a cooperative layer.

9 See Jutta Brunnée, 'The Advisory Opinion on *Obligations of States in Respect of Climate Change*: Harm Prevention under Customary International Law', in this volume; Jahn and Suchantke (n. 6), in this volume; see also Wolfgang G. Friedmann (n. 3), 60 et seq.; Wolfrum, 'Entwicklung des Völkerrechts von einem Koordinations- zu einem Kooperationsrecht', in: Peter Christian Müller-Graf and Herberth Roth (eds), *Recht und Rechtswissenschaft* (C.F. Müller, 2000), 425–429; Rüdiger Wolfrum, 'International Law of Cooperation', in: Wolfrum (ed), *Max Planck Encyclopedia of International Law* (2010), 7, available at: <https://opil.ouplaw.com/display/10.1093/law:epil/9780199231690/law-9780199231690-e1427?rskey=iolEcQ&result=4&prd=MPIL>.

10 Jutta Brunnée, *Procedure and Substance in International Environmental Law*, Collected Courses of the Hague Academy of International Law 405 (Brill, 2019) 87 (115 et seq.).

With the Advisory Opinion, the Court expands its scope to the diffuse phenomenon of climate change which affects the integrity of globally connected environmental ecosystems outside and inside state jurisdiction. At the same time, it extends the rule's temporal dimension by recognising intergenerational equity as an interpretative principle that grants weight to the interests of future generations.[11] This is more than rhetoric: it operates as a doctrinal device through which present-day obligations are assessed in light of their projected future impacts, tightening the standard of due diligence and reinforcing an intertemporal (fiduciary) framing of State obligations.

Substantively, the Advisory Opinion enhances the positive obligations flowing from the rule of prevention. They are structured around obligations of due diligence. Despite their procedural nature, this interpretation cannot be read as a step towards a proceduralisation of international environmental law detached from any substantive goal.[12] Instead, the harm prevention rule drives a proceduralisation that enmeshes substance and procedure through its standard of due diligence whereby the procedural requirements serve the implementation of the substantive stipulations.

Alongside the harm prevention rule, the Court recognises a distinct duty to cooperate for the protection of the environment.[13] By recognising this duty as a self-standing rule of customary international law and refining its normative contours, the Advisory Opinion strengthens its normative force in the context of climate protection. In doing so, the Court positions international law as a proactive normative framework for guiding and structuring collective action.

Moreover, the Court acknowledges the *erga omnes* character of the customary duties to prevent significant harm to the climate system and to cooperate in climate protection in light of the recognition of climate change

---

11 *See* ICJ, *Obligations of States in Respect of Climate Change*, Advisory Opinion of 23 July 2025, paras. 157, 273, 373, despite acknowledging their lack of procedural standing before the Court.

12 For this criticism and concern, see Martti Koskenniemi, 'Peaceful Settlement of Environmental Disputes' NORD 60 (1991), 73-92 (85).

13 ICJ, *Obligations of States in Respect of Climate Change* (n. 11), para. 140. See Jahn and Suchantke (n. 6), in this volume. For a thorough engagement with the ICJ's advisory jurisprudence on duty to cooperate, cf. Khaled El Mahmoud and Natali Gbele, 'When Guidance Becomes Fog: The ICJ and the Normative Uncertainty of the Duty to Co-Operate', EJIL: Talk!, 14 January 2026.

as a common concern (of humankind).[14] Contributions in this volume have underscored the implications of the Advisory Opinion's *erga omnes* recognition as signalling a reallocation of responsibility beyond bilateral relations.[15] Importantly, this gives all States standing to bring respective violations of these common obligations before the ICJ, which in turn enables them to enforce the preventive and cooperative obligations of States.

With the ICJ Advisory Opinion, the trajectory towards an international (environmental) law of cooperation is further consolidated: The Opinion reinforces coordinated action in the management of the climate system.[16] By articulating a self-standing customary duty to cooperate, it overlays international law's coexistential foundations with a more pronounced cooperative orientation.

This normative refinement of the customary international obligations of States proves particularly consequential insofar as it informs and structures the interpretation of the broader framework of international law applicable to climate change. The Court states in its Advisory Opinion that 'at the present stage, compliance in full and in good faith by a State with the climate change treaties [...] suggests that this State substantially complies with the general customary duties to prevent significant environmental harm and to co-operate.'[17] In the reading of the Court, the preventive and cooperative logic of the Paris Agreement as well as its recourse to the regulatory technique[18] of due diligence manifest and mirror the customary rules of harm prevention and cooperation.

This interpretation follows logically from the close enmeshment of customary and treaty law in the field of climate protection. Both share the same overarching goal. As Christina Voigt's contribution intimates,[19] the

---

14 ICJ, *Obligations of States in Respect of Climate Change* (n. 11), para. 440.

15 Jutta Brunnée (n. 9), in this volume; Phillip Paiement and Corina Heri, 'Strengthening International Climate Obligations Beyond Paris: Situating the ICJ's Opinion within a Comparative Legal Context', in this volume; Jannika Jahn and Nele Suchantke (n. 6), all in this volume.

16 ICJ, *Obligations of States in Respect of Climate Change* (n. 11), para. 141; cf. ICJ, *Pulp Mills on the River Uruguay (Argentina v. Uruguay)*, Judgment of 20 April 2010, I.C.J. Reports 2010 (I), para. 77.

17 ICJ, *Obligations of States in Respect of Climate Change* (n. 11), para. 314.

18 On our use of this term, see the Introduction. Heike Krieger, Anne Peters, 'Due Diligence and Structural Change in the International Legal Order', in: Anne Peters, Heike Krieger and Leonhard Kreuzer (eds), *Due Diligence in the International Legal Order* (Oxford University Press, 2020), 351–390 (351).

19 See Voigt (n. 2), in this volume.

Court reads the entire climate regime in line with the UNFCCC's ultimate objective of the 'stabilization of the greenhouse gas concentrations in the atmosphere at a level that would *prevent* dangerous anthropogenic interference with the climate system'.[20] The Paris Agreement temperature target concretises this goal. Moreover, the character of the Paris Agreement's cyclical ambition spiral[21] shares the same regulatory logic as the more abstract customary standard of due diligence.[22] On this basis, the Court holds that both standards inform each other to such an extent that they substantially overlap. This does not signify that 'the autonomous force of customary law'[23] is diluted. Rather, it reflects an overarching consolidation of the applicable international legal rules around the normative refinement of the customary harm prevention rule and the duty to cooperate, geared towards the collective management of the atmospheric commons.

In substance, the Court relies on this interpretative alignment between customary international law and treaty law to further recalibrate the scope of State discretion. The Court interprets the Paris Agreement's provisions in light of the harm prevention rule's due diligence requirements as limiting State discretion in the preparation and implementation of NDCs.[24] It insists that States must satisfy the due diligence standard in determining ambitious and progressive NDCs, which means, in particular, that, when taken together, NDCs must be capable of achieving the temperature goal of limiting global warming to 1.5 °C above preindustrial levels.[25] On this reading, remaining within the 1.5 °C limit is conceived as an inherently collective, yet individualisable obligation incumbent upon all States. The corresponding treaty obligations are owed to the community of States par-

---

20 Art. 2 UNFCCC.

21 On the regime specificity of the due diligence standard under the Paris Agreement, see Lavanya Rajamani, 'Due Diligence in International Climate Change Law', in: Anne Peters, Heike Krieger and Leonhard Kreuzer (eds), *Due Diligence in the International Legal Order* (Oxford University Press, 2020), 163-180. See also Christina Voigt (n. 2), in this volume.

22 Cf. Christina Voigt, '*The Paris Agreement: What is the standard of conduct for Parties?*,' QIL 26 (2016), 17–28.

23 Mario Prost, 'Disaster Passing as Miracle? A Critical Take on the ICJ's Climate Advisory Opinion', EJIL:Talk!, 14 August 2025; See also Andrej Lang and Denise Koecke, 'Rising to the Occasion: The World Court as Architect of a Harmonious International Climate Law Framework', in this volume.

24 ICJ, *Obligations of States in Respect of Climate Change* (n. 11), para. 231.

25 ICJ, *Obligations of States in Respect of Climate Change* (n. 11), para. 241-242, 245.

ties as a whole (*erga omnes partes*), aligning them with their counterparts in customary international law.[26]

The Court furthermore builds on the customary duty to prevent environmental harm to indicate, albeit in a rudimentary manner, the regulatory role of international law in guiding towards a deep transition of the private and energy sectors. In this regard, the Advisory Opinion assumes a forward-looking dimension with potentially transformative implications, justified by the common goal of preventing future harm to the climate system.[27] Several authors point to the far-reaching implications of the Advisory Opinion's finding that a failure to regulate private emissions may constitute an internationally wrongful act.[28] Thus, the Court affirms that under the harm prevention rule States must adopt and enforce 'regulatory mitigation mechanisms' for both public and private operators,[29] implying that a State's climate duty is not satisfied by reducing its own emissions alone but extends to actively regulating the activities of private actors. This places traditional sovereign prerogatives—energy licensing, subsidies, and fiscal incentives—under a new standard of international review, linking corporate emissions to State due diligence duties. Equally significant, and still within the harm prevention rule, is the Court's expansion of environmental impact assessment (EIA) obligations to include downstream and end-use emissions.[30] States are now expected to anticipate and integrate the global carbon effects of projects, such as new oil and gas fields, industrial agriculture, or major infrastructure, into their permitting processes. This innovation shifts EIAs from a localised, site-specific tool to a global emissions filter and embeds private-sector activities squarely within States' climate obligations.[31]

2. Structural Refinement

These normative refinements, it is suggested, manifest an underlying structural refinement of international (environmental) law. This refinement may

26 ICJ, *Obligations of States in Respect of Climate Change* (n. 11), paras. 157, 273, 440.
27 ICJ, *Obligations of States in Respect of Climate Change* (n. 11), para. 427.
28 ICJ, *Obligations of States in Respect of Climate Change* (n. 11), paras. 282, 427.
29 ICJ, *Obligations of States in Respect of Climate Change* (n. 11), para. 282.
30 ICJ, *Obligations of States in Respect of Climate Change* (n. 11), para. 298.
31 ICJ, *Obligations of States in Respect of Climate Change* (n. 11), para. 440.

be conceptualised through intergenerational trusteeship as a conceptual umbrella for the core elements that shape the international legal framework governing climate change: the atmosphere's status as a global environmental commons; climate change constituting a common concern of humankind; intergenerational equity as an interpretative principle; and the refined harm prevention rule together with the duty to cooperate for environmental protection.[32] Taken together, these elements signify that the atmosphere is held in trust for present and future generations, placing States under a fiduciary duty to collectively preserve the stability of the climate system.[33] As a conceptual umbrella, intergenerational trusteeship does not itself constitute a legally binding norm. Rather, it operates as a structural principle[34] that systemises the legal framework under a common purpose, shapes the content of the legal obligations, and guides their interpretation.[35]

This principle builds upon and further develops the principle of solidarity in its intertemporal dimension. According to Wolfrum,[36] solidarity comprises three dimensions: inter-state solidarity (taking into account the

32 Cf. ICJ, *Obligations of States in Respect of Climate Change* (n. 11), paras. 157, 273, 308, 440; Jannika Jahn and Nele Suchantke (n. 6), in this volume.

33 For a conceptualisation of ecological trusteeship, see Klaus Bosselmann, *Earth Trusteeship and the Sovereign State* (Routledge, 2025), both with further references; Trevor Daya-Winterbottom, 'Trusteeship for the environment?', in: Harro van Asselt, Seita Vesa and Kaisa Huhta, *Future-Proofing Law in a Time of Environmental Emergency* (Edward Elgar Publishing, 2025), 251-272; the concept of ecological trusteeship is closely related to the common law public trust doctrine, see Joseph L. Sax, 'The Public Trust Doctrine in Natural Resource Law: Effective Judicial Intervention', Mich. L. Rev. 68 (1970), 471-566 and must be distinguished from certain stewardship models for environmental goods that were critiqued from a postcolonial perspective, see e.g. Surabhi Ranganathan, 'Global Commons', EJIL 27 (2016), 693–717 (714).

34 For the likewise *structural* principle of solidarity, see Rüdiger Wolfrum, 'Solidarity and Community Interests: Driving Forces For the Interpretation and Development of International Law', Collected Courses of the Hague Academy of International Law 416 (Brill, 2021), 300.

35 Armin von Bogdandy, 'Prolegomena zu Prinzipien internationalisierter und internationaler Verwaltung', in: Hans-Heinrich Trute and others (eds), *Allgemeines Verwaltungsrecht – zur Tragfähigkeit eines Konzepts,* Festschrift für Eberhard Schmidt-Aßmann (Mohr Siebeck, 2008).

36 Rüdiger Wolfrum, 'Solidarity amongst States: An Emerging Structural Principle of International Law', in: Pierre-Marie Dupuy and others (eds), *Völkerrecht als Wertordnung / Common Values in international law, Festschrift für Christian Tomuschat* (Engel Verlag, 2006); Chie Kojima and Rüdiger Wolfrum (eds), *Solidarity: A Structural Principle of International Law* (Springer, 2010); Wolfrum (n. 34).

interests of other States), community-oriented solidarity (the interests of the international community as a whole), and intergenerational solidarity (towards future generations).[37] While solidarity itself provides the normative foundation for collective responsibility, trusteeship translates this foundation into a concrete temporal fiduciary logic of State conduct: it defines how States must exercise their powers in light of the shared and continuing interests of humankind.[38] In the climate context, the fiduciary dimension of this principle extends solidarity from its focus on cooperation to a more transformative governance principle, requiring international law to function not merely as a law of cooperation and risk aversion, but as a law that informs and guides structural change, particularly in the economic sector.[39] Moreover, the fiduciary duties flowing from the concept of trusteeship give rise to legal accountability for State conduct, in particular through the justiciability of State duties and the recognition of legal entitlements to hold States to account.[40]

The Advisory Opinion confirms this reading, as the concept of trusteeship appears to permeate the climate regime as a whole, endowing States with fiduciary duties that govern both their external relations and internal obligations. As several contributions to this volume have demonstrated, the rule of harm prevention, especially in its cooperative dimension, now connects internal (prevention within jurisdiction) and external duties (cooperation across borders) with an *erga omnes* effect.[41] It operates as a normative hinge linking domestic governance, transnational cooperation, and the collective maintenance of climate stability. The impact on internal matters is reinforced by the conjunction of environmental principles and human rights, converging in the right to a clean, healthy and sustainable environment as a prerequisite for all other human rights.[42] This, again, is of structural importance.[43] For, the imbuement of an international legal

---

37 Wolfrum (n. 34), 300.

38 For the idea of fiduciary state duties towards humankind, see n. 7.

39 As for instance implied in ICJ, *Obligations of States in Respect of Climate Change* (n. 11), paras. 282, 427.

40 See (n. 7); see also Evan Fox-Decent, From Fiduciary States to Joint Trusteeship of the Atmosphere: The Right to a Healthy Environment through a Fiduciary Prism', in: Charles Sampford, Ken Coghill and Tim Smith, *Fiduciary Duty and the Atmospheric Trust* (Routledge, 2012), 253-268.

41 Jahn and Suchantke (n. 6), in this volume.

42 ICJ, *Obligations of States in Respect of Climate Change* (n. 11), para. 393.

43 Anne Peters, 'Global Constitutionalism: The Social Dimension', in: Takao Suami, Anne Peters, Dimitri Vanoverbeke, Mattias Kumm (eds.), *Global Constitutionalism*

regime with human rights changes the orientation of State responsibilities from inter-state obligations towards obligations which the State owes to the individual. International environmental law is thereby restructured towards being 'built around the central figure of the individual, his rights, and his basic needs'.[44] This, in turn, allows individuals to hold States to account for breaches of their fiduciary duties towards (global) environmental commons.[45]

III. Consolidation of a Public Legal Order of International Climate Protection

In line with the structural principle of intergenerational trusteeship over environmental commons, the Court consolidates the different sources and areas of international law around a common set of concepts, principles and obligations, embedding an orientation of public international law towards environmental protection (1.). It thereby contributes to the construction of an international *public* legal order, a *Völkerrechtsordnung*.[46] To legitimately substantiate the common *public* values, the Court draws on authoritative scientific findings. The 'objectivity' that comes with this allows the Court to demonstrate that it does not commensurate individual State interests with public interests (2.). Aside from formal legal integration, the Court also seeks to build its Advisory Opinion on a solid evidentiary basis which includes civil society briefs so as to embed the legal analysis in real human experiences (3.).

---

from European and East Asian Perspectives (Cambridge University Press, 2018), 277-350 (299–300).

44 Emmanuelle Jouannet, 'How to depart from the existing dire condition of development', in Antonio Cassese (ed.), *Realizing Utopia: The Future of International Law* (Oxford University Press, 2012), 392-417 (398–399).

45 Cf. Fox-Decent (n. 40).

46 Herman Mosler, 'Völkerrecht als Rechtsordnung' HJIL 36 (1976) 6-49; Cf. Hoffmeister and Kleinlein, 'International Public Order', Wolfrum (ed), Max Planck Encyclopedia of International Law (2019), <https://opil.ouplaw.com/display/10.1093/law:epil/9780199231690/law-9780199231690-e1430?rskey=LGJMpt&result=2&prd=MPIL>.

1. Systemic Integration

Several contributions to this book have underlined that systemic integration is a central element of the ICJ's Advisory Opinion.[47] Instead of following a large number of State submissions, which offered a reading of international law as a patchwork of specialised self-contained regimes, depicting the Paris Agreement as *lex specialis*, the Court instead engages in an impressive effort of systemic integration constructing a coherent and mutually reinforcing framework.

To this end, the Court employs Article 31(3)(c) VCLT which directs judges to interpret treaties 'in the light of any relevant rules of international law applicable in the relations between the parties.' Taking this provision seriously, the ICJ situates the Paris Agreement within the broader normative architecture of international law. This allows the Court to read the Agreement's provisions in light of customary prevention duties,[48] UNCLOS obligations on marine pollution,[49] international human rights standards,[50] and the decisions of the COP and CMA as expressions of the parties' subsequent agreements (Art. 31(3)(a) VCLT) and evolving practice.[51] The result is a decidedly public-order conception of international law, in which all 'relevant rules' enter into a conversation with one another.

Against this background, the Court does justice to the principle of systemic integration's hermeneutic qualities.[52] For the principle of systemic integration as an interpretative principle not only requires the insurance of textual coherence, but also an interpretative exercise of hermeneutic harmonisation. A telling example is the Court's determination of the Paris Agreement's regime-specific due diligence standard.[53] Rooted in the

---

47 In particular, Lang and Koecke (n. 23).

48 Brunnée (n. 9) in this volume.

49 Rozemarijn Roland Holst, 'Climate Change Law and the Law of the Sea: Systemic Impacts of the ICJ and ITLOS Advisory Opinions Read Together', in this volume.

50 See Hellen Keller, 'A Right to a Clean, Healthy and Sustainable Environment – or Perhaps not (yet)?', in this volume.

51 See Voigt (n. 2), in this volume.

52 On the hermeneutic qualities of the principle of systemic integration, see McLachlan, *The Principle of System Integration in International Law* (Oxford University Press 2024).

53 On the regime specificity of the due diligence standard, see Voigt, Christina, '*The Paris Agreement: What is the standard of conduct for Parties?*,' QIL 26 (2016), 17–28; Lavanya Rajamani, 'Due Diligence in International Climate Change Law', in: Anne Peters, Heike Krieger and Leonhard Kreuzer (eds), *Due Diligence in the In-*

Agreement's procedural obligations and the qualifiers of progression and highest possible ambition, the Court draws on the customary principle of prevention, as well as on the best available science as manifested in the Agreement's temperature goals in order to arrive at a stringent standard from which concretised duties of conduct and result arise.[54]

Most notable in the Court's exercise of systemic integration is the fusion of environmental and human-rights law. The contributions to this volume have shown in detail,[55] how the ICJ Advisory Opinion bridges these two fields by recognising that environmental protection is a prerequisite for the enjoyment of human and fundamental rights such as life, health, food, water, and self-determination. The Court declares the right to a clean, healthy, and sustainable environment as 'inherent' to other human rights, elevating it from a soft-law aspiration to a core interpretative standard.[56] In this regard, it relies on a broad State consensus as expressed in the General Assembly Resolution 76/300[57], regional human rights conventions, national constitutional documents as well as the case law of regional human rights bodies, such as the IACtHR. At the same time, it exercises restraint and deference in leaving room for other approaches to the enmeshment of environmental needs and human rights, as done for example by the European Court of Human Rights in its *KlimaSeniorinnen* judgment.[58] On this basis, the Court manages to draw a direct link between the climate system and fundamental rights such as life, health, food, water, and self-determination while allowing for leeway in the specific implementation of this link.[59]

The centrality of systemic integration for the Court's envisioned coherent international legal order manifests itself institutionally in its engage-

ternational Legal Order (Oxford University Press, 2020), 163–180; Christina Voigt, Philipp Sauter, Rita Guerreiro Teixeiray, Joeri Rogelj, Carl Schleussner, Carl, Katalin Sulyok, 'The Legal Power of Highest Possible Ambition – Setting Legal and Scientific Benchmarks to Assess Highest Possible Ambition under Article 4(3) of the Paris Agreement', CLLA 15 (2025), 1–24. See also Voigt (n. 2), in this volume.

54 See Paiement and Heri (n. 15), in this volume.

55 In particular Keller (n. 50), in this volume.

56 ICJ, *Obligations of States in Respect of Climate Change* (n. 11), para. 393. See also Keller (n. 50) and Lang and Koecke (n. 23), both in this volume.

57 GA Resolution, The human right to a clean, healthy and sustainable environment, 28 July 2022, A/RES/76/300.

58 Keller (n. 50).

59 See also Jannika Jahn, 'The European Approach to Human Rights-Based Climate Litigation in Global Context: Difference, Deference, Consolidation', Verfassungsblog, 6 December 2025.

ment in cross-judicial dialogue with other tribunals. As several contributions to this volume have highlighted, the Advisory Opinion integrates findings from ITLOS' Advisory Opinion on climate change, which classified anthropogenic greenhouse gases as 'pollution of the marine environment' under UNCLOS and imposed a stringent due-diligence duty on States to prevent, reduce and control such pollution, including by regulating private actors.[60] By weaving these Opinions and judgments into its own reasoning, the ICJ positions itself at the centre of a network of international climate jurisprudence, in which different courts develop complementary doctrines rather than competing ones.

2. Integration Through Science

For the identification of community interests in public international law, courts rely on the articulation of common interests in treaty and customary international law. Additionally, with international law's increasing involvement in scientific risk regulation,[61] scientific expertise and assessments play an important role by giving these common interests an impression of 'objective necessities'.[62] It logically follows that science becomes a central hinge of the normative integration that the Court pursues in its Advisory Opinion. This is why the Court starts with an in-depth overview over central scientific findings on climate change and its negative effects as pronounced by the IPCC. The Court also relies on the assessments of the IPCC to develop legal thresholds and benchmarks such as the 1.5°C goal or to substantiate the 'best available science' which is to inform States' due diligence obligations.[63]

This is particularly interesting in light of the fact that the IPCC has always been conceived of as a producer of politically accepted science

60 Khaled El Mahmoud, 'One Climate, Many Courts: The ICJ Advisory Opinion on Climate Change, Systemic Integration, Cross-Judicial Law-Making, and Interjudicialism', in this volume; Rozemarijn Roland Holst (n. 49), in this volume.

61 Seminally, Jacqueline Peel, *Science and Risk Regulation in International Law* (Cambridge University Press, 2010).

62 On the construction of (regulatory) science as objective and a-political, see Sheila Jasanoff, 'The Practices of Objectivity in Regulatory Science', in: Charles Camic, Neil Gross and Lamont Michele (eds), *Social Knowledge in the Making* (University of Chicago, Press 2011), 307–338.

63 Katalin Sulyok, 'On the Science-Coloured Glasses of the ICJ: Harmfulness, Wrongfulness, and Climate Accountability', in this volume.

specifically *for* the needs of the climate regime (i.e. UNFCCC and following protocols and agreements) in particular (and not for the production of climate science detached from that regime). It is this orientation of the IPCC's work which led to its special report on the impacts of global warming 1.5°C in the first place: The special report on 1.5°C was requested by the COP in 2015 together with the adoption of the Paris Agreement.[64] Remarkably, prior to this request, very little scientific research existed on the 1.5°C temperature goal, as it was widely considered unrealistic and therefore irrelevant by the scientific community. By agreeing to produce a special report on this target, the IPCC created a demand for scientific research that had previously been almost non-existent.[65] In this way, the IPCC became an important actor of scientific policy for the Paris Agreement treaty framework.[66] With the ICJ's Advisory Opinion, this role may have been brought to extend to the area of customary international law. Albeit not made explicit in the Opinion, the temperature target might, due to its scientific grounding, also be interpreted as the current yardstick for the goal of the harm prevention rule.[67] Accordingly, science truly takes on what Jasanoff called 'a constitutional position',[68] as it makes a harmonised, integrated and coherent interpretation of the applicable legal frameworks and norms possible.

64 COP Decision 1/CP.21, para. 21.

65 Provost, 'Rigorous and Relevant: Applying Lessons from the History of IPCC Special Reports to the Post-Paris Agreement World', *Harv. Envtl. L. Rev.* 43 (2019), 507–546, 528 et seq.

66 Marion Lemoine-Schonne, 'Le droit international au défi des évolutions scientifiques: le ole du GIEC', in: Sandrine Maljean-Dubois and Jacqueline Peel (eds), *Climate Change and the Testing of International Law / Le droit international au défi des changements climatiques* (Brill Nijhoff, 2023), 115–143; Jacqueline Peel, 'Imagining Unimaginable Climate Futures in International Climate Change Law', in: Monika Ambrus, Rosemary Rayfuse and Wouter Werner (eds), *Risk and the Regulation of Uncertainty in International Law* (Oxford University Press, 2017), 177–196.

67 Cf. Paiement and Heri (n. 15), in this volume.

68 Sheila Jasanoff, 'Future Imperfect: Science, Technology, and the Imaginations of Modernity', in: Sheila Jasanoff and Sang-Hyun Kim (eds), *Dreamscapes of Modernity: Sociotechnical Imaginaries and the Fabrication of Power* (Chicago University Press, 2015), 1–33, 4.

3. Embedding the Advisory Opinion in Human Experience

Finally, the ICJ's construction of a coherent and integrated international legal order that encompasses the far-reaching impacts of climate change can also be understood as a product of the introduction of terminology into the proceedings which is reflective of the multifaceted lived reality of climate change. Particularly the contributions 'Global and International Court of Justice'[69] and 'Vanishing Yams'[70] illuminate how non-State actors shaped both the process and the substance of the Advisory Opinion. They uncover how civil society groups, Indigenous peoples, and youth movements did not only accompany the proceedings, but substantively influenced them by introducing experiential and moral vocabularies. Through testimony, amicus briefs, and the *Book of Exhibits*, they translated lived vulnerability into legal argument, articulating concepts such as climate-linked cultural loss, Indigenous epistemologies, and children's rights to a stable climate. Although the Court maintains the formal boundaries of standing, human rights and the principles of equity (*infra legem*), it enlarges the group of participants to the proceedings and pays due regard to the fact that climate change is a common concern of humankind and implies potential human rights impairments. At the same time, the Court broadens the audience of its Advisory Opinion which enhances the chances that civil society groups will rely on the Opinion to enforce State obligations through courts. One can assume that this form of civil society participation influences the judges' interpretation by broadening their perspectives on different human experiences with climate change-related developments.

IV. A Structural Transformation Torn Between Cooperative Governance and Distributive Justice?

The Advisory Opinion reinforces international law as a framework for the cooperative governance of the global climate system (1.), and at the same time opens avenues for litigation over climate harms and distributive justice which could arguably inadvertently undermine this collective endeavour (2.). Such proceedings might risk having counterproductive effects if States

69 Lillian Robb and Vishal Prasad, 'Both a "Global" and an "International" Court of Justice', in this volume.

70 Rashmi Dharia, '"Vanishing Yams", A Food Microhistory in the Climate Change Advisory Opinion', in this volume.

were to retract their recognition of climate duties under international law or question the legitimacy of international courts in adjudicating matters with redistributive implications. At the same time, however, they may also strengthen States' commitment to their international obligations by clarifying the legal parameters of responsibility and accountability. Viewed against this background, the ICJ was also tasked with striking a delicate balance: to reinforce international law's authority while signaling where solutions must ultimately be found through political negotiation, including with respect to historical injustices (3.). In this last respect, the Court seemingly remained deeply divided, which foreshadows future struggles over the role of climate litigation.

1. International Law as a Framework for Cooperative Governance

The Advisory Opinion strengthens the role of international law in providing a framework for the protection of the climate system. To this end, it curtails State discretion across conventional, customary, environmental, and human rights law, thereby binding States to shared normative benchmarks. It further consolidates international law around a coherent set of obligations, increasing legal certainty and enabling States to align their conduct with clear standards. The Court bases its reasoning on prior judicial pronouncements and authoritative statements made by other international institutions, such as the IPCC and the ILC, which enhances its authority vis-à-vis States. At the same time, it preserves sufficient leeway for legal pluralism, as is the case in human rights interpretation, thus maintaining the overall coherence of international law.

Additionally, the Court reinforces international law not only substantively but also procedurally by opening new avenues for climate litigation. This includes both inter-state and individual human rights proceedings. The former becomes possible because the Court affirms the applicability of the customary rules on State responsibility, as codified in the ILC's Articles on State Responsibility (ARSIWA).[71] Some States had argued that the Paris Agreement constitutes a *lex specialis* displacing these general rules, but the Court expressly rejected this claim. Inter-state proceedings may therefore help close the enforcement gap in international law, allowing

71 ICJ, *Obligations of States in Respect of Climate Change* (n. 11), paras. 407 et seq.

States to compel compliance with climate obligations. The Court also recognises that claims for reparation—compensation, restitution, or satisfaction—are in principle viable, provided causation and attribution can be proven.[72] Notably, it did not exclude the possibility of establishing such proof, despite the diffuse, cumulative nature of climate causation.[73] For climate governance where reciprocity of State interests is lacking, because the protected goods are community-based and future-oriented, allowing for compensation claims may in fact become one of the few effective mechanisms, alongside human rights litigation, to encourage compliance. By linking enforcement to responsibility, the Court reinforces international law's authority while giving it procedural traction.

2. Tension with Redistributive Justice

It is precisely this part of the Advisory Opinion, however, that appears to have divided the bench. While the Court recognises the potential engagement of State responsibility, it refraines from specifying its technical contours, such as the intertemporal scope of customary law or the evidentiary thresholds for causation and attribution.[74] This reticence can partly be explained by the abstract nature of advisory proceedings, yet it also reflects a deeper divide among the judges. This becomes apparent in the different declarations and separate opinions that all judges but the President and Vice-President added to the Advisory Opinion.

At the core lies a dual challenge: the international legal order must simultaneously address redistribution, both globally and domestically, with respect to harms resulting from past conduct and coordinate future-oriented collective action to protect the global climate system.[75] At first glance, the Advisory Opinion seems to tackle both. In particular, it emphasises the doctrinal foundations for flexible, differentiated forms of responsibility reflecting historical contribution, capacities, and circumstances. Moreover, it opens the door to future litigation and, potentially, to judicially enforced redistribution, whether by States invoking others' responsibility or by individuals and communities challenging insufficient mitigation efforts before

72 ICJ, *Obligations of States in Respect of Climate Change* (n. 11), paras. 436 et seq.

73 ICJ, *Obligations of States in Respect of Climate Change* (n. 11), para. 437.

74 ICJ, *Obligations of States in Respect of Climate Change* (n. 11), paras. 97, 106, 423.

75 Eliana Cusato, 'Progress and Linear Time: International Environmental Law and the Uneven Distribution of Futurity', HJIL 84 (2024), 865–894.

domestic or regional courts. However, it seems that States might face greater difficulties under the framework constructed by the Court than the Advisory Opinion suggests at first glance.

Judge Nolte's declaration illustrates this tension. He emphasises that the Court should have been clearer about the intertemporal, attributional and causal limits of contentious proceedings in climate disputes. The probabilistic and cumulative nature of climate causation, he argues, makes direct attribution of harm among States exceedingly difficult.[76] Nolte also addresses the temporal scope of potential wrongfulness, noting that emissions could only be considered internationally wrongful from the late 1980s onwards.[77] This would raise the question whether the amount of wrongful emissions since that time would be sufficient at all to be considered as having caused significant harm to the climate system.[78] He warns that pursuing redistribution through litigation risks creating 'false hopes' of litigation serving as surrogate for climate policy, potentially undermining the cooperative mechanisms of the Paris Agreement and the legitimacy of international adjudication itself.[79] Outcomes of such climate cases might only have symbolic legal effect.[80] Judge Sebutinde went further, arguing that the Court should have refrained from addressing questions of State responsibility, attribution and causation altogether.[81]

Conversely, Judges Sebutinde and Charlesworth criticise the Opinion for not having properly articulated the various legal consequences and potential remedies available to injured States.[82] They regret its failure to specify what industrialised States might owe to developing and small island States under potential claims for compensation or restitution.[83] More generally, Judge Charlesworth faults the Court for insufficiently differentiating

76 Declaration of Judge Nolte, *Obligations of States in Respect of Climate Change*, Advisory Opinion of 23 July 2025, paras. 19 and 20.

77 Declaration of Judge Nolte (n. 76), paras. 23 et seq.

78 Declaration of Judge Nolte (n. 76), para. 27.

79 Declaration of Judge Nolte (n. 76), para. 31.

80 Declaration of Judge Nolte (n. 76), para. 31.

81 Separate Opinion of Vice-President Sebutinde, *Obligations of States in Respect of Climate Change*, Advisory Opinion of 23 July 2025, para. 13, referring to paras. 421-438 of the Opinion, *Obligations of States in Respect of Climate Change* (n. 11).

82 Separate Opinion of Vice-President Sebutinde (n. 81), paras. 9–12; Separate Opinion of Judge Charlesworth, *Obligations of States in Respect of Climate Change*, Advisory Opinion of 23 July 2025, paras. 13 et seq.

83 Separate Opinion of Vice-President Sebutinde (n. 81), paras. 5, 6, 8, 9; Separate Opinion of Judge Charlesworth (n. 82), paras. 13 et seq.

between those States most vulnerable to climate impacts and those most responsible for emissions.[84]

Overall, it can be said that the Advisory Opinion prioritises collective obligations and a forward-looking framework of cooperation, rather than constructing mechanisms for redistributing past harms. This future-oriented approach reflects broader trends in climate jurisprudence. In recent human rights-based climate litigation, such as *Urgenda*[85] and *KlimaSeniorinnen*[86], courts have been seized for forward-looking orders requiring governments to strengthen mitigation targets or adopt more ambitious legislation. The emerging pattern is one of preventive adjudication, where courts enforce legal obligations including self-imposed goals and targets for the future, rather than adjudicating past wrongs. By contrast, corporate climate litigation, such as *Milieudefensie v. Shell*[87], has yet to yield enforceable reparations. In a similar vein, however, also these proceedings serve as a catalyst for political accountability and public debate.

3. Finding a Delicate Balance between Law and Politics

Against this backdrop, the ICJ's Advisory Opinion can be read as part of an emerging international law of shared, future-oriented responsibility, rather than one of retrospective reparation. Its emphasis on the common concern of humankind and on the duties of prevention and cooperation signals a preference for collective problem-solving over distributive adjudication. A next crucial juncture for the structural transformation of international law will therefore be whether the ICJ will be seized and move towards adjudicating questions of distributive justice in contentious proceedings, acting as an arbiter of competing State interests, or whether it will exercise judicial restraint in this regard, foregrounding its role as an advisory authority and arbiter upholding the future-oriented public order of climate commons governance as established by international law.

---

84 Cf. Separate Opinion of Judge Charlesworth (n. 82), paras. 13–29.

85 Supreme Court of the Netherlands, Urgenda Foundation v. the State of the Netherlands, 20 December 2019, ECLI:NL:HR:2019:2007.

86 ECtHR (GC), *Verein KlimaSeniorInnen and others v. Switzerland*, 9 April 2024, no.53600/20.

87 Rechtbank Den Haag 26 May 2021, Milieudefensie et al/Royal Dutch Shell Plc, ECLI:NL:RBDHA:2021:5339.

V. Conclusion

In its analysis of the international law applicable to climate change, the ICJ constructs a coherent international legal order that provides a clear, future-oriented, and legally binding framework for the global governance of the climate system. At its centre, the Court places the obligations of prevention and cooperation, which serve to systematise and harmonise diverse treaty regimes and disciplinary boundaries through shared concepts such as science-based benchmarks, due diligence, *erga omnes* obligations, and intergenerational equity. It appears, therefore, that the Court has understood its task—at least in part—as one of ordering international law: offering a structural framework capable of coherently managing global climate governance. This vision conceives international law primarily as a regulatory architecture for the cooperative and future-oriented governance of the global commons. Whether the Court will, in the future, succeed in providing practically viable avenues for redistribution, individualised liability, and compensation or instead continue to exercise judicial restraint out of concern for preserving States' collective endeavours and the legitimacy of international adjudication remains to be seen. With the Advisory Opinion, both paths remain open.